A Reign of Terror Begins

When the parcel arrived around 4 P.M. in the ground-floor mail room of Northwestern's Technological Institute, Crist saw immediately that the handwriting was not his. After his secretary confirmed that it wasn't her penmanship either, Crist was troubled enough to alert campus security to the mystery bundle, which through the brown wrapping felt like wood. Campus police officer Terry Marker was dispatched to the mail room, and as a handful of curious onlookers, Crist among them, craned their necks, Marker joked, "O.K., stand back."

Boom!

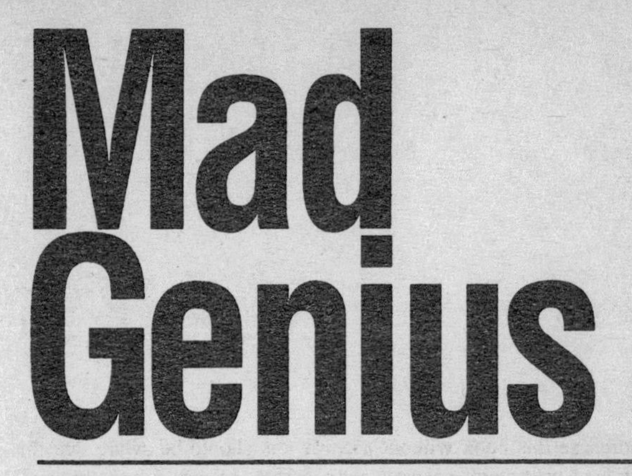

THE ODYSSEY, PURSUIT, AND CAPTURE OF THE UNABOMBER SUSPECT

AWARD-WINNING JOURNALISTS
Nancy Gibbs, Richard Lacayo, Lance Morrow, Jill Smolowe, and David Van Biema
with the Editorial Staff of TIME® Magazine

WARNER BOOKS

A Time Warner Company

WARNER BOOKS EDITION

Cover design by Diane Luger
Cover photograph by Michal Gallacher-Missoulian Gamma Liaison

Warner Books, Inc.
1271 Avenue of the Americas
New York, NY 10020

Visit our web site at
http://pathfinder.com/twep

A Time Warner Company

Printed in the United States of America

First Printing: June, 1996

10 9 8 7 6 5 4 3 2 1

CONTENTS

Mad Genius

Acknowledgments

When major news breaks, it is standard procedure at TIME magazine to dispatch correspondents and photographers to remote places, gather vast amounts of research material and assign writers and editors to pull together accounts that enhance our readers' understanding of often complex events. Typically the journalistic bounty that results from these group efforts is winnowed down to a relatively small number of pages that present only the pick of the informational crop.

On rare occasions, however, the harvest is too bountiful, the tale too compelling, to contain in magazine format. So it is with the story of the Unabomber, the 18-year reign of terror, the Herculean task of hunting down the perpetrator and the arrest of the suspect, Theodore John Kaczynski, on April 3, 1996. When Walter Isaacson, TIME's managing editor, called Warner Books president Laurence Kirshbaum and Warner Paperbacks publisher Mel Parker a week later to propose the idea of expanding TIME's cover story on the arrest to book length, the magazine's correspondents and reporters were already sitting on a trove of facts and knowledgeable contacts. With Warner Books' ready decision to publish the full saga, our journalists returned to their original sources, as well as to a host of new ones uncovered in the wake of Kaczynski's arrest.

Central to the reporting for this book were: Washington correspondent Elaine Shannon, who covers law-enforcement agencies for the magazine; reporter Pat Dawson, on the scene in Montana; Midwest bureau chief James L. Graff and fellow Chicago bureau members Wendy Cole and Julie Grace; Detroit bureau chief William A. McWhirter, plus Midwest stringers Sheila Gribben, Mark Shuman, Josh White and Kelly Williams, all of whom combed through the Kaczynskis' early years; San Francisco bureau chief David S. Jackson, who mined the Bay Area, thick as it was with Unabomber-related material; Los Angeles bureau chief Jordan Bonfante, who with correspondents Elaine Lafferty and Denver-based Richard Woodbury and stringers Anne Palmer Donohoe in Salt Lake City and Ellis Conklin in Seattle probed sites and sources elsewhere in the western part of the country; East Coast–based correspondents Sam Allis, Sharon E. Epperson, Jenifer Mattos and Elaine Rivera, aided by stringers Mary Beth Warner and Mabel Brodrick-Okereke, who followed the Unabomber's trail and delved into David Kaczynski's family life and brother Ted's career at Harvard. Latin America bureau chief Laura López filed on Juan Sánchez Arreola from Chihuahua. The intimate descriptions of Montana's topography and natural beauty is courtesy of national political correspondent Michael Duffy, who flees the nation's capital whenever he can to fish in the state.

In New York, a team led by assistant editor Ratu Kamlani and including chief of research Marta Dorion, assistant editors Ursula Nadasdy de Gallo, Ariadna Victoria Rainert and Susanne Washburn, along with reporters Barbara Burke, Charlotte Faltermayer and Andrea Sachs, reported and culled through voluminous files and other sources. Senior writers Richard Lacayo, Jill Smolowe and David Van Biema, as well as senior editor Nancy Gibbs, then sat down and among them wrote the narrative. The challenge of organizing and editing this considerable work fell to senior editor Lee Aitken.

Copy editing and proofreading a work of this length on an abbreviated schedule was a challenge taken up by copy chief Susan L. Blair, along with Doug Bradley, Bruce Christopher Carr, Evelyn Hannon, Peter J. McGullam, Maria A. Paul, Jane Rigney and Amelia Weiss. Librarians Sandra Jamison, Charles Lampach, Joan Levinstein, Mary Ann Pradt and Angela Thornton gathered additional material to help writers put the story in its full context. Assistant picture editors Bronwen Latimer and Nancy Jo Johnson assembled the photographs that accompany the text. In the end, production editor Michael Skinner managed to pull all the pieces together and deliver a complete package to our colleagues at Warner Books. Start to finish, the book was completed in 11 days, offering readers what we believe is the freshest and most comprehensive account of the Unabomber's story anywhere.

—Barrett Seaman
Special Projects Editor
TIME Magazine

Introduction

The medium—a bomb in a package—was his message. It was loud and sometimes fatal, but inarticulate. It signified . . . what? A nonentity announcing himself to the world. The bombs were what he had instead of a life.

He started sending them in the middle of Jimmy Carter's term of office. A sort of perverted model of saintly patience, the Unabomber labored at the devices through two administrations of Ronald Reagan and four years of George Bush, then three years into Bill Clinton's time. Elsewhere in the larger world, the Shah of Iran fell; the Ayatullah Khomeini took his place, ruled in turn and subsequently died; the Soviet Union crumbled and vanished. History went on. The Unabomber stayed in touch with life by mail.

Invisible, but manifest in his works, he would turn up from time to time in the news, like some demon Forrest Gump—not his face of course, but flashes of his labor, his jack-in-the-box violence. When the smoke cleared, all the FBI would be left with was a sketch of his mysterious terrorist-from-the-funny-papers countenance, the mad monk in hood and sunglasses, a post office icon that did not age. Celebrity in obscurity: off and on, he enjoyed more than the usual 15 minutes of fame. His career went on for 18 years, punctuated by 16 packages, by three deaths, by 22 injuries.

Part of the fascination with the Unabomber—before his somewhat pedantic Luddism came into print, anyway—arose from the mystery of his motive. What made his mind tick? Politics? Ideology? Insanity? The bombs were his only meaningful contact with society, until he blackmailed the Washington *Post* and the New York *Times* to see his 35,000-word antitechnology tract—his megalomanifesto—in print.

In the end, the case of the Unabomber probably belongs more to the history of sociopathic psychiatry than to the history of political ideas. His private violence bubbled up in a culture of paranoia that has always flourished in America. The atmosphere of inflamed suspicion and conspiracy sighting has grown more virulent at home in the years since the cold war ended. Where once the American paranoid impulse had the entire Soviet Union and world communist threat to occupy it (and the threats were real enough), it now can shop around in a multicultural supermarket of bad guys (the government in general; the Internal Revenue Service; the Bureau of Alcohol, Tobacco and Firearms; Exxon; technology as a whole; angry white males; television; secular humanists; homosexuals; Fundamentalist Christians; the radical right; Rush Limbaugh; the media; feminists; immigrants; blacks; liberal Democrats; conservative Republicans). The bazaar of available enemies looks like the bar in *Star Wars*. As that successful paranoid Mao Zedong once advised, "Let a hundred flowers bloom. Let a hundred schools of thought contend."

Paranoia may come in either tribal or private form. It may be an intimate pathology or an aspect of identity politics (racial, ethnic, sexual, for example). In a famous essay in 1965, the historian Richard Hofstadter examined what he called "The Paranoid Style in American Politics." Hofstadter observed, "There is a vital difference between the paranoid spokesman in politics and the clinical paranoic: although they both tend to be overheated, oversuspicious, overaggressive, grandiose, and apocalyptic in expression, the clinical paranoid sees the hostile and conspiratorial world in which he feels himself to be living as directed specifically against him; whereas the spokesman of the paranoid style finds it directed against a nation, a culture, a way of life ..."

Still, it is in the nature of the disease that every paranoid aspires to the universal. He sees himself as target of a vast, malignant conspiracy. Paranoia, after all, is toxic self-importance—a way of imagining oneself to be at the center of the world; that it is a malevolent world is part of the price the paranoid pays for such attention. You invent powerful, satanic enemies and then, in response to them, deploy apocalyptic weapons. Such is the dialogue that the paranoid invents to communicate with the world.

American intellectuals have sometimes taken a certain ain't-we-awful pride in the nation's tradition of political paranoia. But on the whole, Americans' freedom has made them comparative innocents in the world. The great stains on American history (slavery and the near extermination of the Indians) represented the brutality of the overdog, matter-of-factly atrocious; they were not caused by paranoia.

Contrast that to the style of Stalin's regime in the Soviet Union, which was a *Masterpiece Theatre* of the paranoid. His dinners in the Kremlin went on all night. He would sit at a long table and force his ministers and cronies to drink, hour after hour, while he plotted and probed and flattered and terrified them. At dawn, when their brains were numb with fear and vodka and confusion, the NKVD might lead one or two of them away, without explanation, to be shot. Stalin refracted violent fear through alcohol. That was the physics of paranoia under laboratory conditions: for every action, an opposite reaction. Paranoia induces paranoia, a reciprocal mind game. Stalin's chronic and possibly psychotic paranoia—his greatest survival skill, by the way—sent waves of perfectly justified paranoia not only through the Soviet victims within his reach but also out into the world that was within his nuclear range.

Or think of politics in the Balkans: almost a millennium of blood-drenched ethnic and religious paranoia, a form passed down the generations through the flawless fiber optics of tribal memory, every offense committed 400 years ago being as real as yesterday.

America is young, but has done its level best to develop a record of persecution-and-revenge fantasies. They constitute the dark underweave of American idealism. The rhetoric was often riper than the Unabomber's prose. In 1798, for example, the president of Yale, Timothy Dwight, attacked the irreligious Jacobins in these terms: "The sins of these enemies of Christ, and Christians, are of numbers and degrees which mock account and description. All that the malice and atheism of the Dragon, the cruelty and rapacity of the Beast, and the fraud and deceit of the false Prophet, can generate, or accomplish, swell the list."

An anti-Masonic writer in 1829 called Freemasonry the most dangerous institution ever imposed on man, "an engine of Satan ... dark, unfruitful, selfish, demoralizing, blasphemous, murderous, anti-republican and anti-Christian." Virulent anti-Catholicism focused for a time on the Jesuits, who, claimed one writer, "are prowling about all parts of the United States in every possible disguise, expressly to ascertain the advantageous situations and modes to disseminate Popery ... the western country swarms with them under the names of puppet-show men, dancing masters, music teachers, peddlers of images and ornaments, barrel organ players, and similar practitioners."

And so on, through anti-immigrant crusades in the 1920s and McCarthyism in the 1950s.

American paranoias come in waves. The last year or two

brought a surge in the dynamic: Ruby Ridge and Waco convinced some that the Federal Government had become an arm of an international conspiracy—probably rooted in the United Nations. A vivid fantasy of blue-helmeted U.N. troops descending in black helicopters to take over the U.S. by disarming its population was passed from modem to modem around the Internet. The president of the National Rifle Association talked about the government's "jack-booted thugs."

The mood, which started on the fringes, then began to infect the general population. After the 1994 elections, the newly elected Gingrich Congressmen vowed no compromise. Liberals wrote them down as fascists. The Million Man March of African-American men in Washington, otherwise admirable, provided a platform for minister Louis Farrakhan's elaborate numerological conspiracies, the very arithmetic of the universe clicking in conspiracy. The Whitewater scandal and the death of Vincent Foster, deputy counsel to the President, persisted in emitting a low-intensity radioactive glow. And of course, an elaborate police plot framed O.J. Simpson for a double murder.

But then the psychology seemed to change, much for the better, as if, for the moment anyway, the wave of paranoia had exhausted itself. The first anniversary of the April 19 Oklahoma City bombing passed. President Bill Clinton had traveled there in his role as national grief counselor. The victims and their families had come at least some of the way in recovering, while farther to the west, in Denver, the trial of Timothy McVeigh got under way.

And in Montana, the man supposed to be the Unabomber was arrested.

—Lance Morrow

The Hermit's Lair

The majority of people engage in a significant amount of naughty behavior. —Manifesto, paragraph 26

Maybe it wasn't really so lonely at night in the woods at the edge of Montana's Scapegoat Wilderness, where the trees sound like a crowd waiting for the curtain to rise. Theodore John Kaczynski lived at heaven's back door, where the land remained as the explorers had found it, still sealed, unlighted, unwired, resembling most perfectly the place he wanted America to be. It is a place where a man who hates technology and progress and people would have plenty of time to savor the absence of all of them. He could listen to the forest rustle and hum, the larches and ponderosa pines hundreds of years old, hundreds of feet high, the tamaracks and the lodgepoles that totter when the wind rubs up against the Continental Divide. What he didn't know was that for the past few weeks, the trees were listening back.

The agents and explosives experts were everywhere, disguised as lumberjacks and postal workers and mountain men. They had draped the forest with sensors and microphones, nestled snipers not far from the cabin. Some residents of Lincoln, the nearest town, five miles away, thought the guys they had spotted wearing FBI jackets were there to intercept militia types from Idaho on their way to reinforce the rebel Freemen over in Jordan, 320 miles due east on

Montana Highway 200. A Helena FBI agent, known by some town residents, turned up in Lincoln, but locals thought he was there to snowmobile. Some agents staying at the local hotel said they were historians researching old gold mines.

Wayne Cashman, owner of the 7 Up Ranch Supper Club, had seen the agents coming and going for a month; he was told they were on some kind of training mission. They wore green camo pants and a variety of shirts and jackets, heavy hiking or hunting boots and sidearms. By Wednesday, April 3, they had rented all four cabins and 16 motel rooms at the 7 Up. That morning he made them 50 box lunches.

The agents had been asking about the hermit who lived off Stemple Pass Road. But they asked carefully, knowing they were in a small town, where people knew people, word traveled fast, privacy was the local currency. No one could tell them much. Kept to himself. Rarely said much. Didn't look too great, especially lately, his hair matted, his clothes more ragged, riper even than usual. He came down into town only occasionally, to stock up on flour and Spam and canned tuna at the grocery store, maybe pick up some used clothes or spend the day at the library. He walked with his head down, kept his sentences short, but the voice was still noticeable, a cultivated contrast to his shaggy demeanor. He didn't say "ain't," didn't say "yeah, right"; he'd say "quite correct." The dogs in town didn't like him.

Otherwise he stayed in his cabin up near Poorman's Creek, a 10-ft. by 12-ft. shack built of plywood and rolled roofing paper, no wires, no water, three locks on the door. It must have got awfully cold in the winter; the snows came early and stayed late, and he hauled and cut his firewood by hand. He hunted rabbits with a .22-cal. rifle, the same kind his father had used to kill himself. A Census worker had stopped by once and actually got inside, saw the stacks of books, the Shakespeare and Thackeray and Victor Hugo, the tools and boxes, the table and cot. Visitors knew better than to knock. But there were never many visitors.

Ted knew his neighbors, like Butch and Wendy Gehring, who ran the local sawmill. He had bought the land, almost an acre and a half, from Butch's father in 1971. When the agents came to town, they had to tell Butch why they were there, because they rented two nearby cabins from which to keep watch. In fact, so many people knew Ted was being investigated that had he made any close friends whatsoever, in Lincoln or in Helena, he might have been warned, and escaped. Anna Haire at the Helena bookstore said she was amazed that the FBI trusted her and others, because any one of them could have warned him of the closing net. But no one did.

The agents followed Ted's movements day after day, waiting for the moment when he might emerge, with a parcel in his backpack or in his saddlebags, and head into town, maybe catch a ride to Helena, maybe even board a Greyhound headed south, or west, where they could track him to what they had come to believe were the scenes of his crimes: a post office, a campus, a computer store. But days passed, and there was no sign of him except an occasional foray to tend his garden. One day Butch wandered up by the cabin with a Forest Service worker and called out a greeting to Ted. Ted stuck his head out, recognized his neighbor and waved back. But then nothing.

As it turned out, the agents didn't have the luxury of time. Word came from Washington: CBS News was about to break a story that the FBI had finally, after 18 years, tracked down a man they suspected was the Unabomber. There had been some tense negotiations as the feds tried to get CBS to hold off, and the network had agreed to wait a day or two. But it was going to run the story, so there was little hope now of catching their man red-handed. They had to get him outside the cabin; he might have guns, it might be booby-trapped, he might decide to kill himself or one of them, or blow up his shack and all that was inside.

So on Wednesday morning, the same Forest Service official wandered up by the cabin with an FBI agent, holding a map and pretending to be looking for a property line between Ted's land and the national forest. "Ted," they called, "We need to talk." Recognizing the Forest worker from the previous week, Ted opened the door; the air spilled out, dense with woodsmoke and unwashed clothes. The agent then told him who they really were, and that they had come with a search warrant. Ted tried to duck back inside; when the agent and another who had been hiding nearby grabbed him, he tried to shake them off. But he wasn't much of a fighter, and they quickly had him in handcuffs.

The agents took him to a nearby cabin and started asking questions. Wendy heard what happened next from one of the interrogators. "He would just sit and talk about anything, until they brought up the Unabomber," she said. "He said he did not want to talk about the Unabomber case. He said he would like to stay in neutral conversation—that he would like to talk about anything but that."

After about five hours they arrested him. By the time they brought him to the courthouse in Helena, he was wearing a flame orange prison uniform, shackles on his ankles and wrists and a professor's tidy tweed jacket. The reporters flocked about, shouting questions.

"Are you the Unabomber?" he was asked.

"Are you guilty?"

"Why did you do it?"

And for once he didn't hang his head. He flashed the sly

smile that would jog the memory of many old classmates. But as usual, he didn't say a word.

The arrest of Ted Kaczynski brought to an end the longest, most expensive hunt for a serial killer in U.S. history. After 200 suspects, millions of pieces of information, thousands of interviews, a million man-hours, 20,000 calls to 800-701-BOMB and visits with clairvoyants, the agents were not about to rush to judgment and declare that he was the Unabomber. But that didn't keep them from marveling at the finale. For years they had brought all their technology to bear to hunt a man who hated technology. In the end, however, for all their work and patience and skill, it was not a detective story. If Kaczynski is convicted, he will owe his downfall to his own ego and a brother's honor, without which he might have gone on indefinitely, striking and disappearing again, leaving no trace other than a country reluctant to open its mail.

Among the hunters from the FBI, the U.S. Postal Inspection Service and the Bureau of Alcohol, Tobacco and Firearms, there were agents who retired in frustration after failing to solve the ultimate criminal riddle. What kind of man would launch a career as a terrorist with no interest in personal profit, no obvious personal grudges—some bombs were left for random targets—smart and skillful enough to build by hand untraceable bombs, able and willing, right up until the last year, to remain invisible while the legend around him grew? "It was just an incredibly complicated jigsaw puzzle," said a former FBI agent who worked on the case.

Over mugs of coffee in the morning, pizza and beer at midnight, the Unabom task force obsessed about his contradictions. He scraped the labels off batteries so they could not be traced, used stamps long past their issue dates and wires that were out of production. But he made his own screws, built his own triggers, even when cheap parts from Radio Shack would have been much harder to trace. When he began taunting his hunters in letters to newspapers, he said he sanded his bombs down to remove not only fingerprints, but also any oils from his hands that might have seeped into the wood.

The agents imagined a smart, twisted man, carving and fiddling into the night. To kill three strangers and injure 22 others, he had to be powerfully angry. Yet he must have had enormous patience to experiment with explosives and triggers and not blow his fingers off. "When you see this stuff, some of these components bear markings of having been put together and taken apart repeatedly," said Chris Ronay, the FBI's top bomb expert, who retired in 1994. "It's not just that he's creating something carefully. He's played with it for a while. He marks things with numbers so he can put them together again right. He's leaving a little of himself at each crime scene." And each little bit of himself that he left the hunters put into their puzzle. The picture started to focus: a white male, middle-aged, educated, alienated, isolated, brittle, patient, paranoid. And while they got it uncannily right, even in their dreams they could hardly have imagined the life story of the Harvard hermit in the woods.

For years all they had to go on were tiny pieces. A couple of unexploded bombs; remnants of others; some letters to victims. A hair here, a piece of fiber there. But there must have finally come a day when the Unabomber concluded that somehow, his message wasn't getting through. Maybe he had been too subtle. When news came of the bombing of the federal building in Oklahoma City, that horror and its implications brought the country to a halt while politicians and scholars and the oracles of talk radio examined the state of the nation. The Unabomber had been doing this for 17 years, albeit more discreetly, without anyone but the cops paying attention to the pattern of his targets. The next bomb went off five days later; within weeks the letters and writings poured forth. It all began to look like a last, desperate effort to have a conversation.

"If we had never done anything violent," the Unabomber wrote in his 35,000-word manifesto, published, after much soul searching, by the New York *Times* and the Washington *Post* in September 1995, "and had submitted the present writings to a publisher, they probably would not have been accepted. If they had been accepted and published, they probably would not have attracted many readers, because it's more fun to watch the entertainment put out by the media than to read a sober essay." And the message, he believed, was too important to be ignored: industrial society was a plague; it was destroying souls, disrupting community, ravaging nature, ruining the promise of a country in love with its fantasy of the frontier. "In order to get our message before the public with some chance of making a lasting impression," wrote a man who never was able to make a lasting impression, "we've had to kill people."

The manifesto gave the hunters a much clearer sense of what kind of man they might be dealing with; but only one person could read that treatise, hear its message and recognize the messenger. David Kaczynski knew that his brother was strange, his life a walking warning of danger; Ted had grown bitter, shriveled somehow in isolation. When David read the manifesto, he heard echoes of his brother's letters and deepest beliefs and confronted the possibility that he was in possession of the greatest secret in modern criminal history.

What exactly was he supposed to do? Tell his mother? Confront Ted? Wait for more proof? Wait for an arm to be blown off, another timber executive to die? David's decision to launch his own quiet manhunt, and eventually turn his brother over to the FBI, was painfully and perfectly in keeping with the way he lived his life. He was a man with a moral code: blood thicker than water, honor thicker than blood. The agents who swept down on Lincoln, Montana, during Holy Week knew where to go because the brother had shown them the way.

When the investigators arrived at last at the door to the cabin, they were blasted with fumes from the wood stove. Everything was covered with a thick coat of soot. But as their eyes adjusted they saw that they were looking at a mother lode of evidence such as they had hardly dared imagine: books, chemicals, tools, a half-made pipe bomb, 10 looseleaf binders containing detailed diagrams of explosives.

"It's unbelievable," said an investigator. "People had speculated he would save all kinds of crap." But to see it all there, everything the lab guys and the case agents could have wanted, arrayed like Christmas morning ... and that was only the beginning. They set up a generator that hummed through the night, providing the lights and power for their equipment. They sent in a 3-ft.-tall robot to handle suspicious-looking boxes. For a command post, they brought in a long motor home with a dish antenna on the roof and an American flag on a pole outside, near the portable toilet. On the first warm spring day, the voices echoed through the timber, with sudden shouts and bursts of excitement, like an after-work softball team jacked to win.

By Friday night they had found a fully functioning bomb, tucked in a wooden box and ready for mailing. "It was wrapped, armed, assembled and ready to go," said an official. "All you had to do was slap a label on it." After disarming it, the agents told their colleagues they thought it was unmistakably the Unabomber's work, as if he had signed his name on the painting.

But there was more, still more. Maps of San Francisco tucked in a Tater Tots box. Wires and switches in old

Quaker Oats containers. A scrap of paper apparently titled "hit list," with the words "airline industry," "computer industry" and "geneticists." He kept his Michigan diploma in a Samsonite case, his high school yearbooks in a green plastic bag. They vacuumed the floor, gathering up fibers and hairs, cataloging the dust bunnies.

The first two typewriters they found looked promising; their bomber had always used the same one, maybe so the feds would know they were dealing with their real terrorist and not some pretender. But the third typewriter was the lucky one. They found it in the cabin's loft, and nestled next to it, an original copy of the manifesto.

Within a few days the first tourists had arrived—from Costa Rica—to pose by Ted's mailbox and have their pictures taken. He was down in the county jail, on a suicide watch. For the first time in many years, he was living where he could read by a strong light, shoot hoops in the afternoon sun, use a toilet. For Easter dinner he had ham, scalloped potatoes, peas and carrots, lemon coconut pie and coffee.

As for the investigators, they set out on a new mission. They were sure they had their man; now they needed to build an airtight case against him. All across the country they spread, bearing pictures and tracing patterns: how he got around, where he stayed, who might have seen him near the scenes of the crimes. The meticulous search of the cabin went on for weeks. But even as investigators worked at proving what Kaczynski had done, another examination was already under way, conducted by newspaper reporters and armchair psychologists and a country riveted by the tale of a mad genius in the woods. What they all wanted to know was, Why had he done it? And for that story the clues lay elsewhere, starting perhaps in the backyards of Chicago, with a little boy with few friends and a powerful mind.

A Gifted Child

It isn't natural for an adolescent human being to spend the bulk of his time sitting at a desk absorbed in study.

—Manifesto, paragraph 115

One can trace the line of Theodore Kaczynski's early life on a map. It starts in Illinois, then moves through Massachusetts, doubles back to Michigan and shoots to California. From there it takes him finally to the remote woods of Montana. Whatever else that jagged stripe represents—a philosophical wandering, an interrupted career path—it also marks an attempted escape route from the 20th century itself. The man who would find his way to the Scapegoat Wilderness, one of the quietest spots on earth, was born in Chicago, another kind of wild place altogether. Though it's by no means the chief symbol anymore for the overloads of city life—for that we now have New York City and Los Angeles—Chicago is still one of the busiest and most populous cities on earth. And when Kaczynski was born, in 1942, it was still the Second City, a capital of the industrial world. If you wanted an early immersion in all the glories and predicaments of civilization, you could get it there. You might get that even if you didn't want it.

Earlier still, in the first decades of this century, when Kaczynski's parents were coming of age, Chicago was more than the Second City. It was in many senses the First City.

Carl Sandburg's "City of the Big Shoulders" was the hot center of modernity, the great nexus point where all the vectors of invention, money and industry collided. For Americans it was at the heart of their national enterprises—railways, meat packing, timber—the most economically vibrant spot on the continent. For Europeans it was the very essence of America, the place where their writers and intellectuals came for a glimpse of the future. But with the awe it inspired came the uneasy conviction that its headlong development, in which pollution and squalor went hand in hand with prosperity, held a warning about the dilemmas of progress. Even the British author H.G. Wells, an enthusiastic advanceman for the future, was unnerved by the unmanaged expansion he saw there during a visit. Chicago's defining characteristic, he thought, was "the dark disorder of growth."

Kaczynski's parents arrived there in the decade following the First World War. Both of them were children of Polish immigrants, and they were drawn in part by the city's well-established Polish-American communities. Theodore Richard Kaczynski had been born in Pittsburgh, Pennsylvania. Wanda Theresa Dombek had arrived with her parents from Zanesville, Ohio, a pottery-making center 50 miles east of Columbus. On April 11, 1939, less than five months before the start of World War II, they were married. He was 26; she was 21. The newlyweds found an apartment in a two-story brick house at 4755 South Wolcott Avenue in a neighborhood known as the Back of the Yards.

They loved two things: each other and books. Though at this point neither had a college degree, or maybe because of that, they would never stop learning. All his life Ted's acquaintances would be startled by the breadth of his reading. He could joke about the Anabaptists, a splinter group among Reformation Protestants, or discourse on politics. His politics were leftish. So were hers. It was Wanda who, everybody said, loved not only to learn but also to teach. In the late 1960s, after their sons were out of the house, she would even earn a bachelor's degree from the University of Iowa and for two years teach high school freshman English in Geneva, Illinois.

They were also both evidently nonbelievers. Instead of being married in the Roman Catholic Church, the couple exchanged vows before a Cook County judge. "That was highly unusual for a Polish family in those days," says Norbert Gons, 76, a neighborhood historian. And instead of a parochial school, their eldest son would attend the public Sherman Elementary School on West 52nd Street. Says family friend Keith Sorrick: "The boys were raised Darwinian." The Kaczynskis real faith was in the secular trinity of the 20th century: reason, learning, progress.

The Back of the Yards was a Polish-American enclave near the bustling and noxious Chicago stockyards. In his book *City of the Century* historian Donald L. Miller describes how by the 1890s it was "the vilest slum in Chicago." The only open space was "the hair field," where hog's hair and cattle skins were spread out to dry under clouds of buzzing flies. By the time the Kaczynskis arrived the city had made improvements in housing and sanitation, but the Back of the Yards was still nobody's idea of prosperity. On bad days the local air was vivid with the stench from cattle holding pens and the slaughterhouses.

Yet like many a neighborhood of the working poor, it was also upwardly striving, safe and close-knit. Theodore found a job with a first cousin, Felix, whose storefront sausage factory was well known among the shops that lined South Ashland Avenue. Though the place closed in 1969, old-timers will still tell you that Felix Kaczynski and Sons made the best kielbasa on the South Side. Theodore was just a sausage maker, but he was a thinking man's sausage maker: at one point he came up with the idea for a new sausage casing that he attempted, without success, to patent.

On May 22, 1942, the Kaczynskis' first child was born. They named him Theodore John. To distinguish him from the elder Theodore they would take to calling him Teddy. Instead of going to the nearby Evangelical Hospital, Wanda had given birth at Lying-In Hospital, the maternity wing of the University of Chicago Hospitals. Though farther from their apartment it was South Side's best facility. Records there show a normal delivery.

Very soon after, however, something may have gone wrong. Investigators involved with the Unabomber case say the family told them that at age six months, Teddy suffered a severe allergic reaction to medication. It led to a hospital stay of several weeks, during which the family has said he was kept in isolation. Hospital rules did not allow his parents to hold or hug him. When he came home, they sensed a change. The expressive and happy baby they had sent away now appeared listless and withdrawn.

When infants suffer the same kinds of allergic reaction today, the customary treatment is steroids, which weren't available in the early 1940s. Medical practice then prescribed a more complicated regime of ointments and compresses. To keep babies from scratching themselves while they healed, their arms might be partially immobilized with cuffs or splints. Some were even bound in a spread-eagle position. If the treatment required hospitalization, there could also be an emotional impact from the effects of isolation. "To be taken away from Mother at six months is very drastic to a youngster," says Dr. John Kennell of Case Western Reserve University in Cleveland, Ohio, one of the nation's foremost experts on early childhood development.

"Most hospitals at that time didn't allow more than weekly visitation for sick children. To a child of that age, a week without Mother's contact may be totally devastating. They have no appreciation that the abandonment will ever end."

Within a few years it was apparent that there was something else about Teddy. He was smarter than other kids. When he was six he took a Stanford-Binet IQ test that was administered by Ralph Meister, a friend of his father's who was a child psychologist. An average score was 100. His was in the range of 160 to 170. This boy would be more than bright. He possessed gifts of a kind that were granted to very few. It only remained to see how he would display them.

Meister still remembers his surprise when one day the Kaczynski boy asked him for a copy of *Robert's Rules of Order.* The dry handbook of parliamentary procedure was not exactly a Hardy Boys adventure. But Teddy was always hitting the books, even books that were much bigger than he was. It was a discovery that excited his mother no end. Wanda started a special diary. Each new evidence of his budding intellect was lovingly recorded.

Some time in the 1940s, the Kaczynskis moved to a larger place at 5234 South Carpenter Street. They were still in a two-family house, but this time in a house with yards front and back, on a tree-lined street farther away from the foul air of the stockyards. On Oct. 3, 1949, Wanda gave birth to their second child, a boy they named David. Teddy, smart and wary, was seven.

Like many kids he may have reacted coolly to the appearance of a competitor for his parents' attention. Perhaps very coolly. Decades later, after his arrest, one of his aunts told the *Daily Southtown,* a newspaper in suburban Chicago, that before David was born, "he'd snuggle up to me." But not after, she said. "He changed immediately. Maybe we [paid too much attention] to the new baby, like people do." If it's true that Teddy was worried about his hold on his parents' affection, he also would have known by then how to clinch it. Study. Read. Keep on showing the signs of superior intellect that his mother so proudly recorded in that diary.

In 1952 the Kaczynskis made the leap to the suburbs. Evergreen Park, Illinois, was still partly rural when they moved to the three-bedroom brick colonial on South Lawndale Avenue. Truck farms were tucked in among the subdivisions. Teams of horses plowed the nearby cornfields, and the prairie stretched out at the edge of town. But with the postwar combination of prosperity and the baby boom, Chicago was spilling fast into its nearby surroundings. Like America in general, Evergreen Park was a pastoral setting overtaken by civilization, a place that didn't live up to its promise to be ever green.

For a while it was the fastest-growing community in the state, exploding from 5,000 people in 1945 to nearly 16,000 in 1953, eventually rising to a peak of 26,000 in the 1970s. In the same year that the Kaczynskis arrived, so did Evergreen Plaza, one of the nation's first shopping malls. Among its features was an underground conveyor belt that moved groceries from the supermarket to the parking lot, where clerks would carry them to the customer's car. It was one of those machine-age conveniences that in the 1950s seemed the very image of a bright new tomorrow.

The Kaczynskis were well liked in their neighborhood, despite the fact that in some ways they were a breed apart. In a town with 13 established congregations—Evergreen Park called itself the Village of Churches—the Kaczynskis were considered atheists. They were also liberals, an increasingly rare breed among the socially conservative white ethnics of Chicago and its environs. In the 1960s they would revere the Kennedys and the Rev. Martin Luther King. And detest Richard Nixon.

In later years, when they were living in another Chicago suburb, they occasionally wrote letters to the editor of the Chicago *Tribune*. On Oct. 17, 1988, the paper published Theodore's letter defending liberalism, "Isn't it puzzling that lately the 'L' word is used so pejoratively?" he wrote. "That the word 'liberal' is used to evoke something bad? Here are some things that the liberals have given us: Social Security, later the Social Security COLAs, federal deposit insurance, unemployment insurance, the right to join or not to join a union, the G.I. Bill (giving educational opportunities to veterans), Medicare and student loans for education.

"By what twist of the imagination can anyone call the above bad? Let us treat the word 'liberal' with the respect it deserves."

The first of Wanda's two published letters would appear in the *Tribune* on Dec. 21, 1988. That one defended the embattled Soviet leader Mikhail Gorbachev, who had cut short a trip the U.S. to rush to the site of an earthquake in Soviet Armenia: "How cynical can some of our political analysts get? To hear on TV their skeptical comments on why Gorbachev left for Russia, cutting short his agenda in the U.S., they suggest that if it were not for political opposition in his country, he would have stayed in New York basking in the limelight, visiting plush establishments, etc. etc. Please let's give the man some credit for being human!

"Tens of thousands of people were dead, dying or injured in his country. Surely, no matter what, this would take him back home."

On April 20, 1990, Wanda wrote in support of health-care reform, "The most frequent criticism one hears of the Canadian national health plan is that high-tech care is not readily available and that one must wait for elective surgery.

"What is not mentioned is that to millions of uninsured or underinsured people in the U.S., not only are those two aspects of health care unavailable but even primary care and preventive care is out of reach. Are we to deny basic health care to millions of children so that wealthy people can be assured that they can buy expensive medicine quickly and easily?"

But while they might have been more liberal than some of their neighbors, their politics seemed well within the ordinary spectrum. And from the time they arrived in Evergreen Park, the Kaczynskis impressed people there by their kindness and good cheer. When a new neighbor's home was quarantined for six weeks because their infant daughter was stricken with polio, Wanda regularly left hot meals on their front stoop. Joyce Collis, a classmate of Ted's who lived next door, says when she came home from school each day, she often saw Wanda outside waiting for Ted. "She would greet me as I came up the walk in the sweetest way."

The Kaczynskis were familiar figures at meetings of the school board and the PTA, and at the Northwest Boosters, a neighborhood organization that got the local streets paved and a park installed. Years before such things became common, Wanda started a neighborhood preschool. And if the Kaczynskis were smart, they weren't snobbish. "I remember going over there once and there were stacks and stacks of books, mostly philosophy, that Wanda had checked out of the library," says Collis. "Wanda said they were being passed around among family members, and that we were welcome to take any of the books home with us. But we really sort of laughed the suggestion off, because they were heavy, heavy reading."

Next to books, what Ted Sr. loved was the outdoors. He liked gardening, hiking and camping. He used to take the boys into the woods for as much as a week at a time. On some of those trips they would try to live only on whatever they could gather or kill. But he also taught them to love animals. Once he and David came upon a lame rabbit in the nearby woods. They brought it home, where 12-year-old Ted nursed it back to health. Then he took it to the edge of town, where the houses gave way to the open prairie, and released it back into the wild.

But for the Kaczynskis the real focus of their lives was their children. "Wanda and Theodore dedicated practically everything to the kids," says Dr. LeRoy Weinberg, who lived behind them. "When we had parties, they weren't the type to let it go, have a drink, dance, live it up a little." For the Kaczynskis love was bound up with learning. On Sundays there were trips to Adler Planetarium and the Museum of Science and Industry. Neighbors still recall seeing Wanda on the front steps of their house reading to the 10-year-old Teddy from *Scientific American*. "Wanda was a born teacher," says her neighbor Dorothy O'Connell. "She was bound and determined for those boys to do well."

And they did well. David was bright too, though not the standout that his brother was. As for Teddy, O'Connell clearly remembers him at age 11 stopping by her house before he left with his parents for a vacation in the Wisconsin woods. Under his arm was his vacation reading: *Romping Through Mathematics from Addition to Calculus*. A year later, he joined her, his mother and another neighbor in a game of Scrabble. "He beat us all," says O'Connell. "His vocabulary was something."

There was something else that everybody noticed about Teddy. He kept to himself. It worried his parents that whenever a car pulled up to the Kaczynski home, he would dash up the stairs to his room. He didn't like to talk much or to play with other kids. Despite his gifts, he had disciplinary problems in grade school. His parents wondered whether a boy so much brighter than his peers might not feel frustrated in class. As an attempted remedy, he was skipped a grade.

That gave Teddy a curriculum more nearly in pace with his abilities. But as the years went by his shyness seemed to harden into a permanent condition of awkward solitude. He entered his teens with an Elvis pompadour (when his hair was combed at all) and a brown leather briefcase, but few real companions. "He was always a loner," remembers Weinberg. "When he walked, he stared at the ground." His neighbor Joyce Collis recalls that "whenever Ted went out, he was almost pushed out the door by his parents." Her mother sometimes drove her to school and offered rides to the Kaczynski boys. When he got into the car, Ted would offer a curt "Hello," then sit in silence for the rest of the trip. "I don't think Ted was able to build a rapport with anyone," says Collis, "young or old."

David, who was much more outgoing and had more kids his age in the neighborhood, had an easier time. He was the one you might see playing ball in the yard with his father. His mother once said it made her feel young again to have the house filled with the comings and going of David's friends. By the time he got to high school Ted never really seemed to have any of his own, even among the other brains, whom some kids made fun of as the "briefcase boys." As a smart kid in the cliquish world of a '50s high school, he would have been dead meat even if he hadn't been so weird. "He had a pocket protector, the whole thing," says Raymond Janz, a classmate who used to tease him. "We stuffed him in a locker one time just for grins."

Ted did have a couple of hobbies, however. One of them was wood carving. Give him the right tools, and he could craft beautiful and intricate things, like the sewing box he made as a gift for the 13-year-old daughter of a family friend. That was one of the things about him that would cause some raised eyebrows years later among investigators, who knew the Unabomber had mailed some of his explosive devices in handmade wooden compartments.

One of his other schoolboy pastimes was small-scale explosives. No major bursts, just the little ones that have always happened when you bring boys together with chemistry books. With Dale Eickelman, now a professor of anthropology and human relations at Dartmouth College, he used to "blow up weeds" in an open field. "Ted had the know-how of putting together things like batteries, wire leads, potassium nitrate and whatever," says Eickelman. "We would go to the hardware store, use household products and make these things you might call bombs. I remember once we created an explosion in a garbage can."

Wanda once apologized to the neighbors for the noise made by a homemade bomb her son had detonated. Kids remember him setting off a rocket behind the school that rose hundreds of feet into the air. Fascinated by little popping devices called "Atomic Pearls," Teddy had worked out how to make those too. In his senior year one went off in chemistry class when some kids asked him to provide them with the formula, then they botched the execution. The explosion blew out classroom windows. Classmates recall that he was suspended, but there is no record of it at his school.

Evergreen Park high graduate Margaret (Peg) Attridge Giroux remembers Teddy—or Ted, as he was increasingly called—as a "prankster" who had a crush on Joann Vincent De Young. One time he took an animal skin from the biology lab and put it in Joann's locker, Giroux recalls. On another occasion, he handed her a "letter bomb, a little wad of paper that exploded when you opened it. Like a firecracker, but not that powerful." Giroux remembers that Ted always had "a sly smile, like he was saying, 'I'm pulling one over on you.' "

Ted didn't clam up with everybody. Like many bright kids he could be more open sometimes around his elders. "People say that Ted didn't talk," says his neighbor O'Connell. "That wasn't true. If you talked to him, he would have a lot to say." Robert Rippey, who taught math and science at Evergreen Park High School, remembers a "wry" Ted Kaczynski. "I never thought of him as gloomy in any way. He was a clean-cut, nice kid." Rippey always gave him A's. "What made him special was the way he thought. From time to time, he'd go off and work on problems totally independent from what he was learning in class. He'd take a mathematical proof and find different ways of doing it, without any instruction from me. It's the hallmark of a truly penetrating mind."

"I think anyone you talked to who had worked with him would have expected nothing short of extraordinary success," said Lois Skillen, a high school guidance counselor who took him under her wing. "With some students, I have predicted their demise," she told the Chicago *Tribune*. "But with him, never." Ted's high school yearbook also shows him participating in four after-school clubs: math, biology, German and coins. Rippey remembers the boy's excitement at finding a rare copper penny in his pocket change, then happily selling it to his teacher for $75.

During Ted's freshman and sophomore years he joined the high school band, where schoolmates remember him working away at the trombone. Recollections of his talent vary. First-rate is one. Dutiful but uninspired is another. "He played well mechanically," recalls Jerome DeRuntz, who played baritone horn. "But it never sounded like music. He did not have a feel for music." Ever the proud parent, Ted Sr. was a dedicated band booster, recalls Daral DeNormandie, who worked on tag sales with him. "He was like a gentle soul, very much a gentleman," she says. "He was proud of Ted as can be. He was always talking about him skipping a grade and how intelligent he was. He was just a delight."

Even so, by high school Ted seemed deeply out of step with his classmates. Paul Jenkins, who taught Ted algebra in his freshman year and biology in his sophomore year, suggested to the Kaczynskis that he might skip two full grades. They resisted. Whatever his intellectual gifts, Ted had a lot of growing up to do. Already one year ahead of his peers, a two-year leap would land him among classmates who were three years older, physically and emotionally. But holding him back risked deepening his alienation. There was also the satisfaction that came from having a son who could race ahead of others in that way. They agreed to let him skip just his junior year.

That put Ted in the graduating class of 1958. Years earlier, while their high school was under construction, members of that class had begun their freshmen year in a church basement, where the end of classroom periods was marked by the ringing of a cowbell. "That experience made us very close-knit by the time we were seniors," recalls David Kaiser. Kay Jones Stritzel, a cheerleader who was one of Ted's classmates, says he acted like "a frightened puppy dog" whenever she approached him. Even she, at 5 ft. 7 in., towered over Ted, who "looked like a baby." If you talked to him, Kaiser says, Ted would just "turn away and mumble."

So in his senior year, like all the others, Ted didn't fit anywhere. The girls in gingham and headbands wouldn't date him, even if he could have worked up the nerve to ask them. The athletes who roared around in their tail-fin cars were more apt to ignore him than torment him. Even among the other brains, who were mostly two years older, he was the runt of the litter.

But in everything that bore upon the life of the mind he was king. By the time he graduated, he had been accepted to Harvard, a place the more ordinary students of Evergreen High could scarcely aim for, much less get to. But no one was really surprised when Ted was accepted there, anymore than they had been surprised that he was a National Merit finalist, one of five in the graduating class of 183.

It wasn't just that he was brilliant. He was brilliant in the world of numbers, which the cold war had suddenly given a whole new importance. At the start of senior year, in October 1957, the Soviet Union launched Sputnik, the first artificial earth satellite. Suddenly frightened by the prospect of falling behind in the space race—a contest that most people did not even know they were in a few months before—Americans were about to put their children through a crash course in the sciences. For the best and the brightest among them, there would be every opportunity, and not a little pressure, to concentrate on fields that would close the presumed science gap between the U.S. and the U.S.S.R. Teddy was already well along in his training. In one respect at least, he was the perfect specimen of what America needed.

If Teddy was ready. He was just 16, lacking even a driver's license, and he seemed in some ways much younger. There was no doubt that he was ready for the intellectual rigors of college. And the emotional ones? Maybe a life on his own would help to bring him out of his shell. His parents could only hope.

The Untenured Mathematician

The system needs scientists, mathematicians and engineers. It can't function without them. So heavy pressure is put on children to excel in these fields. —Manifesto, paragraph 115

When he arrived at Harvard, Ted Kaczynski did what he had done all his life at home: he ran to his room and shut the door. He was "the ultimate loner," remembered Keith Martin, who lived in the same freshman dorm. Decades later, after Kaczynski was arrested, Andrew Sihler, now a linguistics professor at the University of Wisconsin at Madison, tried to recall who this supposed classmate could be. "I took out my yearbook and said to myself, 'Oh, him.' "

Kaczynski had been accepted at Harvard when the school was in the midst of a long process of change and self-examination. The élite university was opening up to the new winners in the emerging American meritocracy. If his test scores were high enough, a boy from a Polish-American family of modest means could find himself crossing the same quadrangles where Cabots and Lowells used to walk. And where a few Kennedys still did.

But if Harvard was changing, Ted was not. As a freshman, he holed up in a first-floor room at 8 Prescott Street, a light-colored, framed, university residence that housed 15 undergraduates considered poor prospects for group living (most freshman lived two to four in a suite). The three years that followed he spent in the famous and formidable Eliot House, along the Charles River. The preppiest place on campus, Eliot to a large extent was a spill tank for the gene pool of the old Wasp ascendancy. Its legendary house master and philosopher king was professor John Finley, a classicist and the last word in gentlemen. For Kaczynski, a maladroit boy from nowhere in particular, Eliot House might as well have been Buckingham Palace.

It so happens he was assigned to a suite with five other underclassmen who also were outsiders of a kind. "We didn't choose to room together," said Michael D. Rohr, now a philosophy professor at Rutgers University. "I was assigned to a suite of people without roommates. They were mostly loners. One of them seemed more interested in insects than people." The rooms they occupied, the ones approached through the 'N' entry, were "the low-rent wing of Eliot House," said Patrick McIntosh, one of Kaczynski's suitemates. While the classic Harvard suite featured a living room with a fireplace, this "suite" was just a corridor lined by six bedrooms, a bathroom and a walk-in cedar closet that housed a telephone. As everybody knew, the rooms had once been the servant's quarters for the house master's quarters just below. "We felt like we were second class," said McIntosh. "Some of the preppies certainly made us feel that way whenever possible."

Martin, who shared the suite with Kaczynski, remembered him as a blur. "He would walk down the corridor in a forced-march pace and open his door and slam it. And that would basically be it. His goal was not to get stopped by anybody to talk." At a time when Harvard men were required to wear a coat and tie to meals, rumpled Kaczynski complied. But he almost always ate alone, usually at one of the corner tables. "I'd go to his table, and he would not say much," said McIntosh. "He'd smile furtively and leave before he was really finished."

Though he didn't talk much, a lot of people say, like the Cheshire Cat, he left behind his smile. That "great, shy smile" said Gerald Burns, another fellow student. "You should have seen his smile back then." But the other memory he left was a faint bad odor, like the stockyard smell that hung over his old neighborhood in Chicago. His room was filthy. "I swear it was 1 ft. or 2 ft. deep in trash," said McIntosh. "Underneath it all were what smelled like unused cartons of milk. We finally called the house master, who was aghast."

During senior year, McIntosh decided to bunk with Martin. That freed one bedroom, which the group used to create the common room their suite otherwise lacked. The boys moved in a TV, a stereo, a sofa and a few chairs. But Kaczynski never joined them for bull sessions or trips to the movies. While they gathered there, he locked himself away in his room. Sometimes they would ask him to play his trombone more quietly. Said McIntosh: "Why we didn't put two and two together and say this guy needs help, I don't know."

Kaczynski did well at Harvard, but not well enough to make the top of his class. He graduated in 1962, but not cum laude. He didn't write a senior thesis. After leaving, he maintained the same low profile. Since 1982, his mailing address in the Harvard alumni records has been 788 Banchat Pesh, Khadar Khef, Afghanistan. If he was ever there, that part of his life is still to be unearthed.

From Harvard he went on to graduate work in mathematics at the University of Michigan at Ann Arbor. There he made much the same impression as he had at Harvard. "I don't remember anything about him. I don't think I ever even saw him," said Alan Heezen, who spent most of the

1960s studying math at Michigan. "The math department was not very big in those days. I thought I knew everybody in the class, but I guess that I didn't."

Altogether the university had 25,000 students, a crowd where it was easy to get lost. Judging by the university archives, Kaczynski is someone who hardly existed. His name cannot be found in the Michigan yearbook for 1964, when he received his master's degree, nor 1967, when he was awarded his doctorate. He left behind an 80-page doctoral dissertation and some faculty records attesting to the fact that for three years, he served as a part-time teaching assistant. That paid him $2,350 annually.

During his first two years in Ann Arbor, he lived at the East Quadrangle Residence Hall, a vast, brick box that housed 1,100 men. For the next three, he moved to off-campus apartments within walking distance of his classes. Professor Peter Duren remembers Kaczynski as the student who used to show up at his real analysis course wearing a jacket and necktie. "It was unusual in those days," Duren said. The Kaczynski he knew had a passion for math. During lectures he often sat at a front desk, asking one question after another. But outside class the inquisitive student disappeared into himself. "If the topic was math, he was ready and willing to talk about it," said Duren. "He did not go out of his way to make social contact. But he didn't strike me as being pathological. People in math are sometimes a bit strange. It goes with creativity."

One other thing Duren remembered is that when solving problems in math, Kaczynski always offered "much more proof than was really needed." Years later, FBI investigators would note that the Unabomber on occasion built redunancies into his bombs, providing more initiators, for example, than the devices required.

Just as Harvard was changing when Kaczynski arrived

there, so was Michigan. The student movement of the 1960s was gaining momentum; civil rights and antiwar activism were becoming as common on campus as fraternity parties. In 1962, Students for a Democratic Society, which would become the most prominent campus radical group of the era, was founded 98 miles away in Port Huron, Michigan. Men and women studying math or science, like Kaczynski, found themselves under increasing pressure not to undertake work or research that might contribute to the Vietnam War effort.

In 1967, Allen Shields, Kaczynski's doctoral thesis adviser, was one of 60 math professors from around the country who signed an open letter to his colleagues calling on them to refuse involvement in Pentagon research. Published in the *Michigan Daily,* the campus student newspaper, it read in part: "We urge you to regard yourselves as responsible for the uses to which your talents are put. We believe this responsibility forbids putting mathematics in the service of this cruel war."

"There was a gradual loss of faith in institutions," said Michigan State University mathematics professor Joel Shapiro, who studied in the math department with Kaczynski. "And there was a lot of anger on the University of Michigan campus. The whole society was just polarized. Everyone was touched in one way or another by what was going on." Kaczynski, however, remained aloof. Unlike other students, who typically sought weekly sessions with their advisers, he did not meet regularly with his, preferring simply to turn in piles of neatly organized equations. "His strength was his independence," said Duren.

Kaczynski's specialty, "boundary functions," is an area that is familiar to mathematicians and arcane to everyone else. By graduate school, he had moved into a mathematical realm that was utterly removed from human concerns.

Elegant, if you have a taste for abstraction and know the language, but very detached. His doctoral dissertation was closely crafted and presented with carefully argued proof. One typical sentence reads this way: "If *f* is defined in *H*, then the set of curvilinear convergence of *f* is the set of all points *x* ε *X* such that there exists some arc at *x* along which *f* approaches a limit." And so on.

"There is no point in going into his dissertation," said Chia-Shun Yih, one of Kaczynski's thesis advisers, who barely remembers him. "It is advanced and abstract. There is no connection between the violence, the bombs and the work he did on his dissertation. None at all."

If the University of Michigan largely forgot Kaczynski, perhaps Kaczynski did not forget his alma mater. In the fall of 1985, one of the Unabomber's mail bombs went off there, at the home of James McConnell, a well-known professor of psychology and the author of a widely used textbook. The book-size package bomb was opened instead by his assistant, Nicklaus Suino, who sustained flesh wounds to his arms and upper body.

McConnell came to believe he had been targeted because the Unabomber hated one of his fields of research, behavior modification. Years after McConnell's death from a heart attack in 1990, the Unabomber's manifesto appeared to bear out those suspicions. Part of it was devoted to an attack on that same area of study. "The system will therefore be FORCED to use every practical means of controlling human behavior." But when Kaczynski became the chief Unabomber suspect, FBI investigators also began to wonder whether he had zeroed in on McConnell because he knew him, or at least knew of him, from the years when they were both at Michigan.

Toward the end of Kaczynski's years at Michigan, the world of his youth was disintegrating. In 1966, while Ted was finishing up his Ph.D., his brother David moved to New York City to start his freshman year at Columbia University, where he would eventually get a degree in English. His parents moved also, to the small town of Lisbon, Iowa. His father had taken a job there as a supervisor of the newly opened factory of a foam-cutting company, Cushion Pak Inc.

There the Kaczynskis became friends with a crowd of politically active Iowans and got involved in a local controversy over whether children from a nearby Amish community would be required to attend public school. The Kaczynskis became enamored of the Amish and their peaceable ways. Ted Sr. was especially intrigued by their rejection of modern technologies, a position he respected, even if he was not prepared to imitate it himself. "Kaczynski really admired the Amish, the way they lived," said Paul Carlsten, who was then a political-science professor at Iowa's Cornell College. "He saw how technology could subvert the world—just as the Amish did."

In 1968 the elder Kaczynskis moved again, this time to Lombard, Illinois, another suburb of Chicago, and Ted Sr. had a job nearby with another factory. In that year, the compressed forces of the decade suddenly detonated. At Columbia University, where David Kaczynski was a sophomore, the students took over the campus for a week in April. Martin Luther King and Robert Kennedy were assassinated. In France, students and workers nearly toppled the government. In Vietnam, the Viet Cong's Tet offensive made it plain to Americans that victory, if such a thing were possible at all, would be a long and bloody affair.

The elder Kaczynskis, active as they were in liberal causes, found themselves swept into the antiwar presidential candidacy of Senator Eugene McCarthy first in Iowa and then in Illinois, where they both joined the Lombard Democratic

Club (Wanda attended meetings until January 1996). It was a time when all the predicaments of the West boiled down to the word Vietnam, and "the war machine" was a metaphor for the perverse means by which America's industrial and scientific power might subvert democracy and subdue a small nation. When McCarthy spoke of how the best scientific minds were being applied to the service of illegitimate aims, Ted Sr. could only nod in agreement. That summer, at the Democratic Convention in Chicago, the system would appear to melt down before their eyes.

By that time, their eldest son had relocated to Berkeley, another center of the student revolt, but he had not signed up as a soldier in the revolution. He was on his way to a tenured post in the math department, considered by many to be one of the most prestigious in the world. If Ted Kaczynski had wanted it, his skills could have put him in line for a number of private-sector careers that relied upon numbers: aircraft, computers, financial markets. Instead he was pursuing an academic career. After getting his doctorate, he had been hired as an assistant professor of mathematics on a two-year contract that had commenced in the fall of 1967.

The offer required that he teach two undergraduate courses, number systems and introduction to the theory of sets, and two for grad students, general topology and function spaces. "We hired about 10 [assistant professors] a year then," recalled professor emeritus John W. Addison Jr., who was department chairman during Kaczynski's years there. "On average, about one out of three would have got tenure."

Kaczynski stood a good chance of being one of them. Since 1964, he had published three mathematical papers with typically abstruse names: "Another Proof of Wedderburn's Theorem," "Boundary Functions for Functions Defined in a Disk," "On a Boundary Property of

Continuous Functions." While he was at Berkeley, he would publish three more papers. Whatever they were called, it was an accomplishment that would place him well along on the tenure track. An offer could be expected within four to six years of the time he started work.

After he was arrested, everyone would describe Kaczynski's handwriting as meticulous. Childlike would be a better word for the lettering of his faculty biography, the data sheet he provided to Berkeley three days before Christmas 1966. The letters are widely spaced and so painstakingly drawn they look like penmanship samples in a grade-school writing pad. As for information, Kaczynski didn't offer much. One line of the form requested: "Use the following space for biographical data that you desire to have become a part of your official University of California records." He left it blank.

Kaczynski lived in a small apartment at 2628A Regent Street. In a community offering everything from gingerbread Victorians to Arts and Crafts bungalows, his homely stucco residence was the kind of place in which you might expect to find a penniless student, not an assistant professor on his way up in the world. Faculty, even the newer ones, favored the hilly north side of the campus, with its views of the campus clock tower and, further in the distance, the skyline of downtown San Francisco and the Golden Gate Bridge.

The area where Kaczynski settled was flat, viewless and crowded with students. Many people preferred it, however, because Telegraph Avenue ran through the neighborhood like a bolt of lighting. His 15-minute walk to campus took him along all its jagged edges, offering a full dose of the Berkeley carnival. In those days, Telegraph was thronged with long-haired students and street people, dressed in dashikis and ponchos, army surplus and tie-dyes. Life was a costume party, and everybody was invited. It was here you found the shops, cafés and three locally famous bookstores, Moe's, Cody's and Shakespeare & Company. Sidewalk vendors peddled hash pipes and handmade jewelry. In the air, there was incense and marijuana smoke. And music: maybe *After Bathing at Baxter's,* a trippy album by the Jefferson Airplane, maybe *Anthem of the Sun* by the Grateful Dead, who were then still a dustball menagerie and not the institution they would become, or maybe the leftist anthems of Phil Ochs, such as *I Ain't Marchin' Anymore.*

That title was a double-edged joke at the time. Everybody was marchin'. And all roads led to Sproul Plaza. The university's sunlit public forum was the white-hot center of the Big Bang. In 1964 it had seen the birth of the Free Speech Movement, a primal episode of what would be the worldwide student upheaval. By the time Kaczynski arrived at Berkeley, hardly a day went by without a campus demonstration. Most of them started on the steps of Sproul Hall, the main administration building. Classes were routinely canceled because students, too busy protesting, failed to show up. Kaczynski would always show up.

In fact, there is no evidence that Kaczynski was ever involved in any political activity. Still, he would have had to be deaf, dumb and blind not to absorb the message of the student protesters. Certainly the Unabomber did: the manifesto both parrots and pillories much of the leftist rhetoric from this period about freedom, repression, social control and high technology. It also notes that "in any event no one denies that children tend, on average, to hold social attitudes similar to those of their parents." The raucous showdowns in Berkeley had their genteel counterpart in Lisbon, where Ted's mother sewed headbands for the peace candidate's youthful supporters.

Heading for one of his classes in Campbell Hall, where the math department was based at the time, Kaczynski would run a gauntlet of recruitment tables and leafleteers, pacifists, Trotskyists, Hare Krishnas, Black Panthers. The world itself was up for grabs. It could seem sometimes that all of the pieces were being thrown into the air. It only remained to see how they might be reassembled.

Or how the fallout could be avoided altogether. If Kaczynski wanted peace and quiet, there was a bit of that too. Scattered around the surprisingly pastoral Berkeley campus were unexpected pockets of tranquillity. Just outside the back door of Campbell Hall he could walk down 26 steps, pass under an old arch inscribed in Latin and find himself in Faculty Glade, a grove of redwoods. Even now, it remains a place where you can almost imagine shutting out the clatter of history. But not quite. The streets of Berkeley are not all that far away. From there he would have to dip back eventually into the crowd heading for Telegraph.

And back to the classes he hated to face. The boy who could never talk to anyone had no gifts as a teacher. Every year Berkeley students evaluated their instructors in ratings that were printed in a supplement to the college catalog. If Kaczynski were a Broadway show, he would have closed on opening night: "Kaczynski's lectures were useless and right from the book … He showed no concern for the students … He absolutely refuses to answer questions by completely ignoring the students." Undergrads are a tough jury. A lot of faculty fared just as badly. But by now, this notice sounds like the Kaczynski everybody knew. Or didn't know.

His last act was on Jan. 20, 1969. The attention of most people that day was focused on Washington, and the inauguration of a new President, Richard Nixon, the man Kaczynski's father could not abide, the man about whom thousands of passionate young people had said, "If he's elected, I'm leaving the country." On that day, Ted abruptly tendered his resignation. In the two-line note in which he gave the news to math department chairman John Addison, he didn't offer any explanation. Later he told people that he was leaving the field of mathematics altogether. For what? He didn't know.

While some academics leave their posts because they decide they are not going to get tenure, that was not the case for Kaczynski. Addison and Calvin Moore, the department vice chairman, tried to talk him into staying. "Dr Kaczynski has decided to leave the field of mathematics," Addison said in a March 2, 1969, letter to Walter D. Knight, dean of the College of Letters and Sciences, in which he informed him of Kaczynski's "sudden and unexpected resignation." He further told Knight that he and Moore had "tried to persuade him to reconsider his decision but [had] not been successful." Certainly Kaczynski was not the only defector from academics and the sciences in this era. "It was not uncommon," recalled Addison. "One of my advisees went and lived on a farm and did carpentry."

Later Kaczynski's old thesis adviser, Allen Shields, heard that his well-regarded former student had bolted from a job that promised a great deal. Puzzled and concerned, he wrote to Addison, who replied that Kaczynski had told him he was not sure what he was going to do. "He was very calm and relaxed about it on the outside."

Addison added, "Kaczynski seemed almost pathologically shy, and, as far as I know, he made no close friends in the department. Efforts to bring him more into the swing of things had failed."

Montani Semper Liberi

Freedom means having power; not the power to control other people but the power to control the circumstances of one's own life. —Manifesto, paragraph 94

Most people spend some time in the wilderness, one way or another. It is a place one must pass through or perish. Grief is a wilderness, and failure, and regret, and fear. This is where the tests are most private, where success is measured by survival, where rules and rewards are self-imposed, where time loses its formal rhythms. Ted spent 25 years alone in the woods and often had to ask his neighbors what day it was.

The Kaczynski boys may have had a classic '50s suburban childhood, but they also learned from their father how to fend for themselves in the wild, the proper way to eat a porcupine; and as men, both sons sought out places where no one would find them, no one could bother them or judge them or hurt them. Two Ivy League men went off to live in America's last lonely outposts, in shacks with no driveways, no wires, no water. For David, the escape was partial; six months a year in the 1980s he drove a suburban Chicago bus; the other six he spent in a fugitive corner of Texas, in the powdery shadow of the Christmas Mountains, living at first in a 4-ft. hole dug in the ground, covered with tarps or corrugated metal, until he built his primitive cabin. He went there to read and write and think, and there eventually came a day when he was willing to leave. By 1990 he had returned to civilization, shaved his beard, married the girl of his dreams and found a way to do some good, helping runaway kids. For Ted, the retreat began sooner and lasted longer. He went to Montana in 1971 to live on 1.4 acres he and David had bought together, and, apart from a few wanderings and urban interludes he stayed there until the day they came to arrest him. Something must have perished in the wilderness.

Maybe, when he first set off for the woods, there was still hope left in him about the redemptive power of a purer life, some lessons he could learn and even share. There was surely despair as well, hope's twin, but soon after he retreated to Montana, Ted still sought to issue his warnings about the modern world through argument and reason. He began pounding out letters and articles through the long, unpopulated days, articles about what a bad idea it was to fund scientific research, particularly in genetics. He hoped to see one essay published and widely discussed, a catalyst for a new organization of like-minded souls. He sent it off to columnists around the country, musing about the dangers of technology, of what mechanical and mathematical geniuses like him had made of the end of the 20th century. But no one seemed to be listening.

If Ted had brought all his powers of calculus to the question of where to make his stand, he could not have chosen more exquisitely than the high country of western Montana, where the state flower is the bitterroot and people hold festivals in honor of the turkey buzzard. It is a place where a man suspicious of people and progress and technology would have plenty of time to practice what the Unabomber preached. Where the southern end of the 125-mile-long Swan Range meets the tip of the Scapegoat Wilderness is a place where, if you have no light at all when the sun goes down, there is nothing to do but listen to the lodgepole and the ponderosa and the tamaracks sway and bend and aspire as the prevailing westerlies try to climb the Continental Divide.

Lincoln, Montana—little more than a gathering of stores and scrappy homes astride a breathtakingly beautiful two-lane state highway—is a town that sits as close as you can get to the backbone of the western hemisphere and still have a post office and a library within walking distance. There are seven motels, nine restaurants, five churches, one taxidermist, no espresso bars, no hospital. Lincoln sits about 90 minutes west of Great Falls and east of Missoula, just below the largest stretch of untouched, unplugged, unbroken wilderness in the continental U.S. The names are as forbidding as the terrain: inside the Great Bear and the Scapegoat wilderness areas—which together with the Bob Marshall area constitute a landmass larger than Rhode Island—there are no cars, no roads, no buildings beyond a shelter or two, and on any given day more grizzly bears than people. There is a high tolerance for subdued eccentricity. A town with few lawns could hardly expect conformity.

But the world Ted fled chased him even here: western Montana along the Divide became a refuge for many others, known as the "blow-ins"—Californians crowded out of the Pacific paradise, rich Easterners and Washington State retirees, who arrived to build lavish log cabins with whirlpool baths and water softeners and heated garages, scalping the mountainsides to clear enclaves with great views of the Swan and Mission mountain ranges. They didn't work in the lumberyards or the local beef-jerky plant, but on their laptops and modems, if at all. And once they came, of course, especially by the late 1980s, they too wanted all growth to stop, which put them at odds with the folks who had long lived around Lincoln and Ovando and Seeley Lake. Many nailed black-

and-white hand-painted signs to their doors that read THIS FAMILY SUPPORTED BY TIMBER-INDUSTRY DOLLARS.

Ted came long before the big rush, and his cabin had no panoramic view. If he hiked just a ways up Mount Baldy, out his backyard, so to speak, he could see the snowcapped mountain peaks of the west side of the Rockies in one direction and the Blackfoot River Valley in the other. But all around him in the surrounding Helena National Forest, he could also see great white patches of snow marking the logging clear-cuts, a mangled landscape of stumps and scars.

If the aim was privacy and anonymity, no questions asked, he also did the math perfectly. In his book *Out West,* Dayton Duncan noted that the state is the size of Maine, New Hampshire, Vermont, Pennsylvania, Rhode Island, Connecticut, New York, Maryland and Delaware all rolled into one. Take those states, empty them of all the people who live there and replace them with just the residents of Hartford, Connecticut, then add the country's biggest mountains, richest trout streams, majestic forests. That's Montana. Ted lived smack up against the most pristine tract the Big Sky State can boast, a stretch of mountains so impassable and forbidding you can get around it by only two routes more than 150 miles apart: Route 2 along the border with Canada and Route 200.

He was able to get by on a few hundred dollars a year, but it helped to be in a living grocery store. He grew vegetables next to his house, mainly parsnips and potatoes and carrots that would struggle through Montana's short growing season and winter over in the root cellar; the snows can come in September and linger into May. For fertilizer he used his own waste, always recycling. He fought the deer and the rabbits that dug through the garden's chicken-wire fence; for a neighbor he especially liked, he might save his best seeds, complete with growing instructions.

The forests around his home teemed with all manner of rodents and beaver, elk and deer and mountain lions. He hunted squirrels and rabbits, which he'd roast in a pit outside. Occasionally he went deer hunting with Glen Williams, who owned a weekend log cabin on the adjoining property. "One time, I was hunting by myself," Williams remembered, "and he'd just killed a deer, and we got to visiting, and I asked him if he ever killed an elk. Naw, he couldn't afford to buy a tag [elk-hunting permit]. I says, 'I got an idea.' Because he traveled those mountains like a deer, himself. 'I'll take you to Lincoln, I'll pay for the tag, and if you get an elk, you go to the nearest phone, call me collect, and I'll be up there with a four-wheel-drive the next morning.' And he did that. So we got an elk that year. He killed one, called me, I went up there, we got it out and we split it, 50-50. It was way back, about seven miles back in there. We had to go way back in there on a snowmobile and bring it out. We were in there three days gettin' it out."

Williams doesn't think that Ted ever used the hides from deer he killed. In fact, he often offered to take the hides to Great Falls, to sell them to Weissman's hide and scrap-iron business, and then give Ted the money the next weekend. One time, Williams took Ted's deer hide to Pacific Hide & Fur. The company was offering a pair of deerskin gloves as trade for a raw hide, in lieu of cash payment of $3. So Williams decided to take the gloves, and if Ted didn't want them, he'd give Ted the three bucks. He took the gloves up to Ted and offered him the choice. "He didn't know what to do! Boy, he had a heck of a time deciding! Finally, he said he'd take the gloves, they looked pretty good."

The winters were hard on the diet. He would go out into

the woods at night with his .22-cal. rifle, looking for the tracks of the snowshoe hares that foraged at night and relaxed during the day. If it snowed a bit before dawn, the trail was clear; but if it snowed in the evening, the tracks became tangled as the hares doubled back and crossed each other. They were hard to spot, camouflaged white in the snow. Only their black eyes and the tips of their ears gave them away. Ted had to become a very quiet, very careful, very patient hunter.

Summer, on the other hand, was a banquet. Night comes to the Swan and Blackfoot valleys as late as 10, not slowly or all of a sudden but in a parade of almost frenzied animal behavior. Around 8 the temperature starts to drop, which produces just the right change in air pressure so that the mayfly larvae, nymphing in the rocks of the Blackfoot's tributaries, begin to hatch and sprout paper-thin translucent wings, right on top of the water. With so many appetizers appearing as if by magic, the fish start to jump at the bugs. When the fish rise, out come the ospreys and the sea hawks and the bald eagles that make their homes along the lakes and rivers; they have been waiting for a seafood dinner. As the light fades, they concede the airspace to the bats, who don't want fish but are looking for the bugs and are so blind they sometimes dive for the fish. By 10 the fugue is over and the wind picks up and the sun is gone and the owls start hooting, and the loon's eerie call syncopates as the deer wait for the fishermen to leave so they can go feed by the water's edge.

Ted built his cabin out of plywood and rolled roofing paper five miles or so out of town, hunched down in the trees less than a mile from Stemple Pass Road, near Poorman's Creek. Half the year the approach to his door was a block of hard-packed snow and ice, the ground speckled with fresh, Army-green elk scat clustered like small eggs. He included two windows, each a foot square, but no electricity, no plumbing, no clocks, no phone, no outhouse—he used a bucket—only a cot, a table and chair, a Coleman stove and three locks on the door. Out back was a platform with a 5-gal. bucket hanging over it, which probably served as an occasional shower.

There was a mailbox with his name on it clumped among a bouquet of them about a mile from his property, but apart from the occasional letter from his family and some scholarly journals, it didn't get much use. "He's one of the few people who doesn't get credit-card solicitations," a postal worker said. One day Don Shannon, minister at the Lincoln Baptist Church, came upon Ted in the post office, sorting through the junk and the flyers that people had thrown away. He put the piles in his pack and carried them home. Ted instructed his family to use a secret code when they had something "urgent and important" to tell him: if they drew a line in red under the stamp, he would be sure to open the letter. Otherwise he might just ignore it. Sometimes he returned their letters with the grammar corrected. When his father killed himself in 1990, Ted found a letter with the red line in his mailbox. He wrote back in protest: his father's death, he said, did not warrant the urgent code. He did not go to the funeral.

Ted's closest year-round neighbor was a man named Leland Mason, who used to own the beef-jerky plant and lived 300 yds. away. They didn't speak much—"mostly very short, six-word sentences," Mason said, and he visited the cabin only once, around Christmastime some years ago. "I delivered a plate of cookies and candy that the wife fixed up for the neighbors. I took his to him," he said. "That was the only time I was actually at his house. He just opened the door, didn't invite me in. Thanked me for the stuff, we exchanged Christmas greetings, that was it." Mason marveled at the man's endurance. "I was surprised that he could withstand the winters, whenever they got bitter cold."

Of Ted's comings and goings, Mason recalled, "He'd be gone for a week, maybe two, but not real regularly." He could hitch a ride to town, sometimes with the mailman, and catch a bus into Helena, where he stayed at the Park Hotel, on a street called Last Chance Gulch. "When he first started coming here in 1980, I had a little uneasiness," Jack McCabe, the owner, told the Los Angeles *Times.* "Was he going to run right down to the bar and get drunk and then pick up a girl and try to sneak her up here? I don't tolerate that. After a couple of times, I forgot about him. He was always quiet and polite. Didn't smoke or drink, didn't do anything. Wouldn't even talk."

Fourteen dollars a night bought a room with a sink and a chance of catching the morning bus to Butte or Missoula, and from there the Greyhound south to Utah, west over the mountains to the coast, anywhere he pleased. Stacey Fredrickson, a ticket agent at the bus station in Butte, noticed him whenever he passed through. "I saw him numerous times," she said. "He was strange looking, dirty. He looked like someone who should be a transient, ride freight trains, not a Greyhound." When he passed through Helena he often stopped at Aunt Bonnie's used bookstore to replenish his library for a pittance. Most paperbacks went for 25¢. He mainly bought old, obscure politics and sociology books, some math and science. "We have a varied clientele, anyway, so Ted didn't really stand out," said owner Anna Haire. "All types come in here."

Sometimes weeks would pass without his being spotted outside the cabin or heading into town for supplies. For a while he wobbled around on a bike that wouldn't have fetched $5 at a flea market. Then one day Dan Rundell, a 20-year resident of Lincoln, noticed him struggling with it and gave him another one built out of spare parts. "He had to be strong to ride that thing up there," said Rundell. Ted would pedal into town, pants tucked into his boots, a yellow flag warning motorists, to the grocery store and the library. He would load up on staples, Spam and canned tuna, carrying just what he could wedge in his backpack and saddlebags.

Sometimes he would stop in at 2C's Treasures second-hand store to sell owner Cindy Davis whatever he had scavenged; she paid him 50¢ for light bulbs. "He'd take what I gave him and seemed happy. I start low with my offers and he'd take it. I never knew his name until this came out."

Often, local people would drop off stuff left over from garage sales. She set up a clothing rack and table for anyone who needed it, no charge. Ted eagerly took some donated clothes. Davis recalled that he once bought a bag of books for $1. Just before she closed the store, she gave Ted a manual typewriter that she thinks may not have worked very well. She remembered Ted's coming into the launderette, changing his clothes in the rest room, washing and drying the clothes he wore in, then changing back into the clean clothes. "There was a few years there, he wasn't so raggedy and woolly lookin'," neighbor Williams said. "He'd shave there for a few years. I think in the early '80s he started lettin' his beard grow. I remember one time he had a tooth knocked out or pulled out: he went to the dentist and had a filling made for it. He kind of took care of himself for a few years there. But I don't think he bought any clothes for a long time."

He would stop at Becky Garland's Town and Country variety store for small notions, needles and thread, socks and fishing tackle, and she would kid him about the toll on his appearance taken by riding a bike with no rear fender. "In this kind of weather, he would be covered in mud from head to toe. I gave him a bad time, I razzed him, I teased him a bit. On days like this, it was that big mud stripe up the back of his coat that cracked me up," she recalled. "I got a smile from him. You know he had a sense of humor, and it was pretty dry. There was a certain twinkle in his eye when you made him laugh."

Garland was one of the few local residents who seemed to break through to Ted; maybe they shared concerns about the environment, particularly the debate over building a huge gold mine by digging 980 tons of rock out of the Blackfoot River Valley. He once asked her advice about getting a job, maybe with some environmental-research outfit. He brought Becky a letter; he didn't mail it, he handed it to her, a gesture of quiet explanation, like a letter of introduction he had written himself. Ted told what it had been like always being the youngest in his class, missing his childhood, going off to college so quickly. "It was like he was trying to explain why he was socially clumsy, shy," Becky said. "He wanted me to know a little bit about it. He was trying to write on paper what he couldn't express in person. Why he reached out to me as someone to talk to, I have no idea."

He talked of his parents' desire that he get a good education, about a love gone wrong, about the events that had shaped him. "He wrote about things that hurt him in his heart really bad, so that I would understand his feelings, that he was human."

As for that love that went bad, that may have soured Ted on the idea of coming down from his mountain once and for all. In 1978 he needed to earn some money, so he moved back to live with his family in Lombard, Illinois, where his father and David were both working at Foam Cutting Engineers, Inc., a foam-rubber plant in Addison. He developed a crush on a female supervisor named Ellen Tarmichael and saw her socially. Tarmichael has since said publicly there was no romance. They dined once at an unidentified suburban restaurant, she told a crowded press conference. Then, "approximately two weeks later we went to pick apples and returned to his parents' home, where we baked an apple pie. It was on that occasion that I informed Ted that I did not wish to see him further on a social basis." Said a current employee: "The way I understand it, the only thing they had in common was the air they breathe."

But Ted didn't see it that way. He began writing rude limericks about her and hanging them around the plant for all to see and making loud, crude remarks about her. "I understand these were pretty rotten things to say about someone," said the employee. "It must have really hurt her, but she is a strong person." Most of the workers just dismissed him as "a brainy type in the midst of regular working-class guys."

But David, who was Ted's supervisor, told him to leave the woman alone. Ted walked over and slapped a limerick on his machine. So David fired him. Ted went and got a job at a restaurant-machinery plant, where he worked until the spring of 1979. Then he quit and went back to Montana, alone. Family members say Ted wrote a letter saying he had considered harming Tarmichael; she says she never received any correspondence.

Over the years Ted made few friends but few enemies either among his taciturn, tolerant neighbors. Occasionally he would even join a card game. He talked differently from most of the locals, even snobbily, some said, so they mistook him for an artist, invented a romantic past. But he couldn't make friends with the dogs. "All the dogs hated him," recalled Rick Christian, a longtime local. "They'd chase him, bark at him, growl at him when he walked or rode his bike. I had to call them off him." Mason's dogs didn't care for Ted much either. "When I first moved up here, I had a pair of Irish setters, and they would follow him from one corner of my property to the other. They would just raise Cain every time he went, both going and coming."

"He's not the only recluse we have who is strange," said Karen Potter at the Blackfoot Market. "There are people stranger than him." For example, there were the "Sauerkraut Boys," so named because they live out on Sauerkraut Creek. A motley mix of Vietnam vets and once homeless transients, they all moved to a patch of land up in the hills after one of them inherited some money. They didn't much care for visitors, but they did come into town to drink, get in bar fights and ram their cars into trees.

Ted was more inclined to keep to himself, reading, gardening, writing letters. The librarians would special order books for him and save back issues of *Omni* and *Scientific American*. "He liked stuff that was really off the wall and hard to get," said library volunteer Beverly Coleman. "A lot of stuff he wanted was out of print, and a lot of stuff he wanted was in the original. He didn't want to read the English translations." In the back of the library he could find research books, like an *Encyclopedia of Associations,* a *Who's Who* and postal guides from all over the country. There were no national papers, but he did read the local weekly called *Western Spurs*. One week in 1987, the editors issued a challenge to their readers: to "circle with a colored pen spelling, bad grammar, obvious goofs and return your marked copy to us no later than 7 days following publication." The May 21 issue of *Western Spurs* announced, "Ted Kaczynski of Stemple Pass Rd. is the winner of the first Pobody's Nerfect contest. Ted identified (gulp!) 147 undisputed errors. Since this is a one-time-winner only contest, we hope you all will continue to critique our paper and perhaps be the winner next time. Thanks, Ted (we think)."

For most Lincoln residents who don't work for the Forest Service permanently or operate a year-round business, it is a seasonal economy. Some men work on forest-fire crews or building construction in the summer, then maybe guide snowmobile tours in the winter. Women wait tables, tend bar and clean motel rooms—mostly part time. A local plant manufactures Montana Monster Cookies.

Ted got a job early on at a local sawmill, peeling the bark off logs. He quit after one day. He worked for a little while in 1974 at the six-pump Kibbey Korner Truck Stop in Raynesford, but that too soon went awry. He wrote to his boss, Joe Visocan—whom he addressed as "you big fat con man"—"You gave me this big cock-and-bull story about how much money I could make selling tires and all that crap ... 'The sky's the limit' and so forth ... If you had been honest with me I would not have taken the job in the first place."

Ted recently approached Jay Potter, owner of the Blackfoot Market, about getting a job as a grocery check-out clerk. Potter said he didn't have an application handy or any openings at the time. "He'd have to take a bath if he worked here," said Potter.

"Ted was a hard worker," Leland Mason said, "but he was not a smart worker. Short on common sense. Which is typical of a highly educated guy. He was not mechanically inclined. He had one old pickup truck one summer and drove it until it quit on him. It was just a minor thing that was wrong with the truck, but he didn't know how to fix it. He just let it sit up there until somebody bought it from him. It only cost the new owner $25 for the part, and he put it in. Ted had a hard time with everyday mechanical things." Ted tried a chain saw for woodcutting for a while, but that experiment with technology ended in frustration too.

So there was never quite enough to live on. His parents sent an occasional $100 for Christmas, a birthday, but when money became desperately tight, he turned to David. His younger brother provided not only some crucial infusions of cash but also the only real friendship Ted seemed to sustain during his years in the woods. As confidant, correspondent, confessor, Ted chose an uneducated 68-year-old Mexican farmhand named Juan Sánchez Arreola, who entered the brothers' lives because David too had decided he needed an escape hatch.

In the early 1980s, after his brother had already spent a decade largely alone, David set off to find his wilderness. He went to another extreme, the arid Christmas Mountains in West Texas, a stark valley lately baked brown by a drought that drove off the populations of deer, cougar and birds, leaving the snakes and lizards behind. The Spanish conquistadors called the territory *despoblado*—unpopulated. Today, beyond the county seat of Alpine, Brewster County has one person for every two square miles.

The gentle mountains, escarpments and mesas, dulled by the lack of moisture and the dust storms, frame a vast expanse that is one of the most remote regions in the Lower 48. David bought 40 acres on Nine Point Draw, part of the Terlingua Ranch development in the Trans-Pecos, located about 40 miles north of the Mexican border. He was 20 miles from the nearest paved road, five hours from the nearest airport. In the beginning, there was no path or driveway to his lair, so visitors had to make the last 200 yds. on foot through mesquite and greasewood, no easy walk considering the diamondbacks and lizards residing in the underbrush. The ranch sprawled across 200,000 acres of desert and rolling hills, framed by three mountain ranges and bordered in part by Big Bend National Park. What pass for homes are sometimes just encampments, houses stapled together out of trailers and old car bodies.

The town of Terlingua is really a border colony of some 125 recluses, mountain men, assorted eccentrics and hardshell tourists. They while away long days and nights—brutally hot in the summers—holed up in cabins, guzzling beer in dives along the Rio Grande, rafting, painting, writing, communing with nature. No daily newspapers make it this far down into the wild. You can rarely even get a station on the radio dial. There's no doctor, dentist or bank, virtually no stores or groceries. "I'm sure that we've got fugitives living out there," observed computer programmer Alan Baker, taking in the sweeping expanse of mountains from his doorway. "All of us that are here are a bit unusual."

"To come here, you have to want to get away from something," agreed Barbara Ellington, another property owner. "David was a survivor and a loner. He'd come into a store, buy his supplies and then you didn't see him again for weeks." David too was resourceful about his sustenance. A strict vegetarian, he ate berries from the abundant cacti and skinned and fried up the large cactus pads in a skillet. For a time, he cooked over an open fire, then used a propane stove on which he would heat his beans and rice and fashion his meatless chili. "He lived off the land," said his friend Lucille Muchmore. "To live out here, you've got to be self-reliant, and David was especially so. He would never muddy a water hole or break tree branches or kill a rabbit." Once when he was hiking he picked up an old Indian flint knife; when he learned that it would be considered an artifact and that he was wrong to move it, he hiked 40 miles back to return it where he found it.

Unlike his brother, David did not cut himself off from other people during his half-year sabbaticals; he just used his time and chose his friends very carefully. Many nights were spent around a campfire, talking about serious books, philosophy, Gandhi, Thoreau, the solitary life. David seemed almost ashamed that he savored the company. "He said, 'My brother's out there in Montana being a hermit. He's doing a lot better than me,' " recalled his friend Joe La Follette. "Then we had this discussion about what a hermit was. He envied his brother for the purity of it. He was looking up to his brother, the man who went off and divorced himself from the world in a very Thoreauvian way. I think in Dave's eyes his brother was up there figuring out some new math or something."

But both brothers seem to have shared some powerful ideas about what was going wrong: during those long, late desert talks, La Follette recalled, David would argue passionately about the threat of science and progress and materialism. "He worried about computers and other technology and what it would do to humanity. We both worried about the destruction of mankind from too much emphasis on technology." La Follette was so caught up in the arguments that he wrote a novel, never published, about an alienated Berkeley professor at war with the modern world. He called it *Phobia.*

After a while, David upgraded his hole in the ground. With the help of some Mexican friends he built an 8-ft. by 24-ft. cabin nearby, lighted by candles and hurricane lamps. Unlike Ted's mountain hideout, you could see David's place from miles away, a tiny cream-colored structure with a glistening metal roof. This was how he came to meet Juan Sánchez, who would cross the border from Ojinaga to work as a handyman on the ranch. David helped him get a green card; Juan taught him Spanish. And through David, Juan came to know of the other brother in the woods, thus launching what became a long correspondence between Ted and Juan.

The two men never met, despite many letters devoted to planning visits. But Juan did meet the Kaczynski parents, which may have given him some clues about his reclusive friend and pen pal. In 1987 Wanda and Theodore Kaczynski drove from Chicago to the desert to be with their younger son; at the sight of the accommodations, Ted senior decided to check into a motel. "The mama and papa told him he was loco," recalled Sánchez. David apparently revealed that Ted was not on good terms with their parents and "didn't want to have anything to do with them. David once told me that Teodoro called his mother a dog," Sánchez said. "It is very sad when someone doesn't love his parents." Around 1990, Ted said he had developed a heart arrhythmia; he cut off most contact with his family, telling them that the anger he felt when he heard from them was too stressful.

Juan, on the other hand, was able to provide Ted the friendship he never had, through the medium he had come to prize: the mail. For seven years Ted wrote about his life to the Mexican farmhand. The letters, in meticulously grammatical Spanish that Ted learned from books, came on three-ring-binder paper, addressed to "my dear and appreciated friend." He called himself Teodoro Kaczynski and tried hard to offer encouragement and support. In a November 1988 letter, he mentioned that he and his brother had read about a millionaire who gave money to people in need and offered to find the millionaire's address through his local library. "My brother and I will write to this guy to see if he can help you," Ted wrote, "but of course he can't help everybody. However, it wouldn't do any harm to write him. Who knows? It's possible he'll help you."

Juan's greatest concern was with bringing his wife Rosario and his three children into the country, but he was having trouble with immigration officials. Ted sympathized, and his disgust with authority figures of all sorts bleeds through his missives. "It angers me and shames me that those merciless and lying officials want to take away your pension," he wrote in May 1994. "They should live up to their promises. But it is not surprising that government officials do not live up to their promises, because they are either stupid and incompetent, or they are liars who twist the law to be able to commit any injustice. Well, keep me abreast of what happens with these matters of immigration and your pension, so that I can know how things are going."

Along with the anger comes the regret. "Although what the officials are doing is a great injustice," Ted wrote to his friend, "consider that your fortune is not all bad, because you have a wife and three children and all are healthy. Even though you have to endure these difficulties, you will probably overcome them in the end, and your children will thrive and someday they will have children of their own. I wish I had a wife and children! Nevertheless, I know these things are very painful for you. Even though I can do nothing for you now, I never forget you; instead, I think of you and your problems often, and perhaps someday I can help you in one way or another. But I do not have a lot of hope that I can visit you at Christmastime. Things are very bad for me. I still do not have work, and without work there is no money, and without money there is no bus ticket."

The letters chart a slow decline. "I am poorer than ever," he wrote in 1995, "but I am in very good health, and that is more important than anything. As to my poverty, I have $53.01 exactly, barely enough to stave off hunger this winter without hunting rabbits for their meat. But with the rabbit meat and a little flour and other things that I have put away, also a few dried vegetables from my little garden, I will get through the winter very well. And when the spring comes, perhaps I will have better luck with work and money, so that I can visit you. We will see."

By this time Juan had become a surrogate father to both sons; David even asked the older man to try to help his big brother, thinking that if anyone could get through to Ted, it was this one distant, invisible friend. "Juan, give some advice to Teodoro," Juan recalled David's saying. "You are an older man, give some advice." But Juan knew that was little use. "Teodoro wrote me last year, saying, 'If you want to be my friend, don't give me advice.' "

Along with about 50 letters over the years, Ted also sent his friend a bit of his handiwork: a carved wooden cylinder, stained and painted with vines and berries, hollowed out with a cap, rather like a pencil case—or a pipe bomb. He sent it one Christmas, bearing in Latin the motto *Montani Semper Liberi:* Mountain Men Are Always Free. He ended the letter with a benediction: "May God bless you and all your family."

Last fall Juan offered to send Ted $200 for the bus fare to come to Mexico. Ted wrote back that maybe, when the snow melted and spring came, he could come for a visit. There is still hope in the letters, glossy dreams, but also anger and fear of starvation, job rejections, too little money, nowhere to turn. It is not hard to imagine the mind of a hopeful man desperate to make the world a better place and resorting to the most despairing, desperate means to do so.

By the time spring came, Ted was on his way to jail. "I'm not anyone to judge him," said Sánchez. "Only God can do that. If I could talk to Teodoro now, I would tell him he is still my friend. If he writes me and asks me to come visit him in jail, I'll go. Now that I am old, I need my friendships more than ever."

As for David, he eventually left the wilderness. He found what he needed there, including a way out. By 1990 he had decided to marry an old friend; Juan taught him how to write love letters. Under the bright stars of the high desert nights, his friend Mary Ann Dunn gave him dancing lessons. He wired his cabin for a computer. The long hair and beard ended up on a cutting-room floor.

A Pattern Emerges

Almost everyone will agree that we live in a deeply troubled society. —Manifesto, paragraph 6

The parcel had plainly gone astray. Marked with a handwritten address, a return address and ten $1 Eugene O'Neill stamps, there it sat on the morning of May 26, 1978, baking beneath the sun in a parking lot at the downtown Chicago campus of the University of Illinois. Finally, a considerate stranger picked it up and, perhaps reasoning that the sender had not meant to post it quite yet, phoned the name on the return label. "I found your package," she told Buckley Crist, a materials science and engineering professor at Northwestern University in nearby Evanston.

How odd, Crist thought. He had not prepared such a parcel, and he didn't recognize the name of the person to whom it was addressed: a Professor Ed Smith at Rensselaer Polytechnic Institute in Troy, New York. After chatting with the female caller a few minutes, Crist arranged to have a courier retrieve the shoebox-sized package from the University of Illinois campus, just 16 miles away.

When the parcel arrived around 4 p.m. in the ground-floor mail room of Northwestern's Technological Institute, Crist saw immediately that the handwriting was not his. After his secretary confirmed that it wasn't her penmanship either, Crist was troubled enough to alert campus security to the mystery bundle, which through the brown wrapping felt like wood. Campus police officer Terry Marker was dispatched to the mail room, and as a handful of curious onlookers, Crist among them, craned their necks, Marker joked, "O.K., stand back."

Boom! Though pieces of the package swirled around the room, no one was hurt, save Marker, who sustained a small burn on the stretch of skin between his left thumb and index finger. "Everybody all right?" Marker shouted as he struggled to regain his composure. Until that moment, he hadn't suspected that the innocuous package might actually be a bomb. As Marker was treated at Evanston Hospital, where an ice pack was applied to his hand, the local police were called. The shaken witnesses tidied up the 20-ft. by 20-ft. mail room, then Crist returned to work. After an unsuccessful attempt was made to contact the mysterious Ed Smith, Crist decided, that's that. The Bureau of Alcohol, Tobacco and Firearms concluded pretty much the same. Summoned by police to inspect the debris, they sized it up as an amateur job; they made pictures and filed a report. When no leads materialized, they unceremoniously discarded the remnants of the bomb.

Two weeks shy of the one-year anniversary of that seemingly freak explosion, John Harris, a graduate student in applied mathematics at Northwestern, inspected a cigar box resting on a drawing table between two study cubicles on the second floor of the Technological Institute. Harris had been eyeing the box for several days, and on this steamy Wednesday afternoon he decided that it would serve nicely as a pencil holder. He lifted the box and started to peel back the tape that sealed the lid. *Boom!* The explosion was loud enough to startle students from their carrels. In the hallway, they found a shaken Harris covered in black dust. Joel Meyer, an administrative assistant, grabbed an extinguisher to put out the resulting fire. Harris was treated at Evanston Hospital for minor burns.

The campus and local police who inspected the scene found match heads, thousands of them, scattered everywhere. Meyer was able to provide a detailed description of the bomb just moments after the explosion. "It looked like it could have been paper or rags [in the box]," he said. "I smelled sulphur, and I saw a lot of wires attached to flashlight batteries." Meyer also recalled the cigar box on a table between the two carrels. But no one could say how how long it had been resting there without causing any alarm. "I spent a year in Israel," senior Yosh Mantinband told the campus daily, "and whenever they see a [suspicious package] there, they call the bomb squad. But in America no one thinks of that."

Indeed, the bombing itself got scant notice outside the Chicago area. And though it was the second incident at Northwestern's Technological Institute, local officials assumed the two incidents were unrelated, so they neither contacted federal authorities nor tightened security on campus. No one seemed to notice one odd, possibly connecting thread: the cigar box had some twigs glued to it, an echo of the wood box used in the prior incident. Instead, investigators focused on the primitiveness of the latest effort. Matchheads. Rags. Flashlight batteries. "It had to have been an amateur bomb," Meyer told reporters with convincing certainty.

Six months later, on Nov. 15, American Airlines Flight 444 took off from Chicago's O'Hare International Airport at 11:20 a.m., on a course for Washington National Airport. Midway through the flight, there was a loud sucking noise, more like an implosion than an explosion. As the cabin filled with a sweet chemical smell, Captain Don Tynan got on the loudspeaker. Announcing that there was a problem with the sticking valve, he reassured passengers in the calm drawl that seems to be a part of every pilot's training, "It happens from time to time."

Inside the cockpit, the crew had felt what Tynan later described as a "concussion" from the cargo hold; the copilot suggested that perhaps a can of shaving cream had exploded in a piece of luggage. But 20 minutes later, smoke began to seep into the cabin near the ninth row of seats. While flight attendants moved passengers toward the rear of the craft, Tynan determined that he would have to make an emergency landing at Dulles International Airport in Virginia, 25 miles west of Washington.

As the cabin filled with a choking, acrid haze, and oxygen masks descended, the 72 passengers began to panic. Some wept. Others prayed. Many screamed for the attention of the eight crew members. "When I looked back into the cabin, it was like a Stygian scene in hell," Tynan recalled. "Babies were crying all over the place." But he couldn't pause to calm the terrified travelers. He had just 20 minutes to prepare for an unusually rapid descent, which would be from 20,000 ft. at a speed of 600 m.p.h.—twice that of a normal approach.

While passengers were instructed to put on the oxygen masks and place their heads between their knees, Tynan donned his own mask and goggles. "I was worried I was going to get knocked out by the toxic fumes and smoke," he recalled. Worse still, as he approached Dulles, Tynan was unable to make contact with the flight tower. Even without a clearance, he knew he had to land. Then he spotted a light plane on the runway toward which he was headed. With no way to turn back, he continued his descent. The plane moved just moments before the trijet Boeing 727 touched down. Miraculously, no one was seriously injured, though 12 passengers were treated for smoke inhalation. Years later, Tynan would comment with mild aggravation, "The FBI never said a word to me. For all the nitpicking they do, it couldn't have hurt them to have a chat with me."

When fire fighters cut an 18-in. hole through the hold to locate the source of the smoke, they came upon a wooden box measuring roughly 9 in. by 10 in. by 7 in. that was part of the regular mail shipment. The postage on the wrapping totalled $8.50; the postmark was from the Chicago area.

Unlike the explosions at Northwestern University, this blast detonated a ripple of fear across the nation. Eleven days earlier, Iranian militants had seized the U.S. embassy in Tehran and taken 65 hostages—an unprecedented assault on U.S. nationals. Now citizens seemed primed for any manner of terrorism. When a man with a foreign accent phoned several Chicago news outlets 12 hours after Flight 444 landed and claimed the bombing was the work of Iranians, the FBI was contacted. Investigators took seriously the man's threat of further bombings if harassment of Iranians living in the Chicago area persisted. Still, investigators thought it odd that the anonymous caller waited half a day to claim responsibility. More typically, terrorists communicate immediately after an act of violence.

Investigators let it be known that the device had been a "very low yield" bomb, encased in a juice-can container, then placed in the wooden box. Shipped by the U.S. Postal Service and placed directly in Flight 444's mail cargo section, the bomb had evaded the metal detectors that routinely screen passengers. There were indications that the in-flight detonation had been deliberate, not accidental: plucked from the debris was a household barometer, which measures changes in air pressure and had been rigged to trigger the bomb when the 727 climbed to a certain height.

But the explosion had been weak because of a faulty seal of glue and tape on one end of the device. The charge nearest the ruptured seal had caught fire, igniting the mail in the cargo hold. The most toxic smoke had been produced not by the bomb, but rather by the smoldering mailbags in the cargo hold.

Thus James ("Chris") Ronay, one of five agent-examiners in the FBI's Explosives Unit, extracted a nearly intact bomb from the cargo compartment of the Boeing. Ronay had arrived on the tarmac about 10 minutes after the craft landed. Once Virginia state police bomb technicians pulled the charred aluminum mail pod from the hold, Ronay carefully began to bag and label the remnants of the device. He saw that the brown wrapping paper, sealed with filament tape, had been addressed to someone in Washington. All that remained was the partial word *rlines,* probably for *Airlines,* stenciled in green lettering, and the initials NW, which probably referred to northwest Washington, the capital's business district.

Back at his lab in the J. Edgar Hoover FBI Building, Ronay began piecing the fragments together and ruminating about their creator. Ronay, who had spent a year blowing up enemy fortresses and tunnel systems for the Army in Vietnam, then several more disassembling bombs at Fort Benning, Georgia, could see that the bomber had no military training. His invention was crude and employed smokeless powder, a weak explosive available in gun and sporting-goods stores. Moreover, a professional would have known to use a heavy metal pipe instead of a juice can: the stronger the containment vessel, the greater the gas pressure buildup at the moment of ignition, which makes a more powerful explosion. Even so, the bomber had very nearly brought down an airliner. The bomber, Ronay deduced, had aimed to kill, not just make a statement.

Ronay also concluded that the bomber, though self-taught, was sophisticated. He had converted a cheap barometer into an altimeter switch, which meant that he understood some fairly complex concepts about airplanes and barometric pressure. The bomber knew, for example, that when the plane took off and the cabin became pressurized, the barometer needle would leap. He'd inserted a piece of metal in the path of the needle so that its swing would close an electric circuit that linked the power source, four C-cell batteries, to the initiators that, in turn, would ignite the powder charge. Furthermore, in case the barometer failed, he had built in a redundancy, a pull-loop switch, whose contacts would touch, closing the circuit between the batteries and the initiators when the lid on the box was lifted.

The two initiators—more redundancy—also caught Ronay's attention. Each was a wooden dowel measuring about 1/4 in. long. The bombmaker had carved two grooves along the side of each dowel, then run short lengths of wire down each groove. Those wires led to an improvised ignition device. Ronay knew that when the circuit was closed, the surge of power from the batteries would cause the device to ignite the powder. Ronay could see that the wire had been taken from a lamp or some home appliance. The screws had also been used before. Nothing in the bomb, in fact, had been purchased at a store except the powder and batteries.

And that fact struck Ronay as odd. The bomber had put in a lot more work than he needed to. Most bombers used nine-volt batteries because of the ease with which wires can be attached to the two poles. Or they used AA batteries enclosed in battery holders with internal metal contacts and ready-to-wire external poles, which can be bought cheaply at any electronics store. But this bomber had enclosed his C-cell batteries in a handmade wooden box and soldered the wires leading to the initiator directly onto the battery poles. That must have taken a great deal of effort since, as Ronay knew, batteries are heat sinks—they absorb the head of the soldering iron—making it difficult to attach copper wires to them.

Ronay ordered up detailed drawings of the bomb as it would have looked before the explosion, then sent the four-page rendering and other data to both the FBI's Chicago field office and the Postal Inspection Service's lab, which forwarded them to its own Chicago office. There, U.S. postal inspector John A. Ruberti, an experienced bomb investigator known for his tenacity and prodigious command of detail, was assigned to the case. When Ruberti read the report, he understood why the passenger had remarked on the smoke's sweetish smell. The bomber had mixed sugar and potassium chlorate in the smokeless powder. Such a mixture was highly flammable and would have enhanced the blast.

Tracking back from the postmark and routing, Ruberti determined that the package had been mailed at a small postal station located in a grocery store in the Illinois town of Elgin. Then Ruberti and FBI case agent Tom Barrett started calling all the police jurisdictions in the Chicago area. For the first time, there was a flash of recognition. A campus police officer at Northwestern realized that the description matched the cigar-box bomb. It too had involved initiators made of lamp cord, wooden dowels and filaments. Those remnants were plucked from an evidence locker and forwarded to Ronay.

"Once I saw them, I knew we had a serial bomber," Ronay recalled. Beyond the similarity of parts, the loop switches and initiators had been fashioned in precisely the same way. And both bombs had relied on smokeless powder, though the Northwestern blast had been further enhanced by matchstick heads. Ronay knew that none of this could be coincidental: of the hundreds of bombs he had examined, he'd never seen a construction quite like this.

But even now, investigators didn't know how to proceed—and didn't yet realize how much information was actually available. It was 1979, well before the wired age of global cyberspace. As yet, there were no national databases where evidence could be pooled and stored. Several investigating teams had handled—and mishandled—evidence from the three explosions: campus police, town police, the FBI, the ATF and the U.S. Postal Inspection Service. When Ruberti asked Northwestern University if there had been any other bombs, he learned that there had been one in 1978—and that it had long since been destroyed. When the ATF's pictures and report of that bombing finally made it to the FBI's explosives lab, Ronay, like Ruberti, suspected it was the same bomber.

In the winter of 1979, federal agents suspected that bomber was still in the Chicago area. Hoping to get a handle on his motive and where he might strike next, members of the Investigative Support Unit, a small group of profilers at the FBI Academy in Quantico, Virginia, were tapped to devise a psychological profile. The resulting portrait was of a loner with an obsessive-compulsive personality whose sense of insignificance left him feeling like a grain of sand on a vast beach. The bombs represented his longing for power, and were his sick way of imposing order on a cold and chaotic world. Profilers believed this same craving might manifest as an excessively neat house or work space. The bomber was probably poor, holding no better than a marginal job. And, like most serial killers, he was probably driven by a keen sense of revenge, derived from some real or imagined grievance. The target could be anything: an individual, an institution, even an entire industry.

While the profilers rummaged around in the bomber's psyche, the boys in the lab picked through the traces he had left behind. The bomber meticulously fashioned each of his components by hand, from the boxes and hinges to the endcaps and pipes. Every screw was filed to erase telltale tool marks;

every nail was hand-sculpted from wire. "He handmade everything—switches, everything," recalled Ronay, who today is retired from the FBI and heads the Institute of Makers of Explosives, a Washington-based industry group. "Nothing I could see in any of these was store-bought. I called him the 'recycler bomber.'" Postal inspectors and other FBI hands gave him a different nom de guerre: the junkyard bomber.

When the bomber resurfaced, again in the Chicago area, he tried a new tact: he prenotified his victim. During the first week of June 1980, Percy Wood, president of United Airlines, received a letter from an "Enoch Fischer" informing the executive that he would soon receive a book that "you will find of great social significance." On June 10, a warm, sunny day, the promised book appeared in Wood's roadside mailbox in the suburb of Lake Forest. Measuring 5 in. by 8 in. and weighing about 3 lbs., the package bore three kinds of stamps. Wood's 60th birthday had just passed, so perhaps he thought it was a late gift as, at 2:48 p.m., he tore through the wrapping paper and white twine and struggled to open the glued pages of the enclosed book. *Boom!*

The bomb peppered Wood's face with wood fragments, and lodged a portion of pipe in his thigh, requiring surgery at Lake Forest Hospital. It also ripped a gaping hole in the kitchen ceiling. Fortunately for them, neither Wood's wife nor any of his four sons were home at the time.

Postal inspectors soon learned several peculiar things about the package. First, it had been addressed to Percy Addison Wood, though Wood had not used his middle name in years. Second, Wood knew no "Enoch Fischer." (Fischer's return address, agents quickly discovered, was actually an empty lot in Chicago.) Finally, the bomb had been placed inside a hollowed-out copy of Sloan Wilson's *Ice Brothers*, a World War II novel about a Coast Guard boat stationed off Greenland.

Investigators wondered if that title in some way was connected with Eugene O'Neill, who had written *The Iceman Cometh;* the playwright's image had been on the set of stamps that had marked the rigged package back in 1978. The contents of the Wilson novel were scrutinized for possible leads. Ruberti and his team also got hold of a Bible to flesh out the "Enoch" angle. "Enoch was the son of Cain who, even though his father was a murderer, was a very righteous man," Ruberti recalled. "He founded a city, and God took the whole city up to heaven because Enoch was such a good man." The investigators also took a detour into the works of Edgar Allen Poe because the return address on the package had included the street name Ravenswood.

As they combed through Wood's damaged kitchen, investigators turned up traces of a pipe bomb that had been detonated by a pressure-sensitive trip device. Possibly of greater use was the discovery that the smokeless powder used in the device was a special type called improved military rifle, or IMR, powder. Ruberti's team contacted stores in both Illinois and Utah that might carry the powder. No go. The stores only kept records of purchases of black powder.

Investigators also discovered that the package bore no postmark, and its stamps were uncanceled. Yet the mail carrier remembered delivering the parcel. "We had the carrier and Mr. Wood hypnotized to see if they could recall anything else," Ruberti said. The Postal Service offered a $5,000 reward to anyone providing information that would lead to the bomber's arrest and conviction. The promise of a reward drew no meaningful leads, and the investigation went down several blind alleys. Because United Airlines had recently laid off thousands of workers, a search of the company's records was conducted to determine if some disgruntled employee had mailed the bomb.

When the bomb remnants were shipped to the Postal Inspection Service's lab in Washington, forensic chemist James Upton discovered a tantalizing clue: a piece of metal with the initials FC formed of tiny dots punched through with a nail. Clearly, the bomber made them to survive the blast. Was FC a person? A company? An underground group? Was it a religious message? Something like "For Christ"?

If investigators were at a loss about the initials' meaning, they were now convinced of one thing: the bomber was obsessed by wood. Though he was careful enough to erase all fingerprints, he apparently wanted his handiwork recognized. Wood, it seemed, was his calling card. He not only utilized several woods in the construction of each bomb, from the cheap crate variety to the exotic grains used in expensive furniture, he also played with and mocked wood imagery. The most recent victim's name was Wood, he lived in Lake Forest, and the return address had included the word Ravenswood. Moreover, *Ice Brothers* had been published by Arbor House, whose symbol is a leaf.

The Lake Forest bombing also reaffirmed investigators' suspicions that the perpetrator was directing his wrath at universities and airlines. They obtained subpoenas to gather computer tapes of student and employee records from Northwestern University and United Airlines, then cross-indexed, looking for a Northwestern graduate who had been employed by United. They looked for anyone who might bear a grudge against the airline: stockholders, employees, families who had lost loved ones in plane disasters. They also looked at people who had been denied admission to Northwestern or who had been kicked out.

A new psychological profile was devised by Syracuse University behavioral scientist Murray Myron. He concluded that the bomber was a white male in his early 20s to mid-30s, raised in the Midwest and college educated. Ruberti recalled that the profile also suggested that the bomber's "social and sexual life was involved in the creation of these devices."

Though the FBI and U.S. Postal Inspection Service were now on the case, which the FBI crime lab dubbed Unabom—for university and airline, the bomber's two targets—it would be another 14 years before the various federal teams would join together to form a formal task force. And it would be another 16 months, before the Unabomber resurfaced.

As John Wooten stared at the shoebox-sized package wrapped in brown paper, he began to get "that feeling" that comes from years of experience dismantling bombs. Something about its odd position tweaked his caution. Near a window. At the end of a hallway. Nestled against tile walls. And it had gone unclaimed by all the nearly 100 University of Utah students who that Thursday morning were taking classes on the second floor of the computer-sciences building.

"I don't mean to sound like some kind of character. You just get a feeling for the real thing," Wooten said, recalling that day. "Somebody gave some thought to where they placed this thing. It was between two classrooms. If it had gone off, it would have created a tunnel and crisped any living thing in that hallway."

Fortunately, an alert student had notified an employee of the college after she lifted the package and a small wooden lever, measuring no more than 4 in., popped out. The employee summoned campus police who, in turn, phoned an Army base, a short distance from the university campus in Salt Lake City. Within 15 minutes, Staff Sergeant Wooten, an explosive-ordnance-disposal technician, arrived at the scene, and the building was evacuated.

As he inspected the package, Wooten noticed that there was no address on the wrapping, though there were some tiny letters and arrows written with a ballpoint pen. Carefully removing the brown paper, he saw a handcrafted wooden box, the sort of project that might have consumed a whittler's winter. The pieces of wood were connected with handcrafted dovetail joints, and surrounded by pieces of tape. Inside the hollowed box was a rectangular gas can, the top of which was crudely sealed with wax or putty. A household extension-cord wire protruded from a drilled hole in the can, and it was connected to two batteries. Then Wooten saw the 6-in. dowel rod. He understood instantly that this was intended to serve as the swipe switch, a booby trap that would slide down when the box was lifted, detonating the bomb.

Holding the dowel rod in place, Wooten gingerly carried the package to a women's room where the tiled walls would help to contain a blast if the bomb went off. Slowly, he dismantled the device, then X-rayed it. He found that the can, filled with gas, sheltered a pipe bomb that contained smokeless powder. "There was no backup timing device. Nothing," said Wooten. "It was designed to kill whoever happened to pick it up." But the three-wire detonator had failed because the bomber had tried to send too much juice through the middle strand, a miscalculation that caused the bomb to fail to ignite. Had he instead chosen single-strand copper wire, the bomb would have exploded. "People say pipe bombs are crude, but to me they are the most dangerous," Wooten said. "You can't see what's inside."

Briefly, there was speculation that the bomb might be connected to the State Board of Regents meeting being held across campus on that same day in October 1981. The meeting's agenda was well publicized and unpopular: a possible tuition hike for Utah's colleges and universities. Then the ATF inspected the device and ruled it a hoax.

As a result, FBI and postal investigators would not learn of the bomb for another seven months. When Ronay of the FBI and Upton of the Postal Inspection Service finally conducted a joint physical examination of the device, they recognized the Unabomber's imprint. Beyond the signature wood, there was evidence of the enormous patience that went into each of his constructions. "Whoever he was, he was very careful and gave a great amount of attention to detail," Ronay would later observe. "When you see this stuff, some of these components bear markings of having been put together and taken apart repeatedly. It's not just that he's creating something carefully. He's *played* with it for a while. He marks things with numbers so he can put them together again right. He's leaving a little of himself at each crime scene."

Only now, the crime scene had shifted from Illinois to Utah. Then it shifted again, to Nashville, Tennessee. On May 5, 1982, a small package addressed to Patrick Fischer, head of the computer-science department at Vanderbilt University, exploded in the hands of his secretary, Janet Smith, who was handling Fischer's mail while her boss lectured in Puerto Rico. The blast was a weak one, causing only minor lacerations to Smith's hands, arms and chest.

When postal inspectors in Nashville noticed that the bomb had been hidden inside a wooden box, they phoned Ruberti in Chicago, who flew to Nashville and quickly deduced that it was the Unabomber's work. Forensic chemist Upton soon reached the same conclusion: he discovered the initials FC punched in a scrap of metal. Ruberti also noted the three $1 Eugene O'Neill stamps on the wrapping, the postmark from Provo, Utah, and the sender, Leroy W. Bearnson, an engineering professor at Brigham Young University. If that blew a hole in the theory of a United Airlines connection, it opened up new possibilities involving Utah. Ruberti traveled to B.Y.U. in Provo, learned that Bearnson was on sabbatical, and found out that an anonymous sender had dumped the parcel in the campus post office.

On a hunch, he drove to the University of Utah in Salt Lake City and asked police if they had discovered any devices on campus. Soon he was staring at the 1981 bomb. "I looked at the device," Ruberti recalled, "and immediately knew it had been made by the same individual." New records were subpoenaed. Good suspects emerged. But all of them proved to have an alibi on the day of the most recent bombing.

By now, new patterns were beginning to emerge. This was the third of the bomber's six known devices to be set off in the month of May. And, like the peculiar use of Wood's middle name in the 1980 blast, the bomber again seemed to be operating from out-of-date information. He appeared not to know that the alleged sender, Bearnson, was on sabbatical at the time. He also seemed not to know that the intended target, Fischer, had moved from Pennsylvania State University to Vanderbilt two years earlier. The package, addressed to Fischer at Penn State, had been forwarded to Tennessee. Then again, Ruberti reasoned, perhaps the bomb had been intended for Bearnson, and had been misdirected so that it would be returned to the Utah professor.

Two days shy of Independence Day, 1982, a bomb went off on yet another campus, the University of California, Berkeley. The early-morning explosion in a tiny faculty coffee room in Cory Hall, a five-story concrete building that housed the Department of Electrical Engineering and Computer Science, injured the face and right hand of the department's vice chairman, Diogenes J. Angelakos.

Federal investigators were certain it was their man. Again, a pipe bomb stuffed with explosive powder, then suspended in a gas container. Again the trademark wooden handle linked to loop switches. But this time, he had used D-cell batteries. And this time, the Unabomber had left a more teasing trail than usual. A janitor reported spotting a thin, mustached stranger in the building. And the bomber had left a note, probably inadvertently, his first piece of writing since the letter that had previewed the Wood bombing two years earlier. It read, "Wu—it works! I told you it would—R.V."

For the next three years, investigators detected no bombings bearing the terrorist's distinctive signature. Initially, the time was spent checking into the backgrounds of myriad Wus, and tracing both people and organizations that used the R.V. initials. When that yielded nothing, they went back to inspecting and reinspecting the fragments of birch, walnut, cherry and mahogany used by the Unabomber. Maybe he was a woodsman. A lumberyard worker. A crazed environmentalist. As the silence deepened, they began to speculate more hopefully. Perhaps their bomber was in a prison. A mental ward. A hospital. Maybe he had fled the country. Or perhaps he had simply expended his anger.

On May 15, 1985, the Unabomber resurfaced with a device that packed more wallop than any of his previous efforts. As if to jog the minds of investigators, he struck again at Berkeley's Cory Hall, this time with a mixture of ammonium nitrate and aluminum powder

John Hauser, 26, an Air Force pilot and aspiring astronaut studying electrical engineering, was in the computer lab that Wednesday afternoon when he spotted a small white plastic box. Topped by a three-ring binder that was bound by a rubber band, the box looked unsuspicious in the lab setting. Thinking that a colleague had misplaced the two items, Hauser drew closer and lifted the binder. *Boom!* "I thought, 'Why would they do that,' " Hauser recalled years later. "It just seemed such an incredible thing to be happening to me. Then I noticed that my whole arm was on fire. Imagine that you've hit your funny bone on something, and now multiply it by a million or so."

Hauser's injuries were the worst to date for a Unabomber victim. The explosion blew away the fingers on Hauser's right hand and opened a hole in his right arm that severed two major arteries. No longer fit to fly a plane, let alone pilot a shuttle mission, he would settle on a career in teaching.

After this second attack at Berkeley, investigators turned a more vigilant eye to university records to see if they had missed something three years earlier. Given the Berkeley setting, some thought was given to the possibility that campus radicals had been involved. But the research conducted in Cory Hall bore no obvious connection to the students' pet issues at the time: the U.S. military and South Africa's apartheid government. Perhaps, instead, it was the work of a disgruntled student who had been denied admission, or a teaching candidate who had been denied a job. They also retraced links to the other universities that had been hit—Northwestern, Utah, Vanderbilt—looking for possible connections. All trails came up cold.

One month after Hauser's tragedy, a package was found in the mail room of Building 17-04 at the fabrication division of the Boeing Co. in Auburn, Washington. Addressed to no one in particular, it had gone unattended for a month. When clerks finally turned to it, they thought it odd that the package, with a California return address, had been posted to no specific person. After one worker carefully pried the parcel open, he informed the foreman, "I think we got a bomb." The King County bomb squad was summoned, and the 30 mail room employees were evacuated. X rays soon determined that it was, indeed, a bomb. Over the next six hours, the device was slowly dismantled and detonated. "It was a very powerful bomb, and extremely well made," recalled

Tim Shook, who had been on the bomb squad that day and is now its senior bomb technician. "It would have killed anyone within a 20-to-30-ft. radius."

Ruberti was investigating the last blast in Berkeley when he received the call summoning him to Auburn. There, he was met by Upton. The Postal Inspection Service was now giving the Unabom case highest priority. As they probed the evidence, the men noticed that the wooden box containing the bomb had cutouts that bore a likeness to the containers in which prosthetic devices are shipped. That led to a scouring of factories and physicians who dealt in prostheses. Investigators also pondered the question, Had the Unabomber moved from Illinois to Utah to California?

Not exactly, came the answer, five months later, when another deadly package was mailed from Salt Lake City. Six years to the day after the American Airlines explosion, a book-sized parcel arrived at the home of James McConnell, a popular professor of behavioral psychology at the University of Michigan who specialized in theories of human controllability. The package, with no return address, included a note that read, in part, "I'd like you to read this book. Everybody in your position should read this book." McConnell was in a different part of the house when his research assistant, Nicklaus Suino opened the parcel. *Boom!* The pipe bomb, which blew a 6-in. hole in the kitchen counter, was loaded with ammonium nitrate and aluminum powder. Flying metal inflicted minor flesh wounds along Suino's arms and upper body.

The next victim would not be so lucky. Around lunchtime on Dec. 11, 1985, Hugh Scrutton was exiting through the rear door of his computer rental store in a Sacramento, California, strip mall when he bent down beside a Dumpster to move an object composed of wood and protruding nails that looked like a road hazard. The explosion tore a hole in Scrutton's chest, exposing his heart and killing him instantly. The Unabomber had claimed his first fatality. By now the federal bomb technicians knew the Unabomber's signature well, and they instantly spotted his handiwork amid the wreckage. A pipe bomb. Traces of ammonium nitrate and aluminum powder. A handmade wooden box. Four D-cell batteries. A lamp cord.

But this device boasted some improvements. To intensify the explosion, the bomber had used three pipes of equal length and increasing diameter, fitted one within the other like Russian *matryoshka* dolls. Obviously, the bomber now understood that the thicker the containment vessel, the more the gas pressure would build up during ignition, producing a stronger blast. In addition, the plugs that capped either end of the outermost pipe, formerly made from wood, were now fashioned from steel dowel. As before, those dowels were skewered in place crosswise with homemade pins, which meant that the bomber had drilled holes through the steel dowels as well as the pipes. This suggested that the Unabomber had access to a workshop and drill press. In the rubble, investigators found FC, punched by a sharp instrument. Until now, federal investigators had closely held their suspicions of a serial bomber. Tactically, it made no sense to call attention to their investigation. Practically, it might stir alarm. But with a death on their hands and no promising leads, they decided to take the investigation public. Six days before Christmas, Americans learned for the first time that there was a serial bomber on the loose. He had staged 11 attacks in six states across the country, injured 19 people and killed one. The Postal Inspection Service offered a bounty of $25,000, and a 24-hour hot line was established in Washington to handle calls.

Leads poured in. Investigators updated their profile to

embrace any number of possibilities. A disgruntled airline or university employee. A college student or instructor, perhaps living in or around Salt Lake City. Someone laid off from a computer job. A rabid environmentalist. Someone whose job entailed a lot of travel. Perhaps a malcontent postal worker; his packages always seemed to have just the right amount of postage, though they were always self-stamped. Or perhaps a remnant weirdo from one of the radical political groups that used to populate Berkeley in the '60s and '70s, though to investigators, this guy seemed to nurse more of a personal grievance than a political one. But two things investigators felt they knew with some certainly: "He was definitely a loner type, an antisocial individual," recalled Louis Bertram, who at the time was an FBI profiler. "All the signs were the signs of an individual." And bombs were his life.

Investigators updated their assessment of his modus operandi. The Unabomber, they concluded, was obsessional, compulsive and scrupulous about his work. The fact that he created and crafted each piece of each device, repeatedly disassembling and reassembling the parts and varnishing and polishing the wood, suggested a person who exacted some measure of satisfaction from the creative process. But for all his love of wood, he lacked the skills of a trained cabinetmaker. "His angles aren't straight," Don Davis, a top postal inspector in San Francisco, would recall years later. "He spends a lot of time. He does a lot of polishing and sanding to make it feel nice, but they don't look really craftsmanlike."

But though the picture of this loner was coming into sharper focus, investigators closed out 1985 no closer to nabbing the Unabomber than they had ever been.

Hide and Seek

A human being needs goals whose attainment requires effort, and he must have a reasonable rate of success in attaining his goals. —Manifesto, paragraph 37

On the morning of Feb. 20, 1987, the secretary at CAAMS Inc., a computer store at 270 East 900 South in Salt Lake City, looked up from her desk just in time to spot a motion through the small window that overlooked the parking lot behind the shop. A man with a white canvas bag slung over his shoulder was bent over the left-front section of her car, placing some sort of package beneath the wheel. The secretary yelled to another employee, the mother of the store's co-owner, to come take a look. Through the glass, the man heard the yell and looked directly at the secretary through a pair of aviator sunglasses. The mother arrived at the window in time to see the back of the man as he casually sauntered away from the parking lot.

"Nice butt," the secretary cracked.

The two women laughed. Then the phones rang, they moved away from the window, and the incident was promptly forgotten.

An hour later, around 10:30 a.m., co-owner Gary Wright returned from a service call and parked his truck, proudly emblazoned with the store logo, in the back lot. As he hurried toward the store, Wright kicked the peculiar object, which was twin two-by-four boards inexpertly nailed together, nails protruding. *Boom!* Mrs. Wright turned just in time to see the explosion tear into her son's arms, face and legs with a force that would leave one of his hands permanently injured.

Wright's misfortune proved to be the first real break in the Unabomber case. Like the bomb that had killed Hugh Scrutton in Sacramento 14 months earlier, this one had been placed by hand and fashioned to look like a road hazard. One fragment bore the stamp FC, initials known so far only to the bomber and the law-enforcement community, which was keeping them secret. And now, for the first time, someone was able to give investigators an eyewitness description of the Unabomber. The secretary said he was a white male of about 28 years, with blondish hair. She guesstimated his height as 5 ft. 10 in., and fixed his weight at 165 lbs. Three days later, a group of 40 federal agents and area police officers had a local police artist draw a composite sketch of the suspect.

It differed in minor respects from the description offered by the eyewitness. Though the standard police composite sketch was rather crude, it provided the first image of the suspect. The drawing showed a white male in a gray hooded sweatshirt, wearing tear-shaped sunglasses with smoked lenses. On his upper lip was a thin, light mustache. The accompanying description listed the man's age as 25 to 30, and his height as 5 ft. 10 in. to 6 ft. His complexion was described as "ruddy." And his hair was designated "Blond Hair (reddish tint)."

The posted reward was raised to $60,000, with the U.S. Postal Service offering $50,000 and the University of California, Berkeley, handling the rest. A hot line was established to handle tips and leads, and the calls poured in. "We received 300 or 400 telephone leads," recalled Louis Bertram, an FBI official who pursued the Unabomber from

1981 until his own retirement in 1988. "He could have been one of them."

For the first time, federal investigators felt optimistic. "The Salt Lake City witness," said an FBI agent, "gave by far the best information we've had in the case." But none of the new leads panned out. Within two months, the investigating force was severely reduced, and representatives of the FBI, ATF and Postal Inspection Service who had been flown in from San Francisco and Sacramento returned home to their field offices. "There was no way we could justify having that many guys around," said Bertram. "You could say we cut back to a skeleton crew."

Once again, the Unabomber went into retreat—this time for more than six years. Investigators could only speculate. Perhaps the composite sketch had scared him straight. Or perhaps he had had an even closer call. It was titillating to imagine that he might have been one of the dozens of suspects interviewed by agents in the wake of the computer-store bombing.

Though federal agents still had no communiqués or demands from the bomber to guide their search, they had at least established gender, ethnicity, approximate age and rough size. Those few drops were enough to eliminate an ocean of possibilities. They plugged the specifics into many databases, including thousands of criminal records and department of motor vehicles files. Meanwhile, at the FBI's Explosives Unit, where Ronay had by now been elevated to chief, agents kept resifting the physical evidence.

Agents at the FBI's Investigative Support Unit refined the psychological profile. They still perceived the bomber as a loner, probably reared in the Chicago area. Though they would try to bruise the Unabomber's ego and taunt him out of hiding by publicly suggesting that he had only a high school education, investigators were actually pretty sure their culprit was college educated, possibly even the holder of an advanced degree. They further speculated that he was a meticulous man, the sort who dressed neatly, kept careful lists and lovingly maintained an old car in good condition. He was an ideal neighbor, quiet and unobtrusive. He probably had a tough time with women. Almost certainly, his life included no wife, children or career. He wouldn't have had time for them. When bomb-specialist Ronay was asked in one meeting to speculate how long it would take to make one of the Unabomber's devices, he answered, "Ten hours. But I think he took weeks to make it." They were convinced his motive was revenge, and they suspected that he liked both to watch emergency and investigative personnel respond to his bombings, and keep news clips and news videos of his misdeeds.

As the '80s gave way to the '90s, and the Unabomber's silence remained unbroken, the case became what agents call a hummer. It hummed quietly along, neither dying nor flaring up. During those years, investigators reconsidered every possibility. "Maybe he was incarcerated or somehow not available," James Cavanaugh, deputy chief of the explosives division of ATF, would later tell reporters. "Maybe he was overseas. Or in a hospital. Maybe he was just happy." Or maybe he was dead. Perhaps he had even suffered the death that many outraged Americans felt he deserved: perhaps at some remote test site, he had blown himself to smithereens.

On June 22, 1993, Charles Epstein, a prominent geneticist with many awards to his credit, had just returned to his suburban home in bayside Tiburon from his office at the University of California, San Francisco, when he spotted the brown, padded envelope that had been delivered by the mail carrier around 2:30 p.m. and placed on the kitchen table by his daughter Joanna. The return address named a Professor

James Hill of the chemistry department at California State University–Sacramento, known more commonly as Sacramento State. Epstein did not know Hill, but he was accustomed to receiving unsolicited packages from academic colleagues.

He opened the envelope and *boom!*—the Unabomber was back in business. Epstein was rushed to Marin General Hospital, where he underwent five hours of surgery. Though his broken arm and abdominal injuries would eventually heal, Epstein—an expert on genetic disorders such as Down syndrome and Alzheimer's disease—lost three fingers in the blast.

Before the FBI could even catch its breath, another bomb went off two days later in New Haven, Connecticut—the Unabomber's first strike on the East Coast. David Gelernter, director of undergraduate studies in computer science at Yale University, had entered his campus office at 51 Prospect Street around 8 a.m. that Thursday morning. He was just starting to open a parcel that indicated the sender was a computer-science professor at Sacramento State when the bomb went off in his hands. The explosion injured his right eye, chest and abdomen, and smashed his right hand beyond repair.

Dazed but determined, Gelernter crawled down five flights of stairs to the street, leaving bits of clothing and pools of blood in the stairwell, then dragged himself to the university medical clinic a block away. Soon after he was rolled into intensive care and placed on a respirator, FBI investigators descended to pick through his office with tweezers, pulling bomb shards from the walls, floor, ceiling and furniture. Within two hours of the bombing, an anonymous caller phoned the hospital in neighboring West Haven where Gelernter's brother Joel practiced psychiatry. A man's voice warned, "You are next."

Whether that call was a hoax or the real thing, what followed was most definitely a communication from the

Unabomber. In the hours after the bombing at Yale, Kris Ensminger was seated at her desk in midtown Manhattan, opening mail addressed either to herself or her boss, Warren Hoge, an assistant managing editor at the New York *Times*, when one letter caught her attention. "I didn't know exactly what it was," Ensminger recalls. "But the wording was kind of intelligent. We get a lot of crazy letters. But something about it struck me that this may be something serious."

The vigilant secretary was particularly intrigued by a sentence midway through the one-paragraph, typed message: "Ask the FBI about FC." That mention of the FBI persuaded Ensminger to show the letter to Hoge, who in turn summoned the *Times's* security staff. Guards came up to Hoge's office on the third floor, the site of the *Times's* sprawling newsroom, and the letter quickly passed from hand to hand to hand.

By the time the newspaper alerted the FBI, the letter was smudged with too many sets of fingerprints to be of value to the FBI's crime labs. Still, it provided investigators with several useful clues. The envelope had a June 21 postmark and, like the packages to Epstein and Gelernter, had been mailed from Sacramento. Most important, it foretold those two blasts, which occurred on June 22 and June 24, and hinted at more to come.

"We are an anarchist group calling ourselves FC," the letter stated. "Notice that the postmark on this envelope precedes a newsworthy event that will happen about the time you receive this letter, if nothing goes wrong. This will prove that we knew about the event in advance, so our claim of responsibility is truthful. Ask the FBI about FC. They have heard of us. We will give information about our goals at some future time. Right now we only want to establish our identity and provide an identifying number that will ensure the authenticity of any future communications from us." The nine-digit number that followed was laid out like a Social Security number: 553-25-4394. The Unabomber instructed Hoge to keep this number secret, "so that no one else can pretend to speak in our name." Later, FBI agents tracked down its owner, a man in his 20s, and quickly ruled him out as a suspect. The bomber, they figured, must have found the number someplace and appropriated it.

When the *Times* published the contents of the letter on June 25, it withheld the number but published the FC initials that had been a secret up until now. "It's been a long time since we heard from him—or them," Cavanaugh of ATF told reporters. "We don't know what [FC] means, but it's the first time that's been put out there by someone claiming responsibility." Though Cavanaugh had acknowledged the possibility of more than one culprit, investigators had actually long since concluded that the bombs were the work of a single man.

The day of the Yale bombing, FBI Director William Sessions posted a computer message to most universities urging them to be on the alert for suspicious parcels. With 160 billion pieces of mail being moved by the federal Postal Service each year, it was unreasonable to expect the mail service to screen all packages. By the next day, police at several universities, including Yale, Harvard and the Massachusetts Institute of Technology, had alerted their mail handlers. While Gelernter remained in critical condition at Yale–New Haven Hospital, security officials were dispatched to protect his family.

With terror sweeping the academic and scientific communities, Attorney General Janet Reno ordered the creation of a Unabom Task Force on June 28, to be based in San Francisco. FBI managers were instructed to give its chief, FBI Inspector George Clow, everything he needed—the sharpest agents, the latest computer hardware and software, the fastest lab work.

Clow demanded and got a corps of analysts, a great luxury in lean budget times. The Postal Inspection Service and the ATF contributed veterans of earlier Unabom investigations and the best young sleuths. Eventually, the task force would comprise 90 to 100 agents and inspectors and 45 analysts. The increase in personnel mirrored the expanded celebrity now enjoyed by the bomber. By striking at Yale, he had finally excited the interest of the East Coast–based national media, from PEOPLE magazine to CNN and National Public Radio.

When the FBI lab finally got its hands on the letter received by the *Times*, technicians discovered a treasure: a seemingly unintended impression of a handwritten message that read, "Call Nathan R Wed 7 pm." Combing phone books and driver's license records nationwide, the task force searched for anyone named Nathan with a middle or last name beginning with R. In all, the FBI identified 10,000 Nathan Rs in the U.S. and interviewed every one of them. But like FC, Wu and R.V., Nathan R was nowhere to be found.

With the twin bombings in 1993, investigators began to see new patterns. The Unabomber had set off bombs two months apart in 1982; in 1985 there had been two pairs of bombs that went off within a month of each other. Perhaps the guy liked the symmetry of pairs. He also seemed to have an affinity for certain months and dates: four of the bombs had been set in May, four in June, two on Nov. 15.

There were other peculiar pairings. Two times, he had struck Cory Hall at Berkeley. Twice he had selected airline personnel as his targets. Twice he had struck in Salt Lake City. His list of victims included two people who owned computer stores, two computer engineers, two electrical scientists, two graduate students. Two Fischers had been listed on his parcels. Two bombs had struck at Boeing targets. And twice the bomber had used the names of Sacramento State professors for the return addresses.

But what, if anything, did it all add up to? Over mugs of coffee in the morning, pizza and beer at midnight, investigators turned the clues over and over, trying to get a better fix on their prey. Some remained convinced that he was a blue-collar type. Others felt they saw the hand of an educated man, someone perhaps with a Ph.D. While wood experts denounced his unskilled workmanship, metallurgists opined that his soldering was lousy. One theory pegged him as someone who had worked in a machine shop. Another tied him to the aviation industry, after it was noticed that a few of the devices contained a type of wire that was hard to find outside flying circles.

With thousands and thousands of leads, but no short list of suspects, the task force began a series of "immersion conferences." One by one, people who had been connected in any way with the bombings—recipients of packages, alleged senders, unintended victims—were summoned to the task force's San Francisco headquarters for intensive, wide-ranging sessions. Each person was put up in a hotel for the duration of the session, and after each interview, investigators plugged the information into a computer database.

Some interview subjects apparently proved more useful than others. Buckley Crist, the very first professor to have his name appropriated for a package way back in 1978, was interviewed several times. The victim of that bombing, Terry Marker, was interviewed only once. He recalled, "They told me, 'We've been looking for you.' I thought that was strange because I'm easy to find." The bomber's second victim, graduate student John Harris, was also contacted only once.

Chemistry professor James Hill of California State University–Sacramento, who had been listed as the sender of the June 22, 1993, bomb, was interviewed repeatedly. During a 1½-day-long grilling at the end of 1993, he sat at a conference table, surrounded by some 15 federal agents and experts, including a psychologist and a computer specialist, exchanging information and theories. When Hill was shown a series of pictures of explosive devices and reconstructed packages, he was struck by the primitiveness of the designs. The wood had rough edges and looked as if it had been carved with a chisel. The wires had been ineptly soldered.

As Hill and the task force brainstormed, speculation arose that the bomber might be disabled. There was also talk that he might be affiliated with the Sacramento campus. That fit nicely with something Hill had observed earlier that year. In the spring, strange graffiti had appeared on the side of the science building where Hill taught, and on other walls nearby. In each instance, someone had painted a peace symbol–like circle with the letters FC inside. Some of the graffiti had the word ANARCHY painted outside the circle. Like many of the agents, Hill thought FC stood for "Fuck Computers." But others at the conference table thought the letters might refer to some aspect of the popular computer game Dungeons & Dragons. The task force subsequently obtained warrants to scour the records of certain individuals on the Sacramento campus.

The sessions with Hill also reinforced the task force's certainty that the Unabomber tended to have out-of-date information. In Hill's case, the Unabomber had listed the professor's ZIP code as 95819. But the university had recently added a local box number, so it should have read 95819-6057. The package that had exploded at Yale identified the sender as Mary Jane Lee, chairman of Sacramento State's computer-science department. In fact, Lee had vacated that post at least one year earlier, and the new chair was Anne-Louise Radimsky.

In July 1994 the task force decided to create a new sketch

of the Unabomber. The secretary who had seen someone plant a device back in 1987 had always contended that the rendering by a local police artist wasn't quite right. This time the FBI enlisted Jeanne Boylan, a top forensic artist who had produced an uncanny likeness of the man later arrested for kidnapping Polly Klaas in Petaluma, California, in 1993. Boylan was first flown to San Francisco, then she and FBI agent Max Noel traveled to Salt Lake City. "Uncle Max," as Boylan quickly came to call agent Noel, was enthusiastic from the start, greeting the artist at the San Francisco International Airport with a stack of three-ring binders filled with information about the case.

When the pair arrived at the secretary's home, the witness was nonplussed. By now, she had grown accustomed to FBI agents. For years after the 1987 bombing, the FBI had monitored her phone line; for a time, some agents actually moved in nearby. The FBI not only knew that this woman was the only person who had ever seen the Unabomber in action; they knew that the Unabomber knew that fact as well. Since that encounter, the woman and her husband and young son had changed addresses at least three times.

Half an hour into the interview, which was repeatedly interrupted by the woman's son, Boylan learned that the man in the parking lot had been wearing aviator sunglasses. The previous artist had, in at least one of his several renderings, eliminated the glasses and conjured the eyes from his own imagination. "I gave Max a look like, 'What are you, crazy? What am I doing here? A glance of a man with sunglasses and a hood, it's seven years later, and I'm supposed to get something?' " Boylan recalled. "The only good news was that this woman obviously connected this man with the bomb. There was only a short time between seeing him and when the bomb went off. There needs to be trauma for visual information to be imbedded in memory.

The detail of his jaw, the underbite were encoded in her visual memory. It just needed to be pulled out."

For six hours, Boylan talked to the witness about shapes and textures. Not once did the artist ask a direct question about facial features. She knew that people tend to remember images as a whole, rather than in distinct components. "You need to take time to get to the subliminal level of memory," she said. "That's where the accurate information is, not always in what we think we saw." Boylan's sketch was the image that would become fixed in Americans' minds.

Like Percy Wood in 1980 and David Gelernter in 1993, Thomas Mosser was home alone in his kitchen at the moment of impact. This time, the town was North Caldwell, an expensive suburb in northern New Jersey. As with most previous bombs, this one had been cleverly packaged to suggest an everyday item. In this case, it had the size and weight of two videocassettes. It appeared so innocuous, in fact, that the package had been in the house a full day, passing between Mosser's wife and at least one of his two daughters several times without being opened.

Nine days earlier, Mosser had been promoted to general manager of Young & Rubicam, a major advertising firm in Manhattan. There is no chance he recognized the name on the return address: H.C. Wickel, Department of Economics, San Francisco State University, because no one by that name exists. Perhaps, as he unwrapped the package, Mosser was thinking of the Christmas tree he and his family planned to buy later in the day. *Boom!* The blast was so powerful that it blew a crater in the Formica countertop. Mosser's wife Susan ran out of the house yelling, "Help! Help! Help!" But Mosser was already dead.

It was Dec. 10, 1994. (The 11th bomb had gone off on

Dec. 11, 1985.) The Unabomber had been lying low for 18 months, and the task force had dwindled to 30 people. Now as investigators were worried that a companion bomb might be in the offing, Jim R. Freeman, the FBI official who now ran the task force, quickly beefed it up again. He also appealed to the public. "The Unabom suspect has eluded capture for 16 years," he said. "Usually, the suspect will talk to someone, and that will lead to that person being brought to light."

Furious and frustrated, the task force raised the reward to $1 million, established a toll-free number (800-701-BOMB) and went on the Internet to solicit help. Within a week, some 3,100 tips, leads and theories poured into the phone hot line.

Four days after Mosser's death, the Unabom Task Force finally gave a news conference in a federal building in downtown San Francisco. By then scores of corporations, looking to protect themselves, had phoned security firms. The task force had resisted going public for a few days, hoping to have good news to announce. Now, with no real break in the case, investigators felt they should at least provide the panicked public with some pointers about detecting package bombs.

The agents warned the public to be on the alert for unmetered packages, especially those posted to business addresses; few companies used stamps to send parcels anymore. People should also look for packages that seemed to have too much postage on them. Packages that had lumps, bulges and protrusions. Packages with oil stains, odd smells or careless wrapping. Packages addressed erroneously, addressed to generic titles like "Chief of Security," or posted with no return address. If a package was preceded or followed by a note or card asking if the package had arrived, people were exhorted to exercise caution.

The one resonating message that reporters received that day was how common package bombs were—and how difficult it was to guard against them. In the past five years 10,000 bombings had been reported in the U.S., and more than 2,200 attempts. "If somebody has the knowledge and enough hatred to kill you," said ATF explosives-enforcement officer John Caponio, "there's not much you can do about it." It wasn't a very reassuring session.

Two veterans of the Unabomber case found themselves mulling over the elusive quarry. FBI agent John Douglas, who had worked on the agency's original profile in 1979, said, "He has a rigid personality. You have to be a rigid personality to do what he does. Everything is in its place. In order. He may not look perfectly neat, but in his house, all his tools, his possessions, would be in their place, very, very organized." To Douglas, that suggested a special workshop, known only to the Unabomber.

Explosives expert Ronay imagined that workshop as a poorly furnished room where the bomber worked deep into the night, lovingly fashioning bits of wood, copper and steel into cherished but deadly toys. "I think he really gets some gratification or satisfaction in creating and manipulating these bomb components," said Ronay. "If he had a relationship, it was with someone much younger, somebody he could control or be comfortable with. A guy like this is probably not a very accomplished social person."

Beginning in the 1940s, New York City was terrorized by someone called the Mad Bomber. For 16 years, he set off pipe bombs around the city, leaving a long trail of injuries, but no clues. In 1956, after the 47th bombing, the New York *Journal-American* published an open letter, inviting the Mad Bomber to respond. To the surprise of investigators, he did, sending several letters that unwittingly disclosed an age-old grudge against Consolidated Edison, where he had once been employed. That clue was enough to enable investigators to flush George Metesky, 53, out of the shadows and into the safe embrace of a mental hospital. Released in 1973, Metesky died 21 years later at age 90.

The Unabom team desperately wanted such a break—some communication with their prey that would let them see into his mind. So they too issued a not-so-subtle invitation. "The problem is not that there are no leads; there are too many," ATF's Cavanaugh told the New York *Times* in an article that ran eight days after the explosion in Mosser's kitchen. "And Unabomber hasn't told us enough. I feel he wants to tell us more."

The Unabomber did not take the bait immediately. Perhaps he never would have, except for an act of savagery so ruthless and unsettling that it knocked him off the front pages. Four months after that New York *Times* article appeared, on April 19, 1995, a nearly 2½-ton bomb ripped through the Alfred P. Murrah Federal Building in Oklahoma City. The headlines, the grief, the fury, the national bewilderment at the idea that there were people so hostile to the Federal Government that they would murder children, amounted to a national crisis. The Unabomber had been upstaged.

The next day, a Thursday, a shoebox-size package and four letters were posted from Oakland, California. The following Sunday, as these items wended their way through the mails, an anonymous man with a gravelly voice called the Association of California Insurance Companies in Sacramento at 10:52 a.m. and breathed into the answering machine, "Hi. I'm the Unabomber, and I just called to say 'Hi.' "

On Monday morning, a secretary heard the message, but distracted by other chores, waited several hours before she notified police, who quickly passed the information to the FBI. No one knew what to make of the message. The Unabomber had never preyed upon insurance targets.

Perhaps he—or whoever—had misdialed. The insurance association's phone number was 440-1111. The sheriff's office number was 440-5111, just one digit off.

Late that same morning, the parcel mailed from Oakland on June 20 reached the single-story dark brick Sacramento headquarters of the California Forestry Association, just four blocks from the insurance association. Marked with a return address for Closet Dimensions, a custom furniture store in Oakland, the 10-lb. package was addressed to William Dennison, who had vacated the post of CFA president a year earlier. His replacement was Gilbert P. Murray, an affable, quiet-spoken former forester who had quickly earned the affection of his 10-member staff.

Lisa was particularly fond of Murray. Not only had he given her the fancy new title of communications director, but Murray had taken a paternalistic interest in her pregnancy. Now four months along, Lisa was preparing for yet another visit to the doctor when she popped her head into Murray's office and mentioned a videotape she had just had made of her sonogram.

"Bring it in!" Murray responded.

"You want to see my sonogram?" said Lisa, surprised.

"Hey, it'll be neat," he answered. "I'll watch it at lunchtime."

A little later, as the hour approached 2, Murray encountered Lisa in the lobby and asked, "Have you seen Michelle?" referring to the office receptionist.

"No, I haven't," Lisa answered, then headed for her office, 20 ft. away. As she turned into her office, she looked back and saw Murray fiddling with a package in the reception area. "This is heavy enough to be a bomb!" a colleague commented.

"Well," Murray bantered, "at least it's from Oakland, not Oklahoma City."

Boom! Lisa ran into the hallway, but the electricity had been knocked out by the explosion, and there was so much smoke that she couldn't see anything. After calling out Murray's name, she ran back into her office and dialed 911. Then she and four other employees, none of whom had been injured, ran out the back door and stood in the alley, waiting for Murray to join them. When he didn't appear, she begin thinking of his wife and two sons: "What is Connie going to do?"

The bomb, which had exploded in Murray's hands, killed him instantly. It blew two doors off their hinges, blasted a series of hand-size gashes 15 ft. up the walls of a skylight recess and embedded hundreds of pieces of shrapnel in the frame of Lisa's office door. The noise was thunderous. "I once heard an M-80," Lisa recalled. "This was 10 times louder." For blocks around, office workers poured anxiously into the street, their nerves already frayed by the Oklahoma City tragedy. A few hours later, workers in the state capitol shuddered when they spotted a box resting outside a door in a corridor not far from Governor Pete Wilson's office. The next day, an unattended suitcase left in a capitol building washroom stirred alarm. In both instances, the objects proved harmless. On Wednesday, state assembly speaker Willie Brown announced that local police were scouring the capitol building from top to bottom. The search, he explained, was in response to a phone threat: "I want $250,000 or the capitol gets bombed. Give it to me, or I'll blow up the place." The threat proved bogus.

The task force quickly concluded that the Murray murder had no direct connection to Oklahoma City but was the work of the Unabomber, who appeared to have traded up to an even more potent chemical charge, perhaps hard-to-get sodium chlorate. They were worried that their serial killer now had a new motive. "All the reports of the Oklahoma bombing, all the attention that received, may have stimulated the Unabomber to do something he had been planning all along but for which he hadn't picked a date," suggested Fred Rosenthal, a San Francisco psychiatrist. "When someone has a tendency to be violent, and there is a lot of activity and stress and upheaval and chaos, he is then more likely to get involved in violence. It is stimulating, very arousing for him."

The Unabomber, it seemed, wanted to bump the Oklahoma blast off the front pages and reclaim his rightful position as America's pre-eminent terrorist. Cool and calculated for so long, he was perhaps finally losing his legendary patience and discipline.

That same Monday, across the country in Connecticut, 1993 bombing victim David Gelernter was going through the day's mail when he came upon an envelope with the return address Ninth Street and Pennsylvania Avenue, Washington, D.C., 20535. That, he knew, was the address of the FBI headquarters.

Inside, there was a five-paragraph letter from the Unabomber, signed FC and filled with nasty taunts: "People with advanced degrees aren't as smart as they think they are. If you'd had any brains you would have realized that there are a lot of people out there who resent bitterly the way techno-nerds like you are changing the world and you wouldn't have been dumb enough to open an unexpected package from an unknown source." A P.S. added, "Warren Hoge of the New York Times can confirm that this letter does come from FC."

It seemed likely it had, because that same day Hoge received a Unabomber missive himself. Kris Ensminger, the secretary who had opened the letter to Hoge two years earlier, realized immediately that the letter was from the Unabomber, and this time waited for the FBI to open it. What they found inside proved that Cavanaugh of ATF had been right: the Unabomber did want to tell investigators more.

"This is a message from the terrorist group FC," the letter began. "We blew up Thomas Mosser last December because he was a Burston-Marsteller executive. Among other misdeeds, Burston-Marsteller helped Exxon clean up its public image after the Exxon Valdez incident."

Once again, the Unabomber was operating on dated information. Mosser had left Burson-Marsteller nine months before his death to join its parent company, Young & Rubicam. Moreover, though Burson-Marsteller, which he had misspelled, listed Exxon among its clients, the public-relations firm had done no work on the *Exxon Valdez* oil spill. Perhaps he had dug up that bit of misinformation from *Earth First!* a radical environmentalist publication that two months earlier had linked the public-relations firm to Exxon's effort to exert some spin control over the *Valdez* debacle.

"Some news reports have made the misleading statement that we have been attacking universities or scholars," continued the letter, which, single-spaced, filled more than two full pages. "We have nothing against universities or scholars as such. All the university people whom we have attacked have been specialists in technical fields ... The people we are out to get are the scientists and engineers, especially in critical fields like computers and genetics."

That spoke to targets. But what about motive? "We call ourselves anarchists because we would like, ideally, to break down all society into very small, completely autonomous units," he wrote. "Regrettably, we don't see any clear road to this goal, so we leave it to the indefinite future. Our more immediate goal, which we think may be attainable at some time during the next several decades, is the destruction of the worldwide industrial system. Through our bombings we hope to promote social instability in industrial society, propagate anti-industrial ideas and give encouragement to those who hate the industrial system."

The Unabomber also boasted of his growing sophistication as a bombmaker: "Since we no longer have to confine the explosive in a pipe, we are now free of limitations on the size and shape of our bombs . . . So we expect to be able to pack deadly bombs into ever smaller, lighter and more harmless looking packages." Then he offered a threat that seemed a direct response to the Oklahoma blast. "On the other hand, we believe we will be able to make bombs much bigger than any we've made before. With a briefcase-full or a suitcase-full of explosives we should be able to blow out the walls of substantial buildings." Unable to resist a dig at the besieged FBI, he stated, "Clearly we are in a position to do a great deal of damage. And it doesn't appear that the FBI is going to catch us any time soon. The FBI is a joke."

But, the Unabomber confessed, "we are getting tired of making bombs. It's no fun having to spend all your evenings and weekends preparing dangerous mixtures, filing trigger mechanisms out of scraps of metal or searching the sierras for a place isolated enough to test a bomb. So we offer a bargain."

The bargain was this: FC wanted the New York *Times,* TIME or *Newsweek* to publish an article that would run between 29,000 and 37,000 words in length and be followed, each year for three successive years, by 3,000-word articles expanding on its themes. The bombing would stop once the first article appeared in print—unless authorities tracked down the bomber, in which case FC reserved the right to retaliate with violence. Noting that "We distinguish between terrorism and sabotage," the author pledged to stop attacking people, while continuing to target property. "Please see to it that the answer to our effort is well publicized in the media so that we won't miss it," the letter ended. "If the answer is unsatisfactory, we will start building our next bomb."

Bingo! "He's describing his actions and motives for the first time in 17 years," said Jim Freeman, head of the FBI office in San Francisco. "He's made an offer," added Louis Bertram, who had chased the Unabomber for many years before retiring. "It's on the table." Moreover, the Unabomber had referred to the "sierras" in his letter to the *Times*. Investigators took this to mean the Sierra Nevada, whose western slopes were within reach of Sacramento.

Given this flurry of activity, and his penchant for pairs, some veteran hands were worried the Unabomber would strike again soon. "When they feel they're not recognized, that it's a lost cause," warned profiler John Douglas, who had recently retired from the FBI, "they become violent." And one more thing, Douglas said. "When he's finally caught, people will be surprised. He's not going to look odd. He'll be the average next-door neighbor."

Others wondered if their elusive prey was finally weary of his own game. "He is tired and he wants to quit; 17 years has been enough," reckoned Bertram. But, the retired FBI agent warned, "he wants to go out in a glorious way."

The Bomber Speaks

In order to get our message before the public with some chance of making a lasting impression, we've had to kill people. —Manifesto, paragraph 96

For weeks after the death of Gilbert Murray in April, the suddenly talkative Unabomber fell quiet again. Then in June he re-emerged to resume his game at a new level of menace. On June 27, a letter arrived at the office of the San Francisco *Chronicle*. The text was short and to the point. "WARNING: the terrorist group FC, called Unabomber by the FBI, is planning to blow up an airliner out of Los Angeles International Airport sometime during the next six days." So that no one should doubt that this was the real Unabomber talking, the writer cited the first two digits—55—of the nine-digit code he had earlier given the New York *Times*.

Was the killer changing his standard operating procedures? This letter marked the first time he had announced in advance his intention to set a bomb. It also represented an abrupt reversal of his insistence in an earlier letter to the New York *Times* that he targeted only crucial participants in the technological order, such as scientists and engineers. A more perverse twist was still to come. One day after the *Chronicle* received its threat, an anonymous letter arrived at the New York *Times*. The gist of this one was, in effect, "only kidding."

"Since the public has such a short memory," it read, "we

decided to play one last prank to remind them who we are. But no, we haven't tried to plant a bomb on an airline (recently)."

Late in his career, the Unabomber had developed a morbid sense of humor. But had his little joke reached the final punch line? What if he still intended to sabotage a plane? His letter to the *Times* may have been a ruse to persuade authorities to let down their guard. Figuring it could not afford to take chances, the Federal Aviation Administration imposed strict security measures at California's major airports. At Los Angeles International Airport, outbound passengers were required to show identification at every stage of the departure process, from curbside baggage check-in to final boarding. For a week the Postal Service refused to accept any first-class mail in California that weighed more than three-fourths of a pound. A lawyer on a United Airlines flight from San Francisco was briefly interrogated by the FBI because he bore a passing resemblance to the composite sketch of the Unabomber and had been "acting suspicious"—he had been wearing sunglasses throughout the flight.

Then came the most momentous communication of all, the one everybody had been waiting for. On Wednesday night, June 28, a single-spaced typewritten manuscript, 56 pages and 35,000 words long, plus 11 pages of footnotes and other material, arrived at the offices of the New York *Times.* The next day, a similar package arrived at the Washington *Post.* It was the Unabomber's manifesto. It came complete with a page listing corrections to typographical errors—the Unabomber either didn't have access to Wite-Out or didn't approve of it—and a hand-drawn chart: "Diagram of Symptoms Resulting from Disruption of the Power Process," which was the killer's map of the connections between such things as frustration, anger, boredom and abuse. All paths led to a central nexus: "Tendency to Depression."

In letters accompanying the manuscript, the Unabomber offered his cold-blooded deal. He would stop killing if his text was published in the *Times* or the *Post*, along with three annual follow-ups. In a separate letter to Bob Guccione, publisher of *Penthouse*, the would-be-swank skin magazine, the Unabomber added a macabre subclause to his offer. The two papers had "first claim on the right to publish." If they passed, it could be published in *Penthouse*, which had earlier offered to run it.

But since *Penthouse* was less "respectable" than the other publications, "we promise to desist permanently from terrorism, except that we reserve the right to plant one (and only one) bomb intended to kill, after our manuscript has been published." With lawyerly caution, the bomber also reserved the right to go on destroying property even if he quit harming people. Soon after, *Penthouse* publisher Bob Guccione added his own bizarre touch to the episode. He took out a full page ad in the New York *Times* to convince the Unabomber that his magazine was, in fact, a respectable venue—and to offer him a regular column.

The Unabomber's mailings to the *Times* and *Post* created a sensation to compare with anything literally explosive he had ever sent in the past. In his letter to the *Times*, the Unabomber indignantly denied that he had been more active lately to compete with the Oklahoma City bombing. "We strongly deplore the kind of indiscriminate slaughter that occurred in the Oklahoma City event."

He went on: "As for people who willfully and knowingly promote economic growth and technical progress, in our eyes they are criminals, and if they get blown up, they deserve it." Speaking of which, he added that while it was true that the explosive that killed Gilbert Murray had been addressed to someone else, Murray "was pursuing the same goals." But on reflection, the Unabomber was glad that he hadn't destroyed that American Airlines flight in 1979. "The idea was to kill a lot of business people," he wrote. "But, of course, some of the passengers would likely have been innocent people—maybe kids or some working stiff going to see his grandmother. We're glad now that that attempt failed."

If it were not already clear, the Unabomber also explained what motivated him: "anger."

In a sinister side flourish, the letter to the *Times* gave a return address in Davis, California. It turned out be to the headquarters of Calgene Inc., a company best known for the production of genetically engineered tomatoes. Was that his way of saying that he had them in his sights? The return address on the *Post's* mailing belonged to Boon Long Hoe, a San Jose, California, business executive at GSS Array Technology Co. Ltd., a Thailand-based circuit-board manufacturer. A stunned Hoe told the San Jose *Mercury News* that he was "devastated" and bewildered at having been singled out. "I never got any publicity. I'm very low profile and so is the company."

The Unabomber gave the papers three months to decide whether they would publish his text. With that began a furious debate within law-enforcement and journalistic circles. If they published, the papers might be accommodating a serial killer who could simply raise the ante, demanding more space for more public musings. They might also be inviting copycat behavior by other terrorists. Say no, however, and they could appear as accomplices to murder if the enraged Unabomber struck again.

Soon after the manuscripts arrived, a group of executives and editors from the two papers went to the Justice Department for a meeting with Attorney General Janet Reno and FBI Director Louis Freeh. In the *Post* delegation there was publisher Donald E. Graham, president Boisfeuillet Jones Jr. and executive editor Leonard Downie Jr. The *Times* was represented by publisher Arthur Ochs Sulzberger Jr. and executive editor Joseph Lelyveld. According to two *Post* executives at the meeting, they sought the "recommendation" of Reno and Freeh as to whether to publish the text. They were also briefed on the psychological profile of the bomber assembled by the FBI. It dovetailed in important respects with the views of independent behavioral experts consulted by the *Post.*

The government's official policy is that you never make concessions to terrorists. But in this case the Justice Department was anxious to see the text distributed, in the hope of churning up new leads. Journalists believe that, in principle, newspapers aren't supposed to do the bidding of government without the strongest of reasons. Did this qualify? The discussions were intricate and anguished on all sides.

Related arguments were going on everywhere outside. Among psychologists the question was whether publication might satisfy the bomber's desire for public attention and lead him to abandon his killing spree. Or would it simply cause him to escalate his demands? Reid Meloy, a forensic psychologist at the University of California at San Diego who had tracked the Unabomber, told the Los Angeles *Times,* "The next thing you know, he'll demand that all Gideon Bibles in motel rooms across America be replaced with leather-bound copies of his manuscript." Jack Levin, a serial-murder specialist at Northeastern University in Boston, told the same paper: "This is a guy who's got to kill to stay powerful and stay in the spotlight."

In a late September interview with TIME that was then off the record, *Times* publisher Sulzberger recalled that the *Times* collected a group of about a half-dozen staff members to think through what its response should be. "We had three months to figure this thing out," he said. "As we began the process, that group was not of a single mind. But as we got closer to the decision, we really did settle on a course of action that achieved unanimity."

He also defended the decision of the two papers to seek the advice of the FBI. "We wanted the input of people who are considered experts on this," he said. "They've been following this guy for 17 years. Neither [Washington *Post* publisher] Don Graham or I had much experience in dealing with terrorists first hand." Even so, said Sulzberger, at no time did he or his colleagues feel any pressure from the government to publish the manifesto.

In a separate interview, Washington *Post* executive editor Downie concurred that the Justice Department did not plead or twist arms to get the papers to publish. He also insisted that until the very end the executives and editors of the two papers were open to persuasion in either direction. "We didn't make up our minds until we made up our minds," he said.

Meanwhile, the Unabomber was talking again—now with a vengeance, almost a literal one. On June 30, Tom Tyler, a social psychology professor at the University of California, Berkeley, received at his office a flat package that he took to be a student's thesis. What he found instead was a letter from the Unabomber and a copy of the manifesto. The killer wanted to make himself perfectly clear to the professor. Why Tyler? In a May 1 edition of the San Francisco *Chronicle,* he had been quoted in a story that tried to draw comparisons between the bombers behind the Oklahoma City incident and the Unabomber. Tyler thought they shared a fear of monolithic order. "Whether it's the technological élite or the government, it's the same basic idea ... It's an exaggerated idea of a kind of secret, all-powerful group that's controlling people's lives."

"I'm very pleased the Unabomber appears interested in providing education about his beliefs," Tyler said later in a cautiously worded statement released by the university after review by the FBI. "I think discussion about these issues is a far more positive and ultimately much more effective way to bring about change than violence."

Tyler also promised to respond more fully to the Unabomber at a later date. He did it in an open letter published on July 4 in the the San Francisco *Chronicle.* Sometimes sounding like a man trying to placate a very intimidating tiger, he wrote that he agreed with some beliefs expressed by the bomber, but disavowed his means. "Your concerns about widespread feelings of inferiority and oversocialization into conformity with society's rule are widely shared," he told him, "as is your suggestion that many people do not find their lives satisfying." But Tyler said he was not sure he agreed with the manifesto's assertion that "a technological society cannot be reformed."

"People are developing the type of antitechnology ideology that you advocate in your manuscript," he wrote. He cited water conservation and recycling efforts as examples, as well as the movement by many people from cities back to the country. He urged the bomber to seek peaceful change. "My impression is that people react to violence by becoming less willing to change."

While the journalists wrestled among themselves over whether to publish, the FBI sent copies of the manifesto to more than 50 professors around the country. The hope was that, in the cadences of the Unabomber, they might recognize one of their former students. Perhaps the stylistic peculiarities of the text, phrases like "consist in" when most writers would say "consist of," would jog their memories. That decision by the FBI prompted the *Times* and the *Post* to part the curtain a bit on the manifesto. As part of long news stories, each printed 3,000-word excerpts, giving the public its first extended glimpse of the Unabomber's mind at work.

It was not a pretty sight. Even in this condensed version, it was apparent that "Industrial Society and Its Future," as his manifesto was titled, was no page turner. A metastasized term paper in affectless prose, it argued and reargued its central premise: "The industrial revolution and its consequences have been a disaster for the human race." His reflections would have gone unnoticed if he had not found such a deadly way to get the world's attention. In the excerpt's one unforgettable sentence, he said so himself. "In order to get our message before the public with some chance of making a lasting impression, we've had to kill people."

On Wednesday, Sept. 13, roughly two weeks before the bomber's deadline, editors and executives of the *Post* and the *Times* met again in Washington with Attorney General Reno and FBI Director Freeh. Reno and Freeh urged them to go public with the text. The journalists sought the FBI's advice on two questions. Would the bomber keep his word? And how dangerous was the copycat problem? The bureau could offer them no guarantees. But time was running out. They had weighed the pros and cons for three months; it was time to decide. Knowing it would be a controversial decision, especially among their professional peers, they said yes.

To minimize the impact, it was decided that only the Washington *Post* would print and distribute the text. That paper had the mechanical means to produce it as a separate insert, which would keep it out of the main news pages. The papers would split the $30,000 to $40,000 cost of the eight-page section.

"Neither paper would have printed this document for journalistic reasons," the *Post's* publisher Graham said later in an interview with his own paper. "We thought there was an obvious public-safety issue involved and therefore sought the advice of responsible federal officials."

The *Times*' Sulzberger told the *Post*, "It's awfully hard to put too much faith in the words of someone with the record of violence that the Unabomber has." But, he said, "you print it and he doesn't kill anyone else; that's a pretty good deal. You print it and he continues to kill people, what have you lost? The cost of newsprint?" He added: "This is not a First Amendment issue. This centers on the role of a newspaper as part of a community."

On the day that the manifesto appeared, Sulzberger and Graham issued a carefully worded joint statement. Both Reno and Freeh had recommended "that we print this document for public safety reasons," it said. "And we have agreed to do so."

So what exactly was it that the delivery trucks unloaded that day to the newsstands? What is the manifesto, and where does it spring from? A hybrid of grad-school thesis, ransom note and cri de coeur—cry for help—"Industrial Society and Its Future" is in many ways a unique document, at least in the annals of serial murder. But it's by no means as singular as the Unabomber sometimes appears to believe. It may best be described as a blend of some familiar and enduring lines of Western thought, hitched to the author's own idiosyncratic conclusions about history and human nature and filtered through his misery, resentment and fury.

Given its uninviting length and its book-report language, it's unlikely that many people will get to the last of its 232-numbered paragraphs (plus the bonus of 36 footnotes). Yet for all its repetitions and dry patches, the manifesto makes for interesting reading not only as a glimpse into the mind of a killer but also for the way it requires you again and again to disentangle his plausible reflections from his poisonous and hyperbolic conclusions.

The Unabomber's judgment upon technological society is summarized in his opening flourish: "The Industrial Revolution and its consequences have been a disaster for the human race." Its growth has put relentless pressure on the dwindling realm of human freedom, the power to "control the circumstances of one's own life." In this order of things, natural impulses and pursuits are repressed. Science and technology, and the consumer economy they both serve and create, promote false goals—like prosperity and status—that people spend a lifetime pointlessly pursuing. The future will only bring more sophisticated means for controlling people and shaping them to the needs of the technological order through such things as behavior modification and genetic engineering.

In the Unabomber's view, this diseased social order cannot be reformed. "The only way out is to dispense with the industrial-technological system altogether." But he sees no need to attack it frontally now. He expects that it may collapse of its own weight after a period of crisis that is already upon us. What like-minded people need to do is move to ensure that another technological monster doesn't rise from the ashes of this one.

On the whole, this is an apocalyptic reading of current predicaments but one with a few points that reasonable people may agree with. But there is also a second dimension of the manifesto: the long passages of social psychology, especially in the earlier sections, in which we seem to be hearing the author describe the sources of his own unhappiness.

Early in the text, the Unabomber detours into a condemnation of "leftism," which he defines largely, and strangely, in psychological terms, as a tendency toward "feelings of inferiority" and "oversocialization." Oversocialization makes people "feel ashamed of behavior or speech that is contrary to society's expectation." Yet most Americans would be more likely to identify leftism, as do many conservatives, with countercultural hedonism, sexual liberation and doing your own thing. Kaczynski's parents, however, were left leaning in their politics but also, in a way typical of second-generation immigrants, devoted to hard work, study and discipline. When Mommy and Daddy are also leftists, one might well make an association between the left, feelings of guilt and the repression of free impulses.

Elsewhere the Unabomber writes at length about "the power process," by which he means the pursuit of achievable goals and their attainment through "AUTONOMOUS" (his capitals) effort. Technological society thwarts that necessary experience, he says, by promoting false goals. It defeats autonomy by making everyone dependent upon it for the satisfaction of their needs. When the power process is denied, he says, the consequences are "boredom, demoralization, low self-esteem, inferiority feelings, defeatism, depression, anxiety, guilt, frustration, hostility, spouse or child abuse." Is this a diagnosis of humanity as a whole or of the author? In Kaczynski's cabin, the FBI found a bottle of Trazodone, a prescription antidepressant.

Despite his multitude of footnotes, the Unabomber doesn't offer many specific sources for his thinking. Only a few writers are mentioned by name. One is Eric Hoffer, the longshoreman-turned-political-philosopher whose dissection of mass movements, *The True Believer,* was widely read in the 1960s. But much of what the manifesto has to say draws from ideas at large in the West for centuries, starting with the traditions of thought that look upon all the products of human invention as corrupt. It was from the Tree of Knowledge, after all, that Eve took that fatal apple.

> It took the triumph of Romanticism in the late 18th and early 19th centuries for nature to achieve something like its present status as a semidivine and sentimental ideal. This shift roughly coincided with the first stirrings of anxiety about the costs of the nascent Industrial Revolution. Hardly had the new factories appeared across England than the poet William Blake was writing about "dark, satanic mills." Some of the concern was purely economic. In the early

1800's, bands of English workers, the Luddites, spread out across the country, smashing textile machinery that they feared, rightly, was a threat to their livelihood.

But it was in America that the pastoral ideal most powerfully took root. Americans and foreigners alike saw the New World as a chance to begin civilization anew on unspoiled ground. Yet, at the same time, there was no nation that held industry and growth in higher esteem. Very soon the two ideals began to collide. By 1844, when Ralph Waldo Emerson wrote in his journal, "I hear the whistle of the locomotive in the woods," he regarded that sound as the harbinger of a headlong and worrisome force.

In the 20th century, with the nations of the West fully in the grip of industrialization, a sophisticated body of social criticism began to worry about the cost to both the natural world and the human race. As early as the 1920s, social critic Lewis Mumford called for a balance with the needs of nature and community. In the 1930s, a group of Southern intellectuals called the Agrarians argued against the modern world as represented by the North.

In the 1950s, when the general abundance of American life was supposed to dispel all doubts about industrial society, there were still doubts to be heard from writers such as Paul Goodman. His influential book *Growing Up Absurd* was one of the many volumes found in Kaczynski's cabin. By the following decade, which Kaczynski spent almost entirely on campuses, a literature of opposition to the technological and bureaucratic order was in full flower.

One famous critic was Jacques Ellul, the French Protestant theologian whose *The Technological Society* described a world enslaved by its own creations. Another was Herbert Marcuse, the German social thinker who spent most of his career in the U.S. and became a hero of the student left through such books as *One-Dimensional Man,* which accused modern capitalism of a subtle totalitarianism. When the Unabomber writes that modern society is "in certain respects extremely permissive" in areas that don't threaten "the functioning of the system," there is an echo of Marcuse's notion of "repressive tolerance," the means by which society permits just enough freedom to ensure that no serious opposition builds up.

Goodman was a leftist libertarian. Ellul was a Christian who rejected virtually all political orders. The critique of technological society doesn't fit comfortably into any one spot on the standard political spectrum. It's a position with something to offer leftist opponents of corporate capitalism and conservative frontiersmen, as well as religious isolates, nostalgists, environmentalists of all stripes and ordinary lovers of the great outdoors. Likewise, on both the left and the right, there are techno-optimists and cheerleaders for science, industrialization and growth. Newt Gingrich has that in common with the central committee of the Chinese Communist Party.

The Unabomber describes his outlook as "our particular brand of anarchism." "This is not to be a POLITICAL revolution," he writes. "Its object will be to overthrow not governments but the economic and technological basis of the present society." But considered as a blueprint for action of any kind, other than the dismal and murderous actions that the Unabomber took, it has little to offer. And it provides even less in the way of a picture of what kind of society might replace this one. "The positive idea that we propose is nature. That is WILD nature." But just how in this antitechnological utopia would people be forbidden to develop new technologies? And what about such essential areas of progress as medicine and agricultural science?

Living as a hermit, the Unabomber probably had no one to

STEVE ADAMS—GAMMA LIAISON

After an 18-year search, the FBI arrested Ted Kaczynski, a suspect in the Unabom explosions that killed three people and injured 22, at his remote plywood shack in the Montana woods

TODD KOROL—SIPA

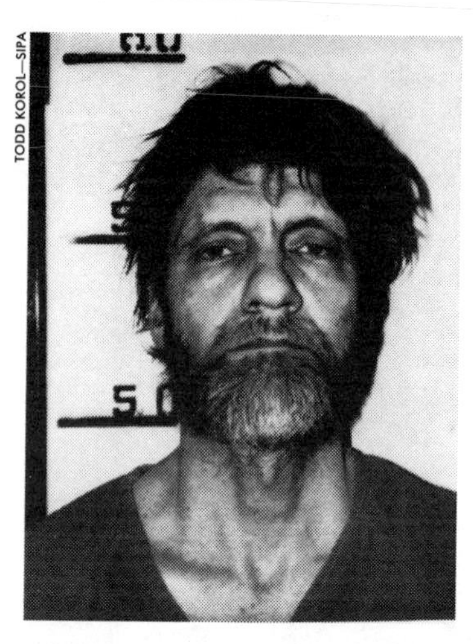

Kaczynski's mug shot from the day of his arrest. He hadn't always looked like this. He is remembered as being clean-cut in his early days in Montana, but after years of living poor, he was described by Lincolnites as "ratty" and "ragged." A Helena hotel owner said he had got much worse during the past year

TOM TREICK—THE OREGONIAN—SYGMA

The "perp walk." FBI agents and federal marshals lead Kaczynski, second from right, up a loading dock to an elevator to the fifth floor of the Helena, Montana, federal building on April 3, 1996

LEWIS AND CLARK COUNTY ASSESSORS—AP

No rnng wtr, no elctrc, mtn view. The 10-ft. by 12-ft. cabin in which the suspect lived on and off for 25 years offered few creature comforts but yielded some 700 pieces of potential evidence

RICK WILKING—REUTERS

Some people in Lincoln said they wouldn't know Kaczynski if he wasn't on a bike, with his pants rolled up and a yellow flag to warn away traffic. On wet days, the fenderless back wheel threw a stripe of mud up his back

SYGMA

An FBI sketch of the Unabomber, left. Perhaps not wanting to be outdone by the Oklahoma City bombing caused the Unabomber to re-emerge—after years of silence—with new threats and demands: he would stop only if the manifesto that he sent to the New York *Times* and the Washington *Post* was printed. In the end, his words, which played a significant role in his capture, betrayed him

AGOSTINI—GAMMA LIAISON

The Washington Post

TUESDAY, SEPTEMBER 19, 1995

118th Year No. 288

Weather

House Plan

Unabomber Manuscript Is Published

'Public Safety Reasons' Cited in Joint Decision By Post, N.Y. Times

By Howard Kurtz
Washington Post Staff Writer

After weighing the question for nearly three months, The Washington Post and New York Times have agreed to publish in today's Post a 35,000-word manuscript submitted by the Unabomber, the serial mail bomber who has promised to halt his deadly attacks if either newspaper ran his lengthy critique of industrial society.

Donald E. Graham, The Post's publisher, and Arthur O. Sulzberger Jr., publisher of the New York Times, said they jointly decided to publish the document "for public safety reasons" after meeting last Wednesday with Attorney General Janet Reno and FBI Director Louis J. Freeh. The papers are splitting the cost of an eight-page insert, which will appear only in The Post because

A SUPPLEMENT TO THE WASHINGTON POST

This text was sent last June to The New York Times and The Washington Post by the person who calls himself "FC," identified by the FBI as the Unabomber, whom authorities have implicated in three murders and 16 bombings. The author threatened to send a bomb to an unspecified destination "with intent to kill" unless one of the newspapers published this manuscript. The Attorney General and the Director of the FBI recommended publication. An article about the decision to publish the document appears on the front page of today's paper.

INDUSTRIAL SOCIETY AND ITS FUTURE

INTRODUCTION

1. The Industrial Revolution and its consequences have been a disaster for the human race. They have greatly increased the life-expectancy of those of us who live in "advanced" countries, but they have destabilized society, have made life unfulfilling, have subjected human beings to indignities, have led to widespread psychological suffering (in the Third World to physical suffering as well) and have inflicted severe damage on the natural world. The continued development of technology will worsen the situation.

9. The two psychological tendencies that underlie modern leftism we call "feelings of inferiority" and "oversocialization." Feelings of inferiority are characteristic of modern leftism as a whole, while oversocialization is characteristic only of a certain segment of modern leftism; but this segment is highly influential.

FEELINGS OF INFERIORITY

his own needs. The leftist is antagonistic to the concept of competition because, deep inside, he feels like a loser.

17. Art forms that appeal to modern leftish intellectuals tend to focus on sordidness, defeat and despair, or else they take an orgiastic tone, throwing off rational control as if there were no hope of accomplishing anything through rational calculation and all that was left was to immerse oneself in the sensations of the moment.

18. Modern leftish philosophers tend to dismiss reason, science, objective reality and to insist that everything is culturally relative. It is true that one can ask serious questions about the foundations of scientific knowledge and about how, if at all, the concept of objective reality can be defined. But it is obvious that modern leftish philosophers are not simply cool-headed logicians systematically analyzing the foundations of knowledge. They are deeply involved emotionally in their attack on truth and reality. They attack these concepts because of their own psychological needs.

TOM HORAN—SYGMA

Attorney Anthony P. Bisceglia contacted the FBI at David Kaczynski's request

DENNIS COOK—AP

FBI profiler Clint Van Zandt, above; private investigator Susan Swanson

STEVE KAGAN—PEOPLE

BRAD RICKERBY—SIPA FOR TIME

David Kaczynski read the manifesto in the hope that he could discount any connection with his brother Ted. But instead it had the opposite effect, confirming his worst suspicion: that his brother might well be the Unabomber

DOROTHY O'CONNELL—AP

David, left, and Ted, center, in 1954 in Evergreen Park, Illinois, playing in the sandbox with their friends, the O'Connell children. "Ted was always the quiet one," said Mrs. O'Connell

JOYCE COLLIS

Well liked in Evergreen Park, the Kaczynski parents impressed the neighbors with their kindness and good cheer; they socialized with friends and actively participated in neighborhood organizations

JEAN MARC GIBOUX—GAMMA LIAISON

In 1952 the Kaczynskis moved to Evergreen Park, a new and growing Chicago suburb, and raised their sons in this three-bedroom house

JOYCE COLLIS

Ted, center back row, the trombone player with the Evergreen Park High School band, in the 1956 yearbook. Recollections of his talents vary: first-rate is one. Dutiful, mechanical and uninspired is another

THEODORE JOHN KACZYNSKI

Born: May 22, 1942 in Chicago, Ill. Prepared at Evergreen Park H.S., Evergreen Park, Ill. Home Address: 9209 Lawndale, Evergreen Park, Ill. Field of Concentration: Mathematics. Scholarships and Prizes: Harvard College Scholarship.

AP

Ted's senior-year page in the 1962 Harvard yearbook. By the late 1950s the élite university was opening up to the new meritocracy

SCOTT MANCHESTER—SYGMA

In the heyday of student revolt in the late '60s, Ted spent two years as an assistant professor of mathematics at Berkeley, remaining above the fray; then he abruptly resigned without giving any reason

Ted earned his graduate degrees at the University of Michigan (1962-67). For a time he lived in one of the dormitories. At Michigan he demonstrated a passion for math, but outside of class the inquisitive student disappeared into himself

WILLIAM JORDAN—THE ANN ARBOR NEWS—AP

F. CARTER SMITH—SYGMA

David and his friend Juan Sánchez Arreola, who helped the younger Kaczynski build a small cabin on his 40 acres of sparsely populated land in West Texas

F. CARTER SMITH—SYGMA

In the early 1980s, David set out to find his own wilderness in Texas. He settled on arid land in the shadow of the Christmas Mountains, 40 miles north of Mexico. He was five hours from the nearest airport, 20 miles from a paved road. Before he built his cabin, he lived in a hole dug in the ground covered by tarps or corrugated metal

Although they never met, Ted had a seven-year correspondence with Sánchez detailing his life in the Montana woods; he wrote mostly of his poverty and isolation

F. CARTER SMITH—SYGMA

PHILLIPPE DEIDERICH—CONTACT FOR TIME

Ted chose Sánchez, a 68-year-old Mexican farmhand, as confidant

F. CARTER SMITH—SYGMA

One Christmas, Ted sent his Mexican pen pal an intricately carved wooden cylinder painted with vines and berries, rather like a pencil case—or a pipe bomb

Ted Sr. and Wanda, left, alongside son David and Linda Patrik, with her parents at the young couple's 1990 summer wedding. A few months later, Ted Sr., suffering from terminal cancer, killed himself

David returned from his Texas wilderness home to marry the girl of his dreams and find a way to do some good, helping runaway kids. At the mostly Buddhist wedding ceremony conducted in a backyard, his smile reflects his good fortune

ERIC MILLER—REUTERS

Looking dapper with a new haircut and clothes, Ted Kaczynski is escorted from federal court in Helena after the judge denied his motion to dismiss all charges because of government leaks

WARREN GOLDBERG—SABA

J.L. BULCAO—GAMMA LIAISON

After Thomas Mosser was killed on Dec. 10, 1994, in his kitchen in North Caldwell, New Jersey, his wife Susan was led away from the house. Earlier, the unopened parcel, delivered to his mailbox, left, had been passed between members of the family. The Mossers and their two daughters had been planning to shop for a Christmas tree later that day

AP

Advertising executive Thomas Mosser had recently been named general manager of Young & Rubicam in New York when a blast took his life in 1994. The Unabomber apparently thought Mosser worked at Burson-Marsteller, an error that did not save Mosser

Gilbert P. Murray was standing in the reception area of the California Forestry Association's Sacramento headquarters when a bomb exploded in his hands on April 24, 1995. The blast, which made a series of hand-size gashes 15 ft. up the walls of a skylight recess, killed Murray instantly, bringing the Unabomber's death toll to three

AP

AP

The explosion at a computer-rental store in Sacramento, California, on Dec. 11, 1985, tore a hole in the chest of Hugh Scrutton, exposing his heart. Though the Unabomber had mailed or planted 10 previous bombs, causing numerous injuries, this was the first incident to claim a life

BARRY STAVER

AP

A June 1980 package exploded in the hands of United Airlines president Percy Wood, above right; engineering professor Diogenes Angelakos, above left, happened upon another bomb in July 1982 in a faculty coffee room at the University of California, Berkeley; graduate student John Hauser, on bike, was injured by a May 1985 blast

David Gelernter, director of undergraduate studies in computer science at Yale University, was the Unabomber's second academic target in the space of just two days. The mailed bomb that erupted in Gelernter's hands on June 24, 1993, injured the professor's right eye, chest and abdomen, and smashed his right hand beyond repair

JAMES KEYSER FOR TIME

challenge his most questionable assumptions. In the end, the most pertinent source for his manifesto may not be Ellul or Mumford but Dostoyevsky and his *Notes from Underground*, with its wretched narrator who despises the claims of rationality but feels their sheer weight pressing in upon him. "Oh no," he cries out at one point as he confronts himself with the possibility that the human race may be boxed into a mechanical arrangement. "In that case man would go insane on purpose, just to be immune from reason." Anyone looking for models of the Unabomber's mind may do well to start there.

Publication of the manifesto only sharpened the fight over whether it was the right thing to do. "It was a huge mistake," Jane Kirtley, executive director of the Reporters' Committee for Freedom of the Press, said in the Washington *Post*. "It really blurs the line between being an independent journalistic enterprise and just being a toady for the government." But William Ketter, president of the American Society of Newspaper Editors, approved the decision in the context of "the history of the press in this country co-operating with the government during wartime."

After Kaczynski's arrest, Warren Hoge, assistant managing editor of the *Times*, said he had no regrets about the decision, especially given that the appearance of the manifesto was a crucial link in the events that led to Kaczynski's capture. "There were people who said, 'How dare you do that? Anybody now can write the New York *Times*, threaten to blow up somebody, and you'll publish 35,000 words.' But, of course, that's not at all what it meant. We published that one because this was a particular individual who had proved beyond a shadow of any doubt that he would do exactly what he threatened to do and that he couldn't be caught. And it was a matter that somebody might die."

The papers also got support from President Clinton. "I applaud them," he told a Pittsburgh, Pennsylvania, television station. "They had acted," he said, "in a good and brave way."

Distribution of the manifesto did not end with the 850,000 copies printed by the *Post*. A day later, the text was published by the Oakland *Tribune*. Time Warner posted a copy on the Internet's World Wide Web, making it perhaps the first epic-length attack on technology to be sent everywhere on a computer network. By December, a small Berkeley publishing house had come out with a paperback edition of the text for $9.95. Kristan Lawson, publisher of Jolly Roger Press, which brought out the book, said the FBI asked him to provide the name, address and phone number of "every single bookstore, company or person that ordered from me." They surmised the Unabomber would order a souvenir copy for himself. Lawson agreed, but with an initial print run of 11,000 copies, he said, the record keeping soon became so burdensome that he stopped taking individual orders and sold only to distributors.

On the day the manifesto was printed, Jim R. Freeman, the special agent in charge of the San Francisco office of the FBI, held a press conference. His main purpose was to urge people to read the thing and to think back to acquaintances from college or even high school, anyone who might have had "similar philosophies." As for the suspect's behavioral profile, Freeman said, "we're basically allowing the manuscript to speak for itself."

Which it did to a lot of people, loudly if not always clearly. In the weeks that followed, the FBI was flooded with thousands of leads. More than 20,000 calls came in to the Unabomber hotline by September. Reports also started to appear that the FBI was looking into the possibility that the suspect had attended high schools in the Chicago area.

A close study of the text also led to revisions—some of them misguided—in the psychological profile of the bomber that the bureau had developed in consultation with psychologists and other specialists. The Unabomber's musings on power structures and social change led them to abandon their earlier assumption that the killer was a student of the physical sciences. Now they concluded that he sounded more like someone who had studied sociology or anthropology. (Though some people with advanced degrees in these fields saw the hand of an unsophisticated autodidact.) But inasmuch as Kaczynski had no formal training in the social sciences, they had it right the first time.

In another area, they appear to have done better. In their earlier profiles, investigators had assumed the Unabomber was best regarded as a terrorist, a man driven chiefly by an ideological agenda. But the manifesto's deep wells of paranoia and rage moved them toward the conclusion that he was better understood as a serial killer, someone acting from a powerful psychological compulsion. In that case, they reasoned, he could not be counted on to keep his promise not to kill again. And on that score they appear to have got it right. FBI agents, in their search of Kaczynski's cabin, turned up a live pipe bomb.

Blood and Honor

You can't eat your cake and have it too.

—Manifesto, paragraph 185

There are places where you can stand atop the Continental Divide and find in the water gathered there—in a pool or a lake or maybe just a snowpack—nature having an existential crisis. Because in many places, well before the headwaters of the Colorado or the Columbia or the Missouri have converged, drops of water are actually dividing and splitting and breaking apart. Against everything you might reasonably expect and believe and imagine, some water along the divide leans gently to the east, tilts over an edge and begins a 2,500-mile trip to the Atlantic. Just a few feet away, water from the same source makes a different choice: banking to the west and spilling into a rivulet, down a gulch, through a draw, into a creek, then a river and on to the Pacific. Nature can be like that: chaotic, capricious, mysterious. This is the story of how two men who sprang from the same pool, the same family, went their own separate and similar ways toward vastly different destinations, only to converge a long time later.

David didn't talk much about his big brother, but good friends knew how he felt. David thought of Ted as the smart one. He was the pure one, true to his beliefs, not only denouncing modern comforts but renouncing them as well. He practiced what he preached all those years in the woods. What David couldn't know, from some bitter letters and occasional glimpses, was just how deep into the woods Ted had gone.

The road forked around 1990, the last time the brothers saw each other. Their father killed himself; David did what Ted could not when he pulled himself back into society. A road was built near his Texas cabin, a friend recalled, and "he jokingly said civilization was starting to move in on him. He said it was getting too crowded." He left his desert hideaway, cut his hair, shaved his beard, joined a softball team and married the woman he had dreamed of since his teens. David had known Linda Patrik at Evergreen Park Community High School and had written and called and stayed in touch. When he went off to Columbia, she went to Carleton College in Minnesota and to Northwestern for her Ph.D. in philosophy, earning her degree a few weeks after the Unabomber struck his first victim, also at Northwestern. David taught school for a while in Iowa; Linda got married, but her husband left her and moved to California. "She was always hoping to have a baby," her mother said, but it just didn't work out.

David was not one to compromise or hurry or lose hope. "She was the only gal he really loved," said Joel Schwartz, David's roommate from Columbia, who was best man at the wedding. "He made a commitment to her way back when he was a young man. But not many people wait 25 years to be with the person they love. He was a patient man. Had it not worked out and they not got back together again, I think he would have accepted that too." In 1989 David went to live with Linda in Schenectady, New York, and they were married the next year. Now whenever he went back to Texas to provision his soul, he didn't go alone; he added a driveway, some lights and a plug for her computer.

Schenectady is an aging Rust Belt city with a growing population of unemployed industrial workers, where neighbors look out for each other and often leave their windows open and doors unlocked at night. It is a sleepy city a few miles west of Albany, the kind of place that drives down statewide violent-crime rates. David and Linda were married in her backyard under a large tent, with about 100 relatives and friends present. She wore a beige dress with lace trim; he wore a casual shirt and light slacks. The ceremony reflected her Buddhist beliefs; the bride and groom, sitting before a large painting of the Green Tara Sudhana, kneeling on pillows decorated with raw rice, clinked finger cymbals and chanted. Later, a Christian minister blessed them. Ted did not come to the wedding.

Now anchored and settled with the woman he had waited for, David found a way to put his energy and his patience to good use. He continued to write. But that wouldn't pay the bills. So he went to work as a counselor for Residential Opportunities Inc., a group of adult-care facilities for the developmentally disabled. "He'd bring his guitar in and play music for the adults once a week," said a co-worker. "He would take them to church on Sundays, to a place geared toward them, where they could be involved in activities, not a place where they would get preached to. Not everyone was so thoughtful." The job could get very stressful. "They need so much attention. But David was very professional and positive." One mute resident was trying to lose weight but hated doing his exercises. "David would joke with him [in sign language] and get him in a better mood. Instead of saying, 'Lie down on the floor and do 20 sit-ups and 30 toe touches,' David would say, 'Let's run around the house three times together. Let's run up and down the stairs together.' It was a positive thing for the client because they could do it together. In two years, I think he lost about 20 lbs. that way."

After two years, David went to work for Equinox, an

Albany agency that helps runaway children; Linda was teaching philosophy at Union College: ancient theories of art in the morning and philosophy and existential literature in the afternoon. The latter class was described as "a philosophical exploration of existential themes in modern literature. Individuality, freedom, the meaning of life and death, social conformity and human relationships." Iman Mafi, a sophomore student of Linda's, recalled one day in class when they were discussing love, and Linda began telling her students about David. "She said in their first year in college in two different cities, her husband once left school to be with her. He basically blew off school and came to be with her and stayed for months. It was very romantic. They wanted to get married back then, and they finally did. She told us the story to show how deep their love was."

It needed to be. By the summer of 1995, the Unabomber had returned, deadlier than ever, and newspapers began running articles about his latest attacks and the trajectory of his 17-year campaign. The map could not be lost on David when he realized where the Unabomber had struck: in Chicago, where he and his brother Ted were raised; in Michigan, where Ted studied; in Berkeley, where he taught; in Utah, where he worked. David read about carefully handcrafted wooden bombs, knowing that his brother was a woodworker. David didn't remember Ted's setting off explosions as a kid but did remember the rockets, the knowledge of propellants. David had sent his brother a money order for $1,000 two months before the New Jersey bombing of Thomas Mosser. He had sent $2,000 a few months later, just before Gilbert Murray's death in Sacramento, California. And then there was the profile: the smart, hostile, educated, alienated loner.

David had a nagging feeling about the crimes, the locations, but he dismissed them at first; the idea was too wild to hang on to. Then in September came the manifesto, and the words that leaped from the page.

He read the manifesto in the hope that he could discount any connection with his brother. But instead it had the opposite effect, and it left David and Linda in a terrible quandary. David thought he could hear his brother in its philosophy and language. "There was tremendous dismay," said someone close to the family. "This is an extremely difficult situation for a family member. This is a close, loving family. I think David wanted very much to believe Ted was not involved." But overriding the blood tie was the thought of more blood spilled. David, observed Joe La Follette's father, Melvin La Follette, a circuit Episcopal priest who came to know David over the years in Texas, "is a straight arrow, very sensitive and moral. He didn't want to hurt his brother. But at the same time, he was scrupulous. He wanted to do the right thing."

David's suspicions forced him to reckon with the changes he had seen over the years and wonder what his brother might be capable of doing. "It was his feeling that his brother mentally went over the edge," said Schwartz, who even went with David to visit Ted in Montana in 1974. David had warned that he might be a little ornery. But Joel didn't see the rough edges. "Ted seemed at ease; Dave had warned me he might not be. My memory of him did not quite fit what we all came to see. He was very orderly, meticulous. He was eccentric, but he was engaging at the same time. We had some lively discussions. He was very much into ecology and very angry at the way the world was going." But over the years, Joel said, David had come to realize something else. "There was a madness there. His isolation opened him to madness. This was why Dave, I believe, felt that Ted had to finally be brought back to the human community. It was his hope anyway."

Schwartz knew David had tried to keep reaching out to his

brother even as Ted slipped further away. Yet the relationship between the brothers grew more strained, particularly after David got married. "I know Dave wrote many letters that were rebuffed in later years," Joel said. "Sometimes, with family members, there can be a kind of distance you can't quite get over."

David knew that if he just dialed 1-800-701-BOMB and spoke directly to the FBI, he would unleash the hounds on his family and never know any peace. Ted had nothing in life except his privacy; one word from David would take that away. On the other hand, he couldn't wake up every morning afraid to turn on the news or read a paper—or open the mail. So he launched what became, in essence, his own private manhunt, hoping it would lead elsewhere than to the man he had known longer than anyone else alive.

In late October, David approached a private investigator named Susan Swanson, a kindergarten classmate of Linda's who worked in the Chicago office of one of the country's premier private-detective agencies, Investigative Group Inc., based in Washington. She and Linda were so close that she knew early on that Ted was the suspect. David gave Swanson typed copies of letters. She started digging quietly, as a friend, for free, learning all there was to know about the Unabomber's career. She went back through old newspaper accounts of the crimes, hoping she would find an alibi for Ted, to no avail.

In late December, as her suspicions grew, Swanson approached the president of her firm, former New York City police commissioner Raymond Kelly. She told him she had "friends who knew someone who, as outlandish as it sounded, might be the Unabomber."

"It sounded kind of sketchy and general," Kelly said. He suggested that she get hold of all the information she could about the case, and if she decided to get the writings analyzed by experts, they should be careful of copycats. He warned her that with all the publicity, there could be other people out there trying to assume the Unabomber's mantle. So Swanson approached Clint Van Zandt, the FBI's former chief hostage negotiator and a behavioral specialist who retired last August after 25 years to set up his own security-consulting firm in Virginia. After receiving age information from Swanson, Van Zandt called in a psychiatrist and a linguistics expert; his team began comparing the Unabomber's manifesto to two of Ted's letters, one 10 years old and about four pages long, the other a single page from a year ago. They were looking for common phrases, wordings, spellings. Right after Christmas, Van Zandt told Swanson his team was convinced the chances were 3 in 5 that the same man had written all three.

The clues lay in the language, its usage, the phrases that echoed in both the letters and the manifesto, phrases such as "primitive peoples," "moral code" and "tend to." "Every time we hit a stylistic, a psychological, a communication comparison—this is one more ounce we put on our scale," Van Zandt said. "Eventually we had a few pounds on our scale." Meanwhile, David had caught a telltale phrase the investigators couldn't have known. Their mother used to say, "You can't eat your cake and have it too." Ted used the phrase in a letter; the Unabomber slipped it into the manifesto.

Van Zandt drew a profile of a highly educated man, probably a Ph.D., between 45 and 55. "He would be living in a very rural setting with limited psychological support, surrounded by books," Van Zandt said. "I had this picture of an individual out there somewhere developing his own philosophies that he chose not to test against anyone else, because he chose to separate himself from society. He became the sole decision maker in his universe, because there was no one there to outvote him."

Van Zandt called Swanson the Friday before New Year's. "We felt very strongly that it was the product of the same individual," he said. "I told her, 'You need to immediately go to the FBI with this. You need to be moving right away.' " Van Zandt did acknowledge that the identification was not dead certain. "I said there could be a lot of 45- to 55-year-old academics who have dropped out of society, who have separated themselves from technology and who may be living a rural existence. Now this has to be resolved by investigation."

Swanson said she understood the gravity of the situation and would make sure the right thing was done. He believed her, but he was concerned that she would not be able to convince her clients to move quickly enough. In Van Zandt's experience with serial killers, their compulsions were never satisfied but actually grew more urgent as the thrill of the last conquest faded.

So he opened his back channel to the FBI. "In the first week of January, I went to two former colleagues at the FBI," he related. "I said, 'I'm working on something with a client that bears strong resemblance to the manifesto. If you don't hear in the next two weeks that there's been a break in the case, let me know.' "

Up to this point he had been paid to consult on the case, but then he did something unusual. Just to be certain, Van Zandt ordered a second analysis at his own expense. He sought out two academic specialists in cultural communications and asked them to examine the manifesto and the letters for common themes and presentation. His second team put the odds at 4 out of 5 that they had their man. "I wanted two separate opinions because of the magnitude of the case," said Van Zandt. "I wanted to be right." He called Swanson again in the second week of January. "I said, 'You really need to go to the FBI. If there is going to be any hesitancy, I'm going, because somebody knows who the Unabomber is.' " But Susan denies he made such a threat and maintains that she and David didn't need pushing. "David was eager to get this painful experience over with," Swanson said, "once he made up his mind to find out the truth about his brother." They had already moved on to the next step.

Rather than approaching the FBI himself, David asked Susan to find him a lawyer, and on Jan. 19, she called an Antioch Law School classmate, Anthony Bisceglie, a white-collar-criminal defense lawyer in Washington. "I wanted him because David needed not only an intermediary but also legal advice and someone he felt comfortable with who had integrity," Swanson said. "Tony was someone I knew well and trusted." At first he didn't even want to know the name of Susan's source, the better to keep his options open. But he quickly became an expert on the Unabom saga and even did his own analysis of the writings.

The private investigators had begun to see patterns and parallels everywhere, as they learned more and more about the unnamed man under their microscope. David told them where the suspect had grown up and studied and how he had been living for the past 25 years. Apart from the geographical coincidences, there were the psychological ones. Their suspect was a highly educated man who held long grudges, who found human contact unbearable, who had been a lifelong loner. The Unabomber called for a return to a primitive life-style; their man lived in an unlit shack in the woods. He was a woodworker, knew about rockets, was able to move about and leave no trail behind him.

But even with such a weight of evidence Bisceglie was leery of approaching the Unabom task force in San Francisco; he knew there were literally thousands of tips coming in all the time, from people beguiled by the million-dollar reward, and he didn't want to get lost in the shuffle. With David's permission, on Jan. 29 Bisceglie called an agent he had known for years who had worked on delicate counterintelligence cases before. "I knew he would know that I was bringing credible information to him," Bisceglie said, "and I knew I could trust him."

Bisceglie's friend helped arrange the first contact, with an agent in the bureau's Washington field office. The lawyer gave the FBI typewriting samples from Ted's writings so that the lab could compare them with the typewriting in the manifesto. The lab's findings were inconclusive. The FBI agent pressed for a meeting with Bisceglie's client. Bisceglie and David resisted, hoping to set a few conditions. "First, we had no desire to have a full-scale investigation launched that would completely disrupt the life of a potentially innocent person," Bisceglie said later. "We had no information whether Ted Kaczynski had anything to do with the making or the use of explosives. The second consideration, which became the driving force, was David Kaczynski's very sincere desire to make sure no further lives were lost if in fact his brother were involved."

Bisceglie demanded assurances "that Ted Kaczynski's welfare would be protected, that his privacy would be protected as long as necessary." The investigation would proceed quietly at first, only approaching people from the suspect's past if some pretext were given, without suggesting he was the Unabom suspect. David wanted to know before agents talked to their mother or Ted's Montana neighbors, so that he could prepare himself and them. He didn't want them to confront his brother directly until it was absolutely necessary; the stress, his paranoia and his mental frailty, David thought, might make Ted hurt himself or someone else. And when and if the moment came to arrest Ted, it would be done humanely. In return, David would tell them where to find their suspect and would hand over the letters and cooperate wherever he could. "When Linda and David went to Washington," Linda's mother said, "their main concern was that they did not want the Unabomber to get the death penalty. Lock him up or put him in solitary, anything—just not the death penalty." Bisceglie told the family the FBI could not make that promise. Sentencing decisions were made by judges and juries, not the FBI. Besides, Ted could be prosecuted for murder in California and New Jersey state courts. The family wanted David's role kept secret; they feared that Ted might strike out violently if he knew they had turned him in. The FBI agreed.

On Valentine's Day, Bisceglie gave investigators the name Theodore J. Kaczynski. "Well," he told them, "this is either a historic moment or the beginning of a wild-goose chase." Three days later, David went to Bisceglie's office and for the first time met with the FBI. Several agents who were members of the San Francisco task force had flown to Washington for the event. They promised to protect Ted's privacy as long as possible, but the mounting evidence unleashed the swarm of agents who had waited so long for just such a break in the case.

Very quietly, fearful of somehow tipping Ted off, they began to go back over his life and travels, searching for clues and confirmation. The FBI began running what they call "administrative background" checks on Theodore Kaczynski. Once David gave the agents the Montana location, they checked the recorder of deeds and found out when he had bought the land and for how much. They checked power-, telephone- and water-company records and found he had none. They tried the department of motor vehicles, tax records and other available indices of his life.

But once again, the most devastating evidence came from the family itself. Unaware of the growing storm in her family, Wanda Kaczynski decided the time had come to leave Illinois and move to Schenectady, closer to her younger son. When she and David began cleaning out the Lombard, Illinois, house to prepare it for sale, he came upon some of Ted's old writings. The echoes of the bomber got louder. Bisceglie spent the winter acting as a liaison between David and the feds, reviewing the case and accumulating more writings. He said, "I spent roughly three months with my office door locked, and we did everything we could to keep a lid on this, to protect, again, Ted Kaczynski's reputation and also to protect the integrity of the investigation."

But even as he provided the investigators with more and more evidence, David requested that his mother not be told, not until he and Linda were ready to tell her themselves. "They didn't want an FBI agent to suddenly be at their front door," said one close to the operation. "They wanted to soften the blow." When Wanda finally learned the truth, Bisceglie said, "her reaction was amazingly strong. She expressed her sincere belief that Ted couldn't be the Unabomber, and she also said, if he were, he had to be stopped."

The agents wanted to take a look around the Lombard home Wanda had just sold. Bill Daeschler, the new owner, had been getting ready to clean out the shed in back and throw out the junk inside. But some FBI agents came and told him they suspected some neighborhood kids had used the shack to build pipe bombs, and they wanted to search it. Among other things, it contained wood, nails and pipes that authorities concluded were bomb components.

By this time it was all out of David and Linda's hands. "They seemed almost exhausted when I saw them," said their friend Mary Ann Welch, who saw them just days before Ted's arrest. "This man had the courage to turn his brother in. This mother had the courage to turn her own son in. They both put the safety of society before their family, for the good of those they didn't know. Wanda handed over all the letters, instead of retreating, and said let this prove them wrong, that Ted is not the Unabomber. And if he is, then let the truth be known. They made the ultimate sacrifice. Who knows who could have got the next bomb?"

Two nights before the news broke, David and Linda went to a friend's home to meditate and find a little peace. They visited Willard Roth, a retired neuroendocrinologist and former chairman of the biology department at Union College, hoping for some spiritual guidance after their torturous decision. Roth had known Linda for years through the college; he and his wife, Laura, are practicing Tibetan Buddhists and helped plan the wedding ceremony. One small room in their house had been converted to a shrine for meditation. In it were big red floor pillows. The walls were adorned with Buddhist paintings and black-and-white pictures of the Panchen Lama. "They came in very briefly, said hello. They took off their shoes and did sitting meditation for an hour," Willard said. "She admitted she was grappling with a difficult personal problem. But she would not talk about it."

Within a week, the doors were double-bolted and curtains were drawn all along Keyes Avenue as a swarm of reporters and camera crews descended on the Kaczynski residence, a two-story, green-and-white bungalow with what would usually be considered a large, inviting front porch. Friends pleaded for the Kaczynski family's privacy. People left flowers. When Wanda arrived one morning, the reporters swooped down on her, asking how it had happened, how her son had gone wrong. And she answered, "You know better than I."

So Many Answers, So Many Questions

Never forget that the human race with technology is just like an alcoholic with a barrel of wine.

—Manifesto, paragraph 203

In the end, technology invaded Ted Kaczynski's little corner of unspoiled wilderness like gangbusters. A week after his arrest, the forest around his tiny cabin reverberated with the rattling hum of a gas-powered generator. Fifty rental vehicles were parked chockablock on the property next door. Nearby the FBI had set up its command post, a long motor home with a dish antenna on the roof and a U.S. flag on a pole outside. Agents strode purposefully to and fro, their voices echoing through the timber in sporadic loud outbursts, like an after-work softball team jacked up to win whenever one of them made a new find. (They even had team uniforms for off-duty hours: someone had printed up T shirts bearing the famous "hooded sweatshirt and shades" police sketch.)

In the days after the raid, that cheery attitude certainly reflected the prevailing understanding of the case against Kaczynski. The original criminal complaint stipulated that his shack contained both bomb components and one partially completed bomb, 10 three-ring notebooks full of bomb sketches, and papers documenting pipe-bomb experiments. That was more than enough to get the hermit of Lincoln, Montana, held without bail under an initial charge of possession of unregistered firearms, "specifically, components from which a destructive device such as a bomb can be readily assembled." During the "perp walk" from the authorities' Ford Bronco to the federal building in Helena, a bit of hoked-up drama during which most suspects direct their gaze at the ground, Kaczynski stared calmly back at the surrounding cameras. Reporters yelled the usual questions, and at least once he directed a sardonic smile over his right shoulder, which was instantly reproduced all over the world in every available medium.

The press, in fact, was reveling in an embarrassment of riches—and some of the revelry got out of control. Someone had leaked David Kaczynski's involvement in the case, and his home in Schenectady was overrun, his wife ambushed on the job. Ted Kaczynski's high school classmates had to disconnect their phones, and the object of his unrequited affections, Ellen Tarmichael, complained that she had photographers hanging off her trees and cash offers from the tabloids. The media chased the story of Theodore Kaczynski's life down every possible road. From the day of the raid on, there was little doubt in the public mind that he and the Unabomber were one and the same.

But the public mind is not the same as a capital-crimes jury. On the late-night panels and the legal talk shows, the professional commentators for the defense were beginning to pipe their traditional counterpoint. The most commonly heard theme was expressed by high-profile attorney Alan Dershowitz. "They are not going to be able to establish every one of the crimes," he told TIME magazine. Kaczynski's defense might be, "There's no such thing as a Unabomber," but equally good might be, "There *is* such a thing as a Unabomber, but I have an alibi for one or two of these things; therefore I couldn't be the Unabomber." Thus, the professor concluded, "The whole falls, if a part falls."

The Justice Department was unlikely to bring a catchall Unabomber charge (and, as long as the case did not involve other suspects, it was legally constrained from doing so). But prosecutors understood that in the hands of a skillful defense lawyer, such an argument could still impress a jury. And in any case, the agency was intent on heading off possible alibis for individual crimes. "Putting him out of that cabin—in Sacramento, Salt Lake City, Chicago—that's going to be key," said one veteran Justice Department prosecutor assigned to the Unabom task force." Ever since David had made his suspicions known to the bureau, members of the Unabom squad had been scattering out across the country, attempting to ascertain that Ted was in the places from which the Unabomber's bombs were mailed, at the times when they were mailed. Of special concern were those postmarked from Salt Lake City and Northern California. If their prime suspect did not live in those regions at the right times, as the authorities had been assuming, could he have visited frequently enough to be a credible suspect?

The feds had no trouble getting Kaczynski out of Montana. Dick Lundberg, a mailman, had given him frequent rides to the state capital of Helena, dropping him at a local $14-a-night hotel. The sleepover is necessary to get to Butte, which offers changes on the Greyhound line for both the Salt Lake City and Sacramento areas. The fiancé of a driver remembered the "very geeky-looking" Kaczynski traveling west or south on Greyhound 15 times in the past five years: "He looked like someone who should be a transient—ride freight trains, not a Greyhound."

It was more difficult confirming that Kaczynski ever reached those destinations. Despite his family's statements that Kaczynski worked as a laborer in Salt Lake City in the early 1970s, checks with motels and blood banks failed to turn up any record of his having been there. A man named Greg Nance told reporters, and the FBI, that he remembered Ted from their time together at the low-rent Regis Hotel. His wife, Rita Nyberg, said she "might be wrong," but she thought she had seen him many times while drinking early-morning coffees at the local Hardee's. More tantalizingly, Nance said he saw Kaczynski waiting for work at the SOS temporary agency. Gary Wright, one of the Unabomber's early victims, used to repair computers at SOS. Yet the federal agents might be forgiven for taking Nance's testimony lightly: a part-time worker in an art supply store with no phone, he also confided to reporters that he was running for Governor.

Northern California, the area from which the Unabomber struck eight times, was proving marginally more promising. Agents canvassed the inexpensive downtown Sacramento area, at times flashing a photo of Kaczynski, who they said might have been using the alias "Conrad." (Enterprising analysts subsequently thought they detected an allusion to *Heart of Darkness* author Joseph Teodor Conrad and his tales of tormented, divided souls.) And several employees at a Tower Books store 20 blocks from the bus station glanced at a newsmagazine cover that week and exclaimed, "Hey, this is Einstein!" That was their name for a wild-haired, ripe-smelling man who, for a few years until 1994, had shown up regularly each spring to browse through science books without buying. But a hotel clerk who told the press that Kaczynski had boarded at his establishment at those same times was less sure of himself when talking to investigators. A federal agent in California was heard to sigh, "I sure wouldn't want to prosecute him yet."

That agent obviously hadn't yet got the word from Lincoln,

where, like a tiny circus car spewing an army of clowns, the 10-by-12-ft. cabin was disgorging an endless parade of incriminating evidence—enough, it seemed, to crush any defense.

The FBI is known for being thorough and deliberate. Teresa Garland, whose sister had received the note from Kaczynski trying to explain his misanthropic views, had herself got a lesser gift: a handmade packet of seeds, marked WILD CARROT: BIG YELLOW 1992, with instructions for planting and harvesting. The agents subpoenaed the seeds. "The real painstaking labor and forensic work is being done now, and that's going to be dog slow," said an investigation source. But as days dragged into weeks, the investigation of the cabin began to strike outsider observers as excruciatingly lengthy, even by bureau standards. With good reason, it turns out.

No one (except possibly some of Kaczynski's old college housemates) could have predicted the encyclopedic density of evidence in that tiny space. Remarked former Unabom task force agent Louis Bertram, "I've been on details serving search warrants before, and we have come across houses full of stuff. But those don't compare to what I'm reading on this list. I'm stunned. The guys at the laboratories are going to have a field day with this. It's like turning kids loose in a cookie jar." The list Bertram was reading, compiled by the FBI for court purposes, includes some 700 items—a little something, it appeared, for everybody.

For those interested in Kaczynski's intellectual life, there were more than 200 books. As expected, they included at least one book quoted at length in the manifesto: *Violence in America: Historical and Comparative Perspectives,* by Hugh Davis Graham and Ted Robert Gurr. There was a biblical concordance, but the presence of Isaac Asimov's somewhat skeptical commentary on the Bible suggested

Kaczynski might not be a conventionally religious man. Also present was Paul Goodman's *Growing Up Absurd,* a best-selling '60s tract that greatly influenced the drop-out generation, and Volumes I and II of Victor Hugo's *Les Misérables,* featuring Jean Valjean, heroic fugitive and victim of social injustice. More chillingly, the bookshelf also included Sloan Wilson's 1979 novel *Ice Brothers,* a hollowed-out copy of which had disguised a Unabomber bomb in 1980.

Observers fascinated by Kaczynski's personal world were not disappointed. There were the sad effects of a life spent alone: "three mittens," "one clear-glass jar containing dental bridge." The avid bicyclist kept his driver's license in a plastic bag. In a Samsonite briefcase, officials found not only his University of Michigan degrees but also "yearbooks in green plastic bag." The man who shot rabbits for food had accumulated five guns: only one, a big-game rifle, was listed as high caliber, but another, intriguingly, was handmade. A bottle of the prescription medicine trazodone, usually indicated for patients who have suffered a major depressive episode, sent some investigators rushing back to the line in the Unabomber manifesto where the author complains, "Instead of removing the conditions that make people depressed, modern society gives them antidepressant drugs." Others set out in search of the doctor who might have prescribed the drug or provided Kaczynski with psychiatric care. There was $32 in cash, and two books of checks from a Helena bank. There was a manila envelope, tantalizingly marked "autobiography." And, ominously, there was a box into which was stuffed a list of corporate executives and maps of San Francisco.

If one box held such dark hints, wondered the investigators, what else would they find in a seemingly endless march of cans, bottles and other humble receptacles?

The answer was a chemistry of terror. Kaczynski had

been an ardent labeler. Receptacles bore notes that their contents were "perfectly clean" or "$BaSO_4$ may be contaminated with a little $MgCl_2$ and smaller amount of $MgSO_2$" or "Al compounds and other crap." And many times those labels indicated the pure ingredients of bomb making: copper sulfate, ammonium nitrate, lead chloride and potassium nitrate. Another container held a thermite concoction that, if ignited, could burn through an inch-thick steel plate. As if to prove it, a Del Monte whole-leaf spinach container held melted metal fragments. A University of Montana chemistry professor, apprised of the inventory, commented dryly, "He certainly had the stuff that will explode." There were also the batteries to set it off, the copper tubing to pack it in and an oats can containing what the FBI called a "trigger switch."

And then there were the finished products. Immediately upon entering the cabin, the agents (and their robot, which a retired official said can do "practically anything in terms of lifting, moving and picking up") had found a partially completed bomb. In a subsequent search, under Kaczynski's bed, they discovered what a tense government communiqué described as a "fully functional device which is yet to be rendered harmless but which appears to have Unabom characteristics."

Indeed it did. Encased in a trademark box, the bomb bore many of the telltale Unabomber "signatures" that FBI and ATF agents had catalogued so painstakingly over the years. NBC News reported that the package bore a fake return address but no sending address. Reflecting on the Unabomber's promise not to kill again if his manifesto was published—and abandoning all pretense that the suspect and the criminal could be anything but one and the same—a source noted that he was "clearly not living up to his agreement." Another agent ebulliently signaled a friend, "We've got him!"

But the pièce de résistance was yet to come. Included in

the detection equipment the agents had brought with them to Lincoln was a small mobile unit for examining documents. When the initial search of the cabin produced two old, manual typewriters, relics of the pre–word processor, pre-Selectric age, speculation was heated that one of them had produced the 35,000-word manifesto and several other Unabomber missives. In straight-faced leaks over the next week, however, investigators let it be known that, alas, the typefaces on the two machines did not correspond to the writings, although they had high hopes for a third typewriter that had been discovered days later. What they did not mention for another four days was that nestled next to that third machine in Kaczynski's loft was a discovery as dazzling, or more so, than the bomb under the bed: a carbon copy of the manifesto itself. Next to it was a copy of one of the bomber's letters to the New York *Times.*

Everything was falling into place. Local merchants recalled having sold Kaczynski the carbon paper. (In a note to one of the manifesto's recipients, psychology professor Tom Tyler, the Unabomber had joked that he couldn't go to a Xerox store because people "would get suspicious if they saw us handling our copies with gloves.") Initial tests suggested that the manuscript had indeed been produced by the typewriter next to it. Most damning of all, if true, was an assertion attributed in *U.S. News & World Report* to a senior law-enforcement official: that tests on the third typewriter indicated that it had typed mailing labels and other material recovered from six Unabomber crime scenes. The cabin was also reported to have yielded up a hooded sweatshirt and sunglasses similar to those in the WANTED poster.

Finally, after vacuuming the cabin, gathering up fibers and hairs that would be compared to filaments found within the

Unabomber's deadly weapons, the agents proclaimed themselves satisfied. Smiled one: "That cabin has never been so clean."

There were, however, still some dangling threads. Just as the cabin search was wrapping up, investigators learned that last summer Kaczynski had ordered 12 cu. yds. of concrete from Helena Sand & Gravel. But when the mixing-truck driver arrived and asked where to pour the load, he was told to stop at the edge of the property. Kaczynski then proceeded to move the concrete, one wheelbarrow load at a time, to an unseen spot. It is possible that in addition to his root cellar, Ted also built a bunker, one that might yet yield even more evidence.

Meanwhile, back in Washington, FBI Director Louis Freeh was furious. Already known to be sensitive about leaks to the media, he had gritted his teeth and issued a terse news release thanking CBS News for holding off on its initial Kaczynski story long enough to allow him to raid the cabin. As news of David Kaczynski's involvement in the case and the early search of the cabin percolated out to the press, Freeh smoldered. Some of the leaks were more specific than government findings filed in court, raising the question of whether, as media reporter Howard Kurtz wrote in the Washington *Post*, "authorities are using the media to convict Kaczynski in the court of public opinion—and, not coincidentally, burnish the FBI's image after years of setbacks and scandal."

Agents, many nervous about the possible compromising of what otherwise looked like a highly promising case, speculated that they would soon have to take polygraph tests to prove they hadn't leaked. After the news of Kaczynski's copy of the manifesto reached the media, the irate director went ballistic, called for an internal investigation and thundered that "unauthorized disclosure of investigative information or other confidential material will lead to immediate firing from the FBI and possible prosecution."

But joy is a hard emotion to contain, and more and more agents had become convinced that the evidence from the cabin was so strong that it would be unnecessary to prove Kaczynski actually went to San Francisco, Oakland, Sacramento or anywhere else to win a conviction. They believed they could prevail simply by showing that Kaczynski created the bombs and that they entered the mails, reached their destinations and exploded. At least two more anonymous "law-enforcement officials" risked all to express what had become a universal sentiment among investigators: "This pretty much ices it for us," said one. "If we lose this one," said another, "we'd better close up and go home."

Robert Cleary is a formidable man. The first assistant U.S. Attorney in Newark, New Jersey, formerly a major-crimes division chief at the prestigious U.S. Attorney's office in Manhattan, he made his name by prosecuting complicated white-collar criminal cases and is known for his "perseverance and diligence," for possessing a mind like the proverbial "steel trap" and as a "consummate team player." He has run the New York City Marathon and climbed Mount Kilimanjaro. But to many observers at the time of his appointment, that was all secondary to the fact that the man chosen to head the federal government's Unabom suspect team, expected eventually to prosecute Theodore Kaczynski, was employed in New Jersey.

By late April, Justice Department officials had still not announced their prosecution strategy, nor were they expected to do so for weeks, perhaps months, depending on how much time Kaczynski's bomb-components-possession case would buy them to consider the evidence and the options. In theory, they could bring federal charges against him in any number of states (including those from which bombs were sent, those they passed through, and those in which they exploded) and state trials were also possible in several venues. The first case brought against him will probably be federal; if only, as Loyola Law School professor Laurie Levenson has pointed out, because "this is a case of clear national interest. This fellow was almost able to bring the country to its knees. The airports stopped flying planes, and people worried about their mail. He published his manifesto in national newspapers. It was very much an attack on the American government system."

The suspect team will probably conduct its initial Unabom prosecution in New Jersey or California. Attorney General Janet Reno, who was criticized for precipitously calling for the death penalty in the Oklahoma City bombing case, will not likely leave herself open to that criticism twice. But her employees will almost certainly bring this case in a state where they can apply a 1994 federal law that makes fatal mail-bombing a capital crime. That will limit them to the two states where the bomber committed murder: New Jersey, home to advertising executive Thomas Mosser, and California, where Sacramento timber lobbyist Gilbert Murray died. (The bomber's first murder, of Sacramento computer store owner Hugh Scrutton, predated the law.)

Robert Cleary led the federal probe into Mosser's murder, which could indicate that the government intends to obey what Dershowitz calls "the first rule of trying people: Don't try the case in California." Many lawyers feel that juries there tend to be more open to defendants' unusual political, religious or social points of view. Or Cleary's home base could mean little; it is worth noting that two colleagues on the team come from San Francisco and Sacramento.

Dershowitz was one of several attorneys who shared with TIME some ideas about possible defense strategies open to Kaczynski. He advanced what might be called Freeh's

Nightmare: "The first thing any lawyer does is challenge the leaking that has been going on. This has not been leaks, this has been hemorrhages. They've clearly been orchestrated leaks, and in clear violation of the defendant's right to a fair trial." Adds Gerry Spence, who led the successful defense of Randy Weaver after the government siege of his home on Ruby Ridge in Idaho: "Every one of those jurors not only will hear the legal evidence against him but has indelibly implanted in his mind the illegal evidence that no just court would permit him to hear."

Ron Kuby, the professional heir to late radical lion William Kunstler and a veteran of several bombing trials, suggests a justification defense, whereby Kaczynski could "try to turn the entire case into a platform railing against modern technology, [or] a prisoner of war defense, refusing to recognize the jurisdiction of the Federal Government. He doesn't strike me as a fellow who will repudiate his views."

Spence argues an oft-suggested route for Kaczynski—insanity—by way of justification, and he does so in a way that almost manages to make the Unabomber look like a populist leader rather than a murderous crank. "What he's saying in the manifesto has a good deal of merit and a good deal of truth in many ways. Many Americans would agree. He is saying the American people have become cogs in the machinery of technology that is destroying people and the earth. He is saying human beings have become alienated and impersonal. Now nobody's talking about that. It's a truth you believe and I believe, but nobody's talking about it because he has become Cassandra.

"What happens when a man who believes the truth and is seeking the truth, whose message is right, but his method is wrong, who believes he is doing the right thing, but is doing the wrong thing—what do we say we have? A man who cannot tell the difference between right and wrong. What do we have then? The insanity defense." Spence adds a caveat. "Let me say I have serious doubts that he wants or would agree to an insanity defense. On the other hand, it's the one point where his viewpoint can be shared with America." (The possibility that Kaczynski might get off due to his mental state found a less polemical champion when Patrick Mullany, a former FBI behavioral specialist who worked on the Unabomber case, suggested eight days after the raid that the evidence collected so far suggested the suspect might be mentally unfit to stand trial.)

The first of these legal strategies to get a test-drive was Freeh's Nightmare. The day after the raid, U.S. District Judge Charles C. Lovell addressed Kaczynski: "I take it you are financially unable to pay for counsel yourself," to which the suspect replied: "Quite correct." But Michael Donahoe, the court-appointed lawyer assigned to the case, is nobody's pushover. Mike McGrath, the Lewis and Clark County Attorney who has appeared against him several times, said, "He's aggressive, innovative, and he comes up with novel defenses." Donahoe made an early splash in the case by asking the judge to enjoin outside lawyers from trying to win his client away from him. One such solicitation, worthy of the television program *Twin Peaks,* came from one Warren Wilson, Esq., and was written in verse: "Together, we are one./ Separately we stand/ In darkness./ Yield to my entreaty./ Come walk with me.")

Thirteen days after his client went to jail on the firearms-possession charge, Donahoe filed a motion in federal court in Helena demanding the dismissal of all charges because of government leaks: "These deliberate disclosures poisoned the entire population of grand jurors within the United States," he added in a memorandum. The leaks, which he said demonstrated the feds' "lynch-mob mentality," had created what he called a "lethal media blitz." In Kaczynski's case, he concluded, "the possibility that he could ever be afforded anything that might remotely resemble [the fair trial] process has been forever lost." In support of this argument, Donahoe submitted 10 pages of headlines from more than 2,204 newspaper articles, many of which he asserted quoted anonymous government sources. In his response, Assistant U.S. Attorney Bernard Hubley, handling the government's case in Montana, felt it necessary to agree that the disclosures were "disgusting" but maintained that they did not require Kaczynski to be set free and given immunity from prosecution. Judge Lovell denied Donahoe's motion, stating that "the defendant is not entitled to perfect treatment. It's not a perfect world. He is entitled to fair treatment. I think he has received fair treatment." Nevertheless, this line of argument could make a potent reappearance at trial time.

Donahoe, however, may not be the one expounding it. Members of his public defender's office were uncertain in mid-April as to whether he would travel with the case to its next venue—or the venue after that. There has been speculation that even if it wins one murder conviction, the Justice Department may want to pile on a few more in other venues in order to assuage the public's desire for justice. But the Unabomber trial will not turn into an all-American circus, in the opinion of former U.S. Attorney Joe Russoniello, who helped supervise the Unabomber case for some years: "There will be no shenanigans. There will be very little histrionics on the part of lawyers. There will be none of that sort of gamesmanship. There will probably be no cameras. There'll be a gag rule on the lawyers, and the jurors will, in all likelihood, be allowed to go home." And yet there is a good chance that Unabomber trials *could* be part of the American legal landscape for some time. Comments Kuby:

"The Federal Government has enough separate charges in separate jurisdictions that they could lose every single case and still keep the guy on trial for the rest of his life."

If so, perhaps one of those trials will help explain how the Unabomber chose his victims.

If the most pressing mystery surrounding the bomber—the establishment of who he was—looked to be solved in early April, and if a sudden outpouring of data had answered the next riddle, which is what would ever bring a man to do such a thing, a third vexing issue remained as clouded as ever: Why these particular people?

At first, the search of the cabin and its contents suggested easy answers. "We're sure that every victim he targeted, every place he bombed—there was a reason for it," said one source close to the investigation a week after the raid. "In one way or another, he ran across them either in person or in readings, or by some attachment. All that remains is to put the pieces together."

But the pieces, at least those available to the public, added up to less than a whole puzzle. During the search of the shack, agents were fascinated by a scrap of paper with the phrase "hit list" written on top, with the words "airline industry," "computer industry" and "geneticists" beneath that. Yet these phrases alone do not reveal anything about the bomber's logic that people hadn't already guessed or that he himself hadn't alluded to in his writings. The Los Angeles *Times* reported that another list, or lists, in the shack included the names of 70 to 80 individuals and groups, but the paper did not suggest that those listed were either past or prospective victims. Both timber-industry officials and a bioengineering program at the University of California, Berkeley, confirmed that the FBI told them Kaczynski had their names. Perhaps most startling, William McInerny, a chemistry professor at the City College of San Francisco who had been a three-sport athlete in Kaczynski's 1958 high school class, told the press the FBI had informed him that his name too had turned up on one of Ted's lists. The bureau advised him to beware of unusual packages or letters. Others reported similar warnings, although it was unclear whether their names had been found in the cabin or elsewhere, or why the bureau would bother warning them if its sole suspect was under lock and key.

Finally, there was an environmental "hit list," which some media sources reported might have influenced the bomber. This remained unproved in the days after the raid. In 1990 a pamphlet at least partly funded by a founder of the radical group Earth First! had produced an "Eco-Fucker Hit List!" whose 110-member roster included the Timber Association of California. Since the bomb that killed Murray was addressed to his group under that outdated name, some wondered whether the list may have influenced Kaczynski's choice of victim. The environmental hit list, however, did not appear, at least by title, on the government's accounting of items in the cabin. Said Earth First! organizer Karen Pickett: "Every environmental group in California has criticized the Timber Association. He didn't need to learn that from this paper. There was no new information there."

Nor was there much more available to the surviving victims. On the face of it, though, they had a new opportunity: to scan their memories not just for someone who might have turned into a homicidal maniac but also for a man named Kaczynski. Patrick Fischer, math professor and former chairman of the Vanderbilt University computer-science department, said FBI agents visited him in Nashville on March 20 and presented him with an array of six photos, six biographies and six names to see whether anything rang a bell. "I think now that I was attending a kind of remote police lineup," he said after the raid on the cabin. The bio that most interested him was the one he later realized was Kaczynski's, but the agents "never matched up the name to a photo or to a bio."

Nor, it seems, did any of Fischer's fellow targets. The Washington *Post* ran a lengthy article indicating that the sudden notoriety of the Kaczynski face and name did not induce great shocks of recognition. Here are some of the correspondences that did pop up.

- Fischer escaped injury in 1982 when his secretary opened a package addressed to him. While Kaczynski was an undergraduate at Harvard, Fischer was studying at the Massachusetts Institute of Technology, also in Cambridge, Massachusetts, and even took one Harvard math class. He doesn't remember the suspect but wonders whether Kaczynski remembered him, and whether Kaczynski regarded him as a "turncoat" for having switched from a specialty in pure mathematics to theoretical computer science. Moreover, Fischer's father Carl was a well-known math professor at the University of Michigan while Kaczynski was there. "For a while I thought he opened up *Who's Who* and threw a dart until he got a computer scientist," said Fischer. "That's probably wrong. There has to be a link."
- Leroy Bearnson, the return addressee on the package that went to Fischer, is now a professor of electrical engineering at Brigham Young University, where he did a lot of consulting work in Salt Lake City. "But if I ran across [Kaczynski], I don't remember it," he said. "My feeling is he chose names at random with certain associations."
- Percy Wood, former president of United Airlines, who was injured by a bomb in 1980, may have been targeted because of his profession. But the word wood had meaning both to the Unabomber and, through his carving hobby, to Kaczynski.

Bearnson's middle name is Wood, Mosser lived on an Aspen Drive, and Murray ran the California Forestry Association.

- Cory Hall, a building at Berkeley, was the site of two unaddressed Unabombs in 1982 and 1985 that wounded Diogenes Angelakos and John Hauser. It is notable for its proximity to Campbell Hall, where Kaczynski taught while at the school. Cory also housed the school's electrical-engineering and computer-sciences department.
- There are other Berkeley connections: Murray, killed in 1995, was a 1975 Berkeley graduate, and the man to whom his package was actually addressed, William Dennison, was a 1959 alumnus who had lectured at the school from 1971 to 1988. Hugh Scrutton, the Sacramento computer store owner murdered in 1985, actually attended Berkeley as a part-time student in 1967, the year Kaczynski began teaching there, though it is unclear whether they overlapped at the school. A federal investigator in California was dubious about even so promising a lead. "The possible connection between Scrutton and Kaczynski, if—repeat if—he's the Unabomber? I don't think we're going to know until he tells us. Both at Berkeley in 1967? Well, it's a big campus. And then to be killed almost 20 years later? That's a pretty damn long grudge, isn't it? There's a weirdness at work here that, in fact, makes you almost not want to know."

Fischer would still very much like to know. Perhaps because he was not injured, he is able to treat the Kaczynski question almost as if it were an intellectual game, played via E-mail with people from his past who might help trace a connection. For now, he has concluded that "the bomber was dealing with a method of abstract selection within a set" but can't figure out why he made the set, while Fischer's brother, who is a colleague of victim David Gelernter at Yale, did not.

While he sleuths, Fischer is also working out his own

psychological profile of Kaczynski, one based on the premise that he had some sort of disillusionment with his scholarly work or academic ambitions while at Berkeley. "He had trained for years," Fischer speculates, "but suddenly there goes your entire value structure ... and he didn't have the cushion of love, close social relationships or even freshman and sophomore bull sessions to thrash it out. Every field has its own definition of crisis, but ours seems particularly vulnerable when things built on neat, tight, logical and complex patterns just fail, for one reason or another. When they come into question, you can get really insecure. That has happened, at one or another time in our lives, to all of us.

"I'm very curious now. The more we know about Kaczynski, the more we'll know about why I was selected. On the other hand, maybe he'll tell me himself."

Maybe he will. He is a model prisoner; Lewis and Clark County Sheriff Chuck O'Reilly attests to that. He reads newspapers and books on ancient history and seems grateful for them. Sometimes he scribbles on a pad, although his jailers won't say what he writes. There is a round-the-clock watch on his cell, but it is pro forma—"not because he has exhibited any tendency toward suicide," said O'Reilly. "He hasn't." Theodore Kaczynski is allowed no contact with the other prisoners, but then solitude has never really bothered him. When O'Reilly noticed him pacing his cell incessantly, he began letting him out once a day for breaks in the prison courtyard, and Kaczynski jogged and shot baskets in his orange prison coveralls.

According to the New York *Times*, which debriefed prison barber Dundee Warden, the prisoner's first haircut in who knew how long went beyond the cordial to the well-nigh jolly. "I never cut it too short because it leaves lines in my hair," said Ted. "You need thinning shears," replied Warden and promised, "When I'm done with you, you'll look like a different guy." To which Kaczynski replied, "Maybe I'll be able to walk right out of here." And the funny thing was, when he next walked into the courtroom—still shackled, of course, but well groomed and better dressed—he looked ruggedly handsome, an eerie reminder of a life that could have been.

Will he talk? Plead insanity? Address those whom the Unabomber maimed or the families of those who were murdered? Will he be found innocent? If he is found guilty and incarcerated for life, will he be happy? After all, his manifesto is now available to millions, and any jail he occupies will have running water and adequate food. If found guilty and sentenced to death, will he be even happier? "It may be better to die fighting for survival, or for a cause, than to live a long but empty and purposeless life," the manifesto declares.

On the World Wide Web, a Unabomber Political Action Committee site drawing 500 visits a day urged people to write in the name Theodore Kaczynski on the November ballot. "This is no joke," asserted its organizer, Chris Korda. At Harvard, Kaczynski was also a campaign presence: posters bearing his 1962 yearbook photo sprang up, exhorting students to VOTE FOR TED FOR U.C. PRESIDENT. TED SEZ ... DON'T VOTE BY E-MAIL. DON'T ACCEPT PACKAGES FROM STRANGERS. DON'T VOTE FOR ANYONE ELSE. That, presumably, *was* a joke.

In a telephone interview from the New York *Times* building, assistant managing editor Warren Hoge reflected again on the publishing of the manifesto: "It was the right decision when we did it. I'm probably even more satisfied now, since it was the publication of the manifesto that seems to have led to his capture. Also, no one else died. How would we have felt if we had refused to publish it, and somebody else had died?"

From the safety of retirement, former FBI supervisor Ken Thompson, who left the bureau last year after 25 years and now helps run a security firm, was still intrigued by the culprit who outlasted him. The Unabomber is "beyond classic," he says. "The boys in the basement at Quantico [the bureau's Academy] are going to spend years studying this case."

In Ojinaga, Mexico, Kaczynski's erstwhile pen pal Juan Sanchez Arreola, upon seeing his own image on a television screen, told one reporter, "My head is full of thorns." To another, he added, "I told David for a long time to get over his fear of women and get married, and he listened to my advice not to be alone. Ted did not. And if I could meet Ted even now, I would tell him what I always told David: a man alone isn't worth anything."

In southern Texas, a phone rang. It was David Kaczynski calling Mary Ann Dunn, his oldest friend there. He said of his brother, "I don't understand what he did. I love him, but I want to see that things are done right."

A Victim Replies

David Gelernter is an author and computer scientist at Yale University. On June 24, 1993, he received a package, presumed to be from the Unabomber, that exploded, severely wounding him in the abdomen, face, chest and hands. Following the arrest of Theodore J. Kaczynski, he wrote this piece for TIME.

The first time I was honored beyond deserving was on a tour of a Hollywood studio as a child. For some reason, I was chosen to go onstage and pet a fake gorilla while it growled dramatically. I got a big hand. For several months after I was badly hurt by a mail bomb, it was the same story, roughly speaking: gratifying but undeserved applause. The public figured that computer technology had been (in some sense) the intended victim, and so I became Mr. Computer Science. I was proud to represent a field that has contributed so much in the way of knowledge, jobs, wealth and space-invader games over its brief history, but it was an honor I didn't deserve. There are computer scientists far more distinguished than I, and to tell the truth, I don't even like computers very much. They pose technical problems that are deep and engrossing, but when there is playing to be done, I'd much rather play with my young boys or my wife. I will make time to untangle the minor problems the boys' computer is prone to only when I am up against a wall and Prince of

Persia has ground to a dead halt. I don't want any kidnapped princesses on my conscience.

I was especially unworthy to take on the role of representing computer science, because I had written pieces that many colleagues regarded as traitorous. The aspect of my first book, *Mirror Worlds,* that attracted the most attention was the debate between pro- and antitechnology alter egos; my skeptical side won. I'd also published attacks on the use of computers in school. Parents plead for a decent education in the basics, reading and writing and history and arithmetic, and too many teachers respond with vacuous fun and games with computers.

As for the suspect to whom (evidently) I owe the distinction, I will pass over in silence the fact that he is a Harvard man, and otherwise he doesn't interest me. The tendency among some intellectuals and journalists to dignify with analysis the thinking of violent criminals has always struck me as low and contemptible. I couldn't care less what the man's views on technology are or what message he intended to deliver; the message I got was that in any society, no matter how rich, just and free, you can rely on there being a certain number of evil cowards. I thank him for passing it along, but I knew that anyway.

When I made it back to my office several months after the explosion, it was immaculate for the first time in my career. There had been a fire and the sprinklers triggered, but my friends, colleagues and graduate students had lugged everything to a new office and set things up beautifully. At the bottom of one crate, I found my battered but legible copy of essays by E.B. White. I knew immediately what it was doing there and why it had survived the blast; it included a short piece called "What Do Our Hearts Treasure?" White tells in his unsentimental, concrete way about a Christmas he and his wife had to spend in Florida, about their vague unhappiness and forced cheer—and their pleasure when a box arrived from back home in Maine, out of the blue, and proved to be full of fir branches, whose scent filled the room.

The bright side, so to speak, of grave injury, discomfort and nearness to death is that you emerge with a clear fix on what the heart treasures. Mostly I didn't learn anything new but had the satisfaction of having my hunches confirmed. I emerged knowing that, as I had always suspected, the time I spend with my wife and boys is all that matters in the end. I emerged as a practicing Jew. (Admittedly, I had always been one.) In the "miscellaneous" department, I emerged with great admiration for Senator Dole, whose battlefield injuries were a little like mine; I cribbed my lefty handshake from him, and his example cheered me when things were bad. I'd admired him anyway but without any sense of personal connection.

I emerged no longer diffident about lining up incorrectly with conventional career categories. By inclination I'm a writer and painter; I got into computer science because of the Talmudic injunction to learn a useful trade and support your wife and family. Shoemaking was more what the rabbis had in mind, but I had never shown any aptitude for shoes and don't regret my choice. The explosion smashed my right hand, and for several months, I was under the impression I would never paint again; I bitterly regretted the work I had never put down on canvas. But I learned to paint with my left hand and will never again neglect my duties as a painter. By the same token, I'd been planning a book about the 1939 New York World's Fair. It was to be such an abnormal book—part history, part novel—that I figured it would be years before I worked up enough courage to write the thing. But when I got home from the hospital, it was clear that I ought just to sit down and do it. To my surprise it was a success; one critic who is quoted in praise of White's book on its cover is quoted on the cover of mine too—a thing the heart treasures. A number of people even bought copies.

And maybe in the end I might *not* have been a bad choice for Mr. Technology. It doesn't take a great scientist to embody the nobility of the basic enterprise; a man who doesn't see technology as the world's most important proposition and would rather be playing with his children than making discoveries might conceivably be a good representative of the whole quintessentially human quest, our continuing attempt to learn and build new things. My response to April's arrest is to congratulate the FBI on its fine work, thank once again the many people who helped us generously when we needed it, remember and honor the men who were bestially murdered and drink *l'chaim*—to the life of mind, to the human enterprise that no bomb can touch.

The Evidence

Editor's note: The list below was compiled in the presence of Special Agent Tony Maxwell of the FBI and subsequently released to the public by order of Judge Charles Lovell in Helena. Without direct access to the original document, TIME *had to rely on its reading of what was a finely printed document, reproduced by copying machine. We have indicated those parts where the print proved illegible. For the sake of clarity, we also corrected what we determined to be purely typographical errors.*

Inventory of items seized at the residence of Theodore Kaczynski, HCR# 30, Box 27, Lincoln, Montana:

DEV 1 (control sample) one Winchester Super X shotgun round
L 1 ng misc. pipes and cordage
L 8 Northwest Territory hiking shoes
L 9 black pepper can containing several metal pieces and a plastic bottle labeled "strychnine oats"
L 10 one Aldrich box containing misc. papers, newspaper clippings, a bus schedule, addresses of corporate officials and maps of San Francisco
L 11 misc. cans, string, plastic and metal
L 12 pieces of lock in a cornmeal container
L 13 toolbox in green bag
L 14 piece of pipe (possible piece of rifle)
L 15 radio sonde measuring temp., humidity, etc.
L 16 metal parts and pieces
L 17 welding-type mask
L 18 Tater Tot box containing misc. books and maps
L 19 tan duffel bag containing clothing and two additional duffel-type bags
L 20 metal parts and pieces, chains, locks and possible traps
L 21 wire screen
L 22 bow strings and arrows in a quiver
L 23 one steak knife

L 24 pipes (misc. sizes)
L 25 pipes and a bowl
L 26 L-shaped pipe
L 27 section of pipe
L 28 section of pipe
L 29 plastic bag containing black jacket
L 30 bomb components
L 31 two rolls of brown paper marked "3qq," can containing wire marked "qq" and documents
L 32 box marked all "1 or 10 q or qq" (handwritten), metal tubes, wiring, springs, ball trigger in tinfoil, stapler, 9V battery and small copper-colored tubing
L 32a copper-colored tubing removed from Item L-32
L 33 books with "5q" marked on container
L 34 letters
L 35 Samsonite briefcase containing University of Michigan degrees, etc.
L 36 gray case containing typewriter
L 37 large green ammo can that contained Item L-4
L 38 TV wire with cord around it
L 39 yearbooks in green plastic bag
L 40 green tarp and twine
L 41 box of clothing and towels
L 42 rain-poncho-type material
L 43 typewriter parts
L 44 section of pipe
L 45 various paper and twine
L 46 Sears box containing arrows
L 47 12 saw blades
L 48 a section of rope
L 49 a section of wood
L 50 five bottles labeled "saltpeter"
L 51 five bottles labeled "saltpeter"
L 52 five bottles labeled "saltpeter" and plastic bag marked "3q"
L 53 glass container with off-white drills
L 54 Calumet bottle containing white powder
L 55 plastic container with white clumpy powder
L 56 plastic bottle with black chunky material in paper and hand-labeled "wezela [unreadable] #2, nuevo lote exp 103"
L 57 container of white powder labeled "$KClO_3$ [unreadable] potassium 99.95% pure"
L 58 container of white powder
L 59 container of yellow crystals with plastic bags

L 60 container of white powder
L 61 six sealed bottles labeled "sulfur"
L 62 plastic bag and container of yellow powder labeled "sulfur"
L 63 plastic bag containing two pieces of wood and makeup
L 64 solder wire and plastic bag
L 65 container labeled "salt"
L 66 jar of white crystalline substance and note "ammonium nitrate"
L 67 1-gal. jug labeled "abietic acid," and sample taken from the jug (two plastic bags)
L 68 bottle labeled "ammonium nitrate NH_4NO_3"
L 69 two cans in bags labeled "abietic acid"
L 70 two bottles labeled "aluminum" and box lid with experiment info.
L 71 various containers marked "aluminum materials"
L 72 This item number was not used.
L 73 piece of wire
L 74 piece of wood
L 75 two steak knives
L 76 large plastic container labeled "$NaCl_3$ + NaCl"
L 77 two pieces of wood and three strips of wood
MA 1 box of 52 books
MA 2 box of 41 books and 23 index cards
MA 3 pair of gloves
MA 4 metal pan and stick
MA 5 appears to be hand-done calendar
MA 6 can with paper addresses
MA 7 can with matches and wood fragments
MA 8 three tools
MA 9 part of radio
MA 10 documents
MA 11 tin with wire across top
MA 12 tools in Tide detergent box
MA 13 container of fine twine
MA 14 small ratchet, tweezers and a pocket knife
MA 15 four measuring spoons
MA 16 tools in a can
MA 17 blue zippered sweatshirt
MA 18 blue hood and old towel
MA 19 two pair of plastic glasses
MA 20 blue jacket
MA 21 green hooded jacket
MA 22 metal pot

MA 23 plastic bag containing cans and hoses
MA 24 a cutting of green jacket
MA 25 one plastic container labeled "citric acid" containing white powder
MA 26 magnet
MA 27 one plastic bottle containing metallic granular material
MA 28 wood and screws
MA 29 red-colored vise
MA 30 pieces of metal
MA 31 medallion
MA 32 drawings and documents
MA 33 clamp
MA 34 bottle of white powder labeled "$NaCl$"
MA 35 Item numbers MA-35 through MA-54 were not used.
MA 55 wood pieces and screen
MB 1 74 books
MB 2 29 books and documents
MB 3 folded papers with chemical residue
MB 4 recorder and case
MB 5 two empty metal cans
MB 6 three arrows
MB 7 one rock
MB 8 four copper tubes
MB 9 plastic jar containing triggering devices, each numbered with masking-tape tag
MB 10 three pairs of scissors
MB 11 one plastic bottle of glue, label "Elmer's Mucilage"
MB 12 one tube of Duro Super Glue
MB 13 one metal can containing three tubes of paint in the following colors: medium cadmium red, raw umber, deep permanent green
MB 14 one metal can containing wicks and strings with a piece of newspaper inside to keep contents from moving about
MB 15 two paint kits: small one in black metal container labeled "Prang Water Colors"; larger one in yellow and clear plastic container
MB 16 one wood-handled knife, contained in a sheath made of newspaper
MB 17 one T-shaped metal pipe or bracket with serial number GH-4 and partial serial number 3658391.
MB 18 two small metal tins
MB 19 one metal can
MB 20 one white plastic shopping bag containing steel wire; hand-

written notation on outside of bag "S ..."; and handwritten notation on packages of wire, "coast to coast, Helena, July, 1994."

MB 21 one metal can labeled "Del Monte Whole Leaf Spinach," containing melted metal fragments
MB 22 one paper bag containing white electrical extension cords; bag wrapped in strapping tape
MB 23 one small metal can
MB 24 nine metal cans
MB 25 two small metal cans
MB 26 one small white ceramic crucible
MB 27 two off-white-colored ceramic crucible lids
MB 28 one brown clasp envelope marked "autobiography"
MB 29 Grip-Line rubber-stamp kit
MB 30 plastic bag containing several notebooks, envelopes and misc. handwritten documents
MB 31 one brown paper bag containing two packages of notebook filler paper
MB 32 one brown paperback book titled *Growing Up Absurd,* by Paul Goodman
MB 33 misc. maps
MB 34 one box of Reynolds aluminum foil with red rubber band around it
MB 35 three metal bottle caps labeled "Mazola Corn Oil"
MB 36 piece of cut pipe
MB 37 bottom portion of unfired cartridge
MB 38 one Hanson, Model 1509 scale, wrapped in brown paper with masking tape
MB 39 brown plastic jar "Nature's Best", containing fired cartridge casings
MB 40 one brown wood-handle pocket knife
MB 41 pick-hatchet tool
MB 42 knife in sheath of tattered white cloth
MB 43 hunting knife in leather sheath
MB 44 wood-handle file
MB 45 seven large drill bits
MB 46 Great Neck #50 hacksaw
MB 47 one drilling base
MB 48 one handsaw
MB 49 one handsaw
MB 50 one brown plastic oblong Hershey canister with lid
MB 51 three brown thin cardboard paper trays
MB 52 three brown thin cardboard paper trays

MB 53 two brown thin cardboard paper trays
MB 54 one coil of wire and metal parts
MB 55 one package of Mead brand typing paper, with bottom half in paper and strapping tape
MB 56 student guides and publications from the University of Montana and Carroll College
MB 57 one brown plastic oblong Hershey canister with lid
MB 58 numerous containers (metal, plastic and cardboard) containing a variety of nails and metal fasteners
MB 59 numerous containers (metal, plastic and cardboard) containing a variety of bolts, screws and metal fasteners
MB 60 two white plastic butane cigarette lighters
MB 61 one Calumet Baking Powder canister containing one red Le Watch brand watch, watch parts and misc. metal parts
MB 62 one brown plastic oblong container, containing one mousetrap, one piece of inner-tube valve, and one orange plastic bag containing wire
MB 63 one yellow plastic pail
MB 64 six cast metallic objects
MB 65 cone-shaped metallic casting
MB 66 one cast metallic object
MB 67 ten canisters containing various metal samples and one round metal object
MB 68 one metal can containing nuts, bolts and other metal objects
MB 69 one cardboard canister containing small amount of white powder and labeled "Shopper's Value Quick Oats"
MB 70 one cardboard canister containing small amount of white powder and labeled "Shopper's Value Quick Oats"
MB 71 one plastic bottle labeled "Chateau 70% Rubbing Alcohol" and containing springs and other metal objects
MB 72 one Calumet Baking Powder canister containing machined metal parts
MB 73 one Calumet Baking Powder canister containing parts of a pocket-knife blade and other assorted metal parts
MB 74 Johnson & Johnson Medicated Band-Aid metal can containing various metal parts
MB 75 one metal can containing wire and other metal parts
MB 76 one cylindrical Quaker Yellow Corn Meal cardboard canister containing two spools of solder
MB 77 one cylindrical Quaker Oats cardboard canister containing wires, a switch and an alligator clip
MB 78 bottom half of cardboard instant-milk box containing tube of Trubond clear silicone caulk, a clear plastic box of screw-

drivers with masking-tape label "254," a wire brush, a level, three paintbrushes, a paper bag containing small square magnets and misc. metal parts

MB 79 hand drill with blue and red wooden handle

MB 80 nine pieces of wood approximately 8 in. long (appear similar to paneling strips)

MB 81 misc. pieces of metal, including tin-can lid, ball of aluminum foil, two pieces of blue hacksaw blade, pipe fittings in T formation and pair of pliers

MB 82 group of metal fasteners, bundled together with blue rubber band

MB 83 two white homemade envelopes, one with handwritten notation "wire," the other "dump."

MB 84 three yellow rubber gloves: one labeled "Ansell" brand; another labeled "Large, Playtex, Dover, Del."; all three with wrist area cut off

MB 85 one cut portion of a battery, "Radiosonde, NSM-6135-01-054-2098, VIZ Mfg. Co., 335 E. Pierce St., Philadelphia, PA, 19144, USA, Patent No. 3205.096," wrapped in a piece of newspaper dated Nov. 22, 1995, page 4 of the *Consumer Press*

MB 86 small plastic container with strip of black tape around it and torn white handwritten label, "Lima Duras de Hierro Parcialmente Limpias," containing brownish-black powder believed to be aluminum

MB 87 two plastic bottles of glue: one labeled "Ross Mucilage for Paperwork," the other "Ross Kangaroo Mucilage"

MB 88 one metal nutcracker

MB 89 one metal Hershey's Cocoa can containing misc. nuts and bolts

MB 90 Quaker Yellow Corn Meal container with handwritten notation "transformer" on top, containing electrical wire and misc. electrical parts

MB 91 one metal Hershey's Cocoa can containing misc. metal parts

MB 92 one brown plastic container containing trace metal

MB 93 Calumet Double Action Baking Powder metal container containing a lump of metal

MB 94 one small Shopper's Value Tomato Paste can containing resisters and a tan plastic shopping bag containing resisters

MB 95 seven rolled-up maps

MB 96 homemade olive green cloth pouch containing a tan plastic shopping bag with three matchbooks with playing card symbols on it, two plastic bags with small pieces of wood in them, and a compass on a string, and a red rubber band. Blue denim patches and various pieces of string all over outside of pouch

MB 97 misc. pieces of curved wire, metal cap in doughnut shape, and round piece of metal cut in strips around the edges

MB 98 Gold Medal flour sack containing misc. debris (to include soil, wood and hair)

MB 99 tan plastic shopping bag containing various types of cord and twine

MB 100 Flavorite Large Pitted Ripe Olives can containing large amount of screws and handwritten note "burned and soaked in corroding solution—clean"

MB 101 glass jar with red metal lid and handwritten note attached with masking tape that says, "aluminum from some type of paint—type of paint unknown." The jar contained clumps of a silver-gray substance.

MB 102 two small orange plastic containers covered with pieces of newspaper, one secured with a tan rubber band

MB 103 one metal ring and a spool of brown thread labeled "American Thread Co., Stamford, CT., 100% Polyester"

MB 104 metal files wrapped in orange and clear plastic bag, with a white piece of paper attached with a black rubber band. There appear to be some kind of mathematical equations on the paper.

MB 105 one metal can containing misc. pieces of copper

MB 106 brown cardboard box containing misc. [grinding] wheels and pieces of metal

MB 107 Quaker Yellow Corn Meal cardboard container containing pieces of screening material

MB 108 one hacksaw blade with red color on each end

MB 109 one metal can containing misc. screws, metal parts and a white envelope with silver coin pieces in it

MB 110 two pieces of splintered hardwood, wrapped in a sheet of newspaper, front page of *Missoulian*, dated Friday, Sept. 16, 1988

MB 111 three pages of handwritten notes attached together with a metal paper fastener and rolled up using a large tan rubber band

MB 112 one spool of twine secured with a piece of masking tape

MB 113 one small brown plastic bottle labeled "Nature Made Therapeutic M [unreadable]," with a piece of masking tape around it, with handwritten notation "coarse aluminum filings"

MB 114 one small metal can containing small clumps of metal. The can is covered with a piece of newspaper and secured with a dirty white rubber band

MB 115 one Calumet Baking Powder can containing soldering wire

MB 116 one small metal container (appears empty)

MB 117 one small metal can with wire handle through it and one piece of metal

MB 118 seven metal casings

MB 119 one small brown plastic bottle labeled "Nature Made Therapeutic M [unreadable],"with paper label attached with masking tape, with handwritten notation "aluminum filings from our big block of cast aluminum 5.1 oz."

MB 120 one Carnation Dry Milk cardboard container

MB120a small orange plastic bottle with white plastic cap, with piece of masking tape around it with handwritten notation "AgCl, slightly photo-decomposed"

MB120aa one whitish plastic bottle with black cap, label "manganese dioxide (technical) contact with other material may cause fire. Do not grind. Do not breathe dust. 8J28D, 1/4 lbs. Analytical & Research Chemicals, Inc."

MB120b small brown plastic bottle with black cap, with piece of masking tape around it, with handwritten notation "lithorgetminium & free lead not very pure"

MB120c small plastic orange container with white plastic cap, with a piece of black tape around it securing a white label with handwritten notation "Fe_20_3, .347 units, Exp. 51, Lot [unreadable] without H_2So_4"

MB120d small plastic tube containing blue powder. The tube had masking tape around it, with the handwritten notation "$[CuS0_4]$ $5H_20$ copper sulfate."

MB120e small glass jar with red and white checkered metal cap containing white flaky substance, with masking tape around it, with handwritten notation "NH_4Cl [ammonium] chloride Exp. 136"

MB 120f small plastic bottle labeled "Supreme Brand Aspirin Tablets" containing pink-colored strips of paper and white label reading "litmus paper neutral"

MB120g one small white plastic bottle with white metal cap, labeled "Bayer Aspirin," with masking tape around it, with handwritten notation "lead chloride—contaminated with some hydroxide, oxide, or carbonate of lead"

MB120h whitish plastic bottle with red plastic cap, containing a grayish powder

MB 120i small gray plastic box labeled "[pH Hydrion] vivid, double roll 5.5 to 9.5, catalog no. 168"

MB 120j small brown plastic bottle with white plastic cap, with notebook- paper label taped on with masking tape with handwritten notation "Na_2CO_3 from Red Devil lye. Should be reasonably pure, if Red Devil lye is. (No, not very pure)"

MB120k white paper envelope wrapped with masking tape with handwritten notation "Elmer's Brand Mucilage"

MB 120l whitish plastic bottle with white cap labeled "orange." The bottle had a white paper label secured with masking tape. The label contained the following handwritten notation: "$Fe(OH)_2$ partially (or wholly?) oxidized to $Fe(OH)_3$ Exp. 51, lot E"

MB120m small brown plastic bottle labeled "therapeutic M" with masking tape around it, with handwritten notation "lead acetate, lead hydroxide, lead carbonate, unknown proportions, not very pure"

MB120n one Calumet Baking Powder can with paper label secured with masking tape, with handwritten notation "black sand presumably consist[s] largely of [$Fe0_{45}$]"

MB120o white plastic bottle with white plastic cap labeled "NDC 0923-0371-03 powdered alum (ammonium alum) astringent, Whiteworth"

MB120p white plastic bottle with white metal cap. Bottle contained a label, "McKesson boric acid crystals NF," and had a small white price tag "112-1755, K3MME, Bergums 1.93."

MB120q small tan cardboard box labeled "Fuel compressed, trioxane, ration heating, F.S.N. 9110-263-9865, 3 bars, specification: MIL-F-10805C, Can-Tite Rubber Corporation, Inwood, L.I., New York, 11696"

MB 120r one brown plastic Osco Castor Oil bottle with white plastic cap

MB 120s one Grape Super Sip plastic bottle with paper label secured with masking tape bearing handwritten notation "Fe_20_3 Exp. 51, Lot (di)"

MB 120t small clear glass Folger's jar with gold-colored plastic cap containing greenish-gray crystals. The jar has masking tape wrapped around it with the handwritten notation "greenish precipitate (presumably a copper compound) from Exp. 241."

MB120u white plastic McKesson Boric Acid Powder NF bottle with white metal cap. The bottle has a small white price tag bearing the following information: "112-1797 H3HG Bergums 1.77"

MB120v one whitish plastic Raspberry Super Sip bottle with white plastic cap with masking tape across and around cap and masking tape around bottle with handwritten notation "AgCl, heavily contaminated with [unreadable] compounds and other crap"

MB120w white elongated plastic bottle with white plastic cap, label "laxative" (brand name not visible) with white paper label secured with masking tape, with handwritten notation "mixture of [litharge] and minium, possibly contaminated with other oxides of Pb, also perhaps carbonate and nitrate of Pb, hydroxide, and a little free lead"

MB120x clear glass jar, with whitish plastic stopper type cap, with white paper label secured with handwritten notation "amorphous carbon (made by heating sucrose)"; containing a black powdery substance

MB120y metal can covered with a piece of newspaper, secured with masking tape with handwritten notation "alder charcoal"

MB120z oblong whitish plastic container with black cap, with black tape and masking tape around the cap; label "Aldrich Scientific, P3191, 500g, Potassium Carbonate, Anhydrous Granular Technical, K, Co, FW 138.21, Aldrich Scientific, 5415 Jackwood Dr., San Antonio, TX 78238-1897, Lot 9C06G"

MB 121 rod-shaped pieces of dark-colored/blackish powder, wrapped in a handwritten note inside a red and white checkered bread bag

MB 122 three bundles of clear glass tubing; one wrapped in a page of *Consumer Press* newspaper dated June 21, 1995, and secured with yellow and white rubber bands; another is wrapped in a large-pocket bubble wrap, with handwritten notation "5 mm pyrex tubing"; another is wrapped in large-pocket bubble wrap with handwritten notation "10 mm pyrex tubing," all wrapped together in a *Missoulian* newspaper dated Jan. 16, 1991

MB 123 one white porcelain mortar and pestle, wrapped in *Consumer Press* newspaper dated April 5, 1995, page 26, and secured with a yellow rubber band

MB 124 metal can with handwritten notation "12:00 AM," containing two metal castings

MB 125 round cardboard canister, label "Old-Fashioned Quaker Oats," with handwritten notation on the top "rubber tubings, funnels, bulbs, etc." The canister contains assorted pieces of rubber tubing, a small piece of glass tubing, a black rubber stopper, two metal clips and one smaller round cardboard canister. The smaller canister is a Quaker Yellow Cornmeal container with handwritten notation on the top "plastic and glass tubing, short pieces." This smaller container contains assorted pieces of plastic and rubber tubing, several black rubber stoppers and two metal clips.

MB 126 one stainless steel .22-cal. revolver and nine .22-cal. rounds of ammunition. The revolver is further described as an "H&R Inc., U.S.A., Model 930, serial # AE 1935." The revolver has a black handle, which is wrapped in masking tape

MB 127 one package of Gillette Super Blue Blades and a variety of string and twine bound together with a blue rubber band in a white piece of paper. The paper has the handwritten notation "additional ties for big shelter cloth"

MB 128 one yellow and black plastic True Value flashlight with light bulb in it but no batteries

MB 129 cardboard box with U.S. Post Office metered mail "Kansas City, MO, Oct. 27, '76," containing various spools of twine, bundles of string and numerous strips of leather

MB 130 one cardboard box that had contained Items MB-79, MB-84 and MB-86"

MB 131 one metal can containing pieces of carved wood and carved bone

MB 132 one Band-Aid Brand Plastic Strips metal can wrapped in a plastic bag, secured with a blue rubber band, containing five strands of copper wire

MB 133 one piece of wavy wire bent in the form of a circle

MB 134 tan plastic shopping bag containing one cut brass bracket/pipe fitting, two small pieces of copper tubing (one piece has masking tape around it), four plastic containers (two whitish plastic with white metal tops, one whitish plastic with a red plastic top, and one orange plastic with a white plastic top), each containing copper and/or other metal fragments

MB 135 one round cardboard Old Fashioned Quaker Oats canister containing an electronics tester, serial number 800341385, with handwritten note on masking tape on front "note: when on 'high' the ammeter gives incorrect reading. See Exp. 242."; and a second handwritten note on top of canister, "ammeter," between two intersecting pieces of masking tape.

MB 136 one clear plastic box containing one long flathead nail, one piece of wire, and assorted pieces of metal

MB 137 one small clear glass jar, with red and white checkered metal cap, containing two staples (for wood) and a small amount of gold, shiny [granules] and flakes

MB 138 one orangish-yellow elongated plastic container/box containing nails, small pieces of wood, and sewing instruments and materials

MB 139 one roll of Gould Quikstik brown packing tape; label inside roll "Gould Packaging, Inc, Vancouver, WA 98666"

MB 140 one pair of pliers

MB 141 one unopened package of Coghlan's Waterproof Wooden Matches, "Coghlan's Ltd., Winnipeg, Canada, made in Australia," containing four boxes of matches

MB 142 one white plastic bag containing a white plastic face mask, with string and rubber band attached to it, and an empty package of "Flexo Products, Inc. replacement micro-foam filters for protective mask"

MB 143 one piece of copper tubing

MB 144 one metal can containing a white toothbrush, bottle caps, balls of aluminum foil, pieces of screening material and various metal pieces

MB 145 one small round cardboard Quaker Yellow Cornmeal canister, containing numerous hose clamps and metal brackets, with handwritten notation on the top of the canister "Hose clamps, etc."

MB 146 two blue and two orange plastic funnels, and one white homemade cloth filter for funnel

MB 147 one paper Gold Medal Whole Wheat flour bag, containing several large nails, secured shut with a dirty tan rubber band

MB 148 one white plastic jar with white metal cap; label "Rexall Sublimed Sulfur, N.F. (Flowers of Sulfur), Parasiticide-Scabicide"

MB 149 one small, square, yellow tin labeled "John Wagner & Sons, Rare Flowery Jasmine Tea," containing one small metal washer and several small pieces of wire

MB 150 one plastic bread bag, secured with a shoelace, containing five small containers: 1) an orange plastic bottle with white plastic lid, with masking tape around it, with handwritten note "Thermite laced with chlorate mixture"; 2) an orange plastic container, with white plastic cap, with masking tape on it, with handwritten notation "Exp. 118"; 3) an orange plastic bottle with white plastic lid, with masking tape around it, with handwritten notation "KCl03 + S + charcoal + mucilage"; 4) an orange plastic container with white plastic cap, with masking tape around it, with handwritten notation "Al + S"; 5) a small metal container, silver color, with masking tape around it, with handwritten notation "Smokeless powder from Remington 30.06 bronze points"

MB 151 one tan plastic shopping bag, containing three aluminum-foil envelopes/pouches; each with masking-tape labels with handwritten notations: 1) "Restos parcialmente cuajados de mezcla 206-1(a) de Exps 225, 228, 245, mezcla 206-1(a)"; 2) Mix 158-4 (slightly modified) from Exp. 244 clean and can be used."; 3) "Mix 158-4 Exp. 244. Clotted with acetone"

MB 152 one metal can with white paper label attached with strapping filament tape, with handwritten notation "Exp. 126 Pittsburgh container #2"

MB 153 one clear plastic jar with white metal lid, with masking tape around it, with handwritten notation "(Al + S) + thermite"

MB 154 one paper container of "[unreadable] Fine Granulated Sugar," secured with two large rubber bands

MB 155 one paper Gold Medal Whole Wheat flour sack with handwritten notation "dump in Lincoln" at the bottom, containing miscellaneous debris (to include soil, small pieces of wood, metal, screws and bolts), secured with a rubber band

MB 156 white plastic bag containing one large round cardboard Quaker Old-Fashioned Oats canister, with handwritten notation, "class 1 no rust," on intersecting pieces of packing tape on top and containing a large variety of metal pieces and wire

MB 157 one white plastic bag containing one small round cardboard Quaker Yellow Corn Meal canister, containing one aluminum-foil envelope/pouch, containing "flash powder"; handwritten notations on top of canister "spoons" and "Exp. 220" (crossed through)

MB 158 round metal Calumet Baking Powder can with white paper label secured with masking tape, with handwritten notation "Na_2CO_3—impure. Probably contaminated with [$NaHCO_3$], NaCl, and $NaClO_3$. This is the first lot of crystals removed March 23. And second lot."

MB 159 one brown plastic bottle with clear plastic lid, labeled "Osco Drug Vitamin Mineral Formula," with masking tape around it, with handwritten notation "Crude $KClO_3$, medium $KClO_3$, content. Must be filtered."

MB 160 blue powderlike substance

MB 161 white plastic bottle labeled "RIT Liquid Dye," with masking tape around it, with handwritten notation "$CaSO_4$ (not dry)"

MB 162 brown plastic bottle with white metal cap and pink-colored plastic twisted under cap, with masking tape around bottle, with handwritten notation "mostly KCl, with modest amount $KClO_3$, tare with cap=0.6 oz."

MB 163 one metal can with aluminum foil pressed over the top, with white paper label secured with masking tape, with handwritten notation "Cuidado muy sensibilizado nezcla c de Exp. 90 esta la misma que la mezela #5"; contains large black particles

MB 164 one glass bottle with white metal cap; labeled "McKesson glycerin USP, #21315, McKesson Laboratories, Dublin, CA 94566"

MB 165 liquid sample from bottle marked "sodium tartrate"

MB 166 liquid sample from bottle marked "KCl"

MB 167 whitish plastic bottle with white metal cap, with clear plastic twisted under cap, with label "McKesson saltpeter (potassium nitrate)," with small bright-yellowish-green price tag, "Bergum Drug, Why Pay More? $1.73"

MB 168 small brown bottle with white plastic cap, with masking tape around bottle, with handwritten notation "crude $KClO_3$. Good purity, except that it must be filtered. Tare with cap=0.6 oz."

MB 169 one clear plastic bottle with clear plastic cap, with pink plastic twisted under cap, with masking tape around bottle, with handwritten notation "crude $KClO_3$—good purity" (twice)

MB 170 one round cardboard and metal canister labeled "Clabber Girl Baking Powder," containing silver-gray powdery substance

MB 171 two small white cardboard boxes labeled "Potassium chromate K. CrO, for lab use only, Hagenow Labs, Inc., Manitowoc, Wis.," in a white plastic shopping bag

MB 172 one white plastic shopping bag containing a white powdery substance, and containing a small clear plastic baggie with an aluminum-foil envelope/pouch, containing a powdery substance (possibly "flash powder")

MB 173 one small plastic orange container with white plastic cap, with white paper label secured with masking tape, with handwritten notation "$BaSO_4$ may be contaminated with a little $MgCl_2$ and smaller amount of $MgSO_2$"

MB 174 small white plastic jar with white metal cap, with handwritten notation "smallest," containing metal screw/bolt and nut

MB 175 one whitish plastic bottle with white metal cap, with masking tape around bottle, with handwritten notation "pure sucrose ground fine"

MB 176 one clear glass jar with white metal cap, with picture of a lion on the cap and the name Wagner, with masking tape around jar, with handwritten notations "curic hydroxide?" (crossed out) and "probably basic carbonate $Cu_2(OH)_2CO_3$"; contains blue powdery substance

MB 177 whitish plastic bottle with white metal cap and clear plastic twisted under cap; label "McKesson boric acid crystals NF,

NDC 0022-0144-85" and small square bright-yellowish-green price tag, "Bergum Drug Why Pay More? $1.93"

MB 178 one white plastic bottle with white plastic cap; label "Flowers of Sulfur USP, Whiteworth Inc., Gardena, CA. 90248, NDC 0923-3500-03," with masking tape around the base, with a small square white price tag, "Bergums 217-6956 L5GJB $5.17"

MB 179 small orange plastic container with white plastic cap, with masking tape around container, with handwritten notation "silver oxide Ag_2O"

MB 180 one small clear glass jar with white metal cap, with handwritten notation "washed charcoal very finely ground"; contains black powdery substance

MB 181 one small orange plastic container with white plastic cap, with black tape around it, securing a white paper label, with handwritten notation "Fe_2O_3 Exp. 51, [unreadable] (bi), with H_2SO_4"

MB 182 one round metal can labeled "Calumet Baking Powder," with a piece of newspaper over the top, secured with masking tape around the can, with handwritten notation "perfectly clean"; and one round brown cardboard canister, with silver-colored metal lid, containing powdery substance (possibly "flash powder")

MB 183 unknown powder

MB 184 glass bottle containing pure liquid

MB 185 rubber bands and ties

MB 186 two pieces of metal

MB 187 small piece of cut metal

MB 188 (3) razors, (1) thermometer

MB 189 cordage

MB 190 two plastic containers with white crystalline material

MB 191 (5) pairs of glasses and (1) clear lens

MB 192 long piece of inner tube

MB 193 two cans of adhesive

MB 194 .25-cal. gun (Raven Arms), magazine containing six bullets, and one bullet

MB 195 vacuum debris

MB 196 vacuum debris

MB 197 dust and debris

MB 198 vacuum debris

MB 199 vacuum debris

MB 200 screws

MC 1 three blue binders

MC 2 two binders
MC 3 two binders
MC 4 two binders
MC 5 misc. documents in yellow envelopes
MC 6 36 books
MC 7 gloves
MC 8 shoe insoles
MC 9 nylon and cord
MC 10 rifle scope wrapped in plastic
MC 11 greenish-colored coat
MC 12 vitamin jar containing steel pins
MC 13 rag pillow
MC 14 blanket
MC 15 three mittens and two boots
MC 16 two wood planks (one with aluminum covering)
MC 17 blue scarf
MC 18 scarf (turquoise and green)
MC 19 red hat
MC 20 strapping
MC 21 bolt action .22-cal. rifle
MC 22 Remington model .700 30.06 #6292650
MC 23 straw hat and strings
MC 24 information on white paper re. 30.06
MC 25 wooden/metal contraption
MC 26 one hand-bowed wood saw
MC 27 bookshelf
MC 28 metal bracket
MC 29 screen sample
MC 30 wood and nails
MD 1 two check boxes. One contains a toothbrush; the other contains a dental instrument.
MD 2 envelopes, handwritten documents and misc. documents
MD 3 two books of checks #135-159 and #160-184; account number 001-04219-12, in the name of Theodore J. Kaczynski, from the Western Federal Savings Bank
MD 4 envelopes containing misc. documents
MD 5 brown box containing misc. documents
MD 6 padded envelopes and self-adhesive labels in tan plastic Osco Drug shopping bag
MD 7 one box of Mead envelopes, one package of self-adhesive labels and one package of hole reinforcers
MD 8 one blue spiral notebook and one black vinyl notebook

MD 9 plastic shopping bag containing Montana driver's license, $32 cash and misc. handwritten notes
MD 10 one small tomato-paste can containing 87¢ and a black watch and receipt
MD 11 two metal cans containing "secrets" box, paper clips and keys
MD 12 two metal cans containing pipe cleaners, writing instruments, rulers and a watch
MD 13 stack of maps rubber-banded together
MD 14 two small cardboard boxes and typewriter ribbons
MD 15 plastic container with assorted maps and matchbook from Limited System Stores, Lombard, Illinois
MD 16 six books: Eastern mysticism, Basimov's *Guide to the Bible, Holy Bible–Dictionary Concordance, Comes the Comrade, Les Misérables,* Vols. 1 and 2
MD 17 plastic K-Mart shopping bag containing carbon paper and misc. paper
MD 18 three notebook binders and a pad of colored construction paper
MD 19 notebook and misc. papers
MD 20 can opener
MD 21 metal container/can (appears empty)
MD 22 metal container/can labeled "Veg-All" (appears empty)
MD 23 metal container/can (appears empty)
MD 24 black oblong metal can (appears empty)
MD 25 black oblong metal can (appears empty)
MD 26 black oblong metal can (appears empty)
MD 27 one clear glass jar containing visible residue
MD 28 one clear glass jar containing dental bridge
MD 29 one plastic jar labeled "Honey USDA Food" (appears empty)
MD 30 one black oblong metal can (appears empty)
MD 31 four brown oblong plastic lids
MD 32 one small plastic jar with partial label (appears empty)
MD 33 one small plastic jar, brown with orange label "Nutri-Plus calcium, magnesium and zinc" (appears empty)
MD 34 one small plastic jar labeled "calcium hydroxide, USP" (appears empty)
MD 35 one metal can (appears empty)
MD 36 one metal can covered with paper and rubber band
MD 37 one metal can labeled "Veg-All" (appears empty)
MD 38 one small metal can (appears empty)
MD 39 one container of Morton salt
MD 40 one white Mix 'n Drink plastic cup
MD 41 one white Mix 'n Drink plastic cup

MD 42 one white Mix 'n Drink plastic cup
MD 43 one white Mix 'n Drink" plastic cup
MD 44 one white plastic cup
MD 45 box of Proverb Series matchbooks, containing 21 matchbooks
MD 46 razor blades wrapped in aluminum foil
MD 47 one small tin can containing visible residue
MD 48 one glass jar with blue metal lid
MD 49 one metal frying pan without handle
MD 50 one metal can
MD 51 one glass jar labeled "Adams Unsalted 100% Natural Peanut Butter" and extra lid (appears empty)
MD 52 bottom half of plastic water jug, partial label "Distilled Water"
MD 53 one metal can (appears empty)
MD 54 one metal can (appears empty)
MD 55 one metal can (appears empty)
MD 56 one metal can labeled "Del Monte Diced Tomatoes" (appears empty)
MD 57 one metal can labeled "Veg-All" (appears empty)
MD 58 one small metal can (appears empty)
MD 59 one cardboard box full of misc. documents, envelopes and leather portfolio
MD 60 green canvas U.S. Army backpack
MD 61 khaki-colored cloth, somewhat deteriorated and resembling a ski mask
MD 62 wood-handled hammer
MD 63 one package of saw blades
MD 64 one long-bladed black handle knife
MD 65 saw (handsaw)
MD 66 one wooden, apparently handmade, measuring instrument
MD 67 one small brown glass bottle
MD 68 metal can containing spent cartridge casings
MD 69 one baking-powder canister with handwritten masking-tape label, "trigger spring for .22 rifle"
MD 70 two packages of waterproof matches and one matchbook
MD 71 one red metal box containing gun-cleaning kit labeled "Sears, cal.30 6 20253"
MD 72 one piece of metal with curled end
MD 73 one coil of rope
MD 74 one small, round, cardboard Quaker Yellow Cornmeal canister, containing a white powdery substance
MD 75 one white plastic jar with black plastic cap; label "2919 tartaric acid N.F., Humco Laboratory, Texarkana, Texas 75501," with portion of red tamper-resistant tape across the cap and a

small white square price tag "247-9996 IEUR Bergums $8.83"; label states "fill Aug. 3-83, Exp. May-88"

MD 76 one large whitish plastic jar with white plastic cap; label "NDC-0395-2285-01 Humco Laboratory, plaster of Paris (dental)"; contains white powdery substance
MD 77 wood pieces
MD 78 staples
MD 79 wire ring
MD 80 scabbard
MD 81 feathers
MD 82 This item number was not used.
MD 83 shelf
ME 1 steel/metal screen with wood frame
ME 2 wood brace and screw
ME 3 screws and nails
ME 4 two pulleys
ME 5 screws
ME 6 staples
ME 7 cordage
ME 8 screws and wires
ME 9 strainer, hooks
ME 10 wire
MF 1 vacuum sweepings of main floor
MF 2 filings/debris
MF 3 file (tool)
MF 4 file with red handle
MF 5 metal files
MF 6 brushed debris
MF 7 package of Manlo envelopes
MF 8 brown bags/newspapers
MF 9 debris/cardboard
MF 10 folded cardboard box
MF 11 plastic bottle (cut in half) with rolled notebook papers
MF 12 improvised explosive device (IED) contained in a cardboard box, wrapped in plastic bags with various tape and rubber bands
MF 12a pipe bomb
MF 12aa outer pipe with attached metal fragments
MF 12ab pipe shaving and filter
MF 12ac end plug/metal fragments
MF 12ad tape and twine, outer wrap of pipe
MF 12ae improvised detonation and filler
MF 12af bulk filler

MF 13 This item number was not used.
MF 14 small blue spiral notebook containing handwritten notes in [unreadable] plastic shopping bag with rubber bands
MF 15 six twigs from paper container
MF 16 pliers/vise grip
MF 17 cardboard cylinder container
MF 18 hatchet
MF 19 traveling kit—nylon bag with contents, with list of items
MF 20 nails
MF 21 shoes, with double sole of different sizes (contained in a plastic bag)
MF 22 aluminum rectangular pan
MF 23 batteries (size C, two batteries)
MF 24 box of wax paper
MF 25 piece of wood with a piece of wax paper
MF 26 brown sweater rolled in plastic bag
MF 27 dirty green tarp in plastic bag
MF 28 hat, brown bag, camouflage jacket, green/brown pants and canvas jacket contained in plastic bag
MF 29 plastic rain gear (poncho)
MF 30 brown plastic raincoat
MF 31 knife
MF 32 maps of local area (two maps)
MF 33 canvas green/brown face mask and black canvas face mask
MF 34 radio and map of Lincoln, Montana, area
MF 35 white rags tied together
MF 36 plastic bag with two fish hooks, string and two boxes of matches
MF 37 pocket knife
MF 38 pieces of wood in plastic
MF 39 plastic garbage bag, and bag containing clothing strips
MF 40 iodized salt in bottle
MF 41 ammo pack and waterproof matches
MF 42 pipe approximately 6½ ft. long
MF 43 handmade gun with spent cartridge
MF 44 wood boards in foil
MF 45 debris
MF 46 misc. wood with screws and nails, to include pieces from the wood bin itself, bed and bed frame
MF 47 one large piece of wood bin
MF 48 one bottle of Trazadone antidepressant
MF 49 wood fragments
MF 50 wood fragments in plastic container

MF 51 tin containing hand tools
MF 52 two spades/hand shovels
MF 53 six metal bars
MF 54 long piece of metal
MF 55 newspaper articles
MF 56 cornmeal box containing spools, wood and foam
MF 57 two axes
MF 58 piece of cable
MF 59 plastic bag of stitching hoop and thread
MF 60 plastic bag containing filter paper to measure burn and documents explaining it
MF 61 misc. metal pieces, screws, bolts, etc.
MF 62 pair of forging pliers
MF 63 pieces of wood
MF 64 springs and note on envelope in Quick Oats box
MF 65 misc. metal and brass in Quick Oats box
MF 66 tin-can lids in Quick Oats box
MF 67 metal can
MF 68 cardboard can with trace
MF 69 metal pot and lid
MF 70 Calumet can containing wax-type substance
MF 71 piece of sheet metal
MF 72 a cut portion of axe blade
MF 73 metal can containing unknown residue
MF 74 metal can containing unknown residue
MF 75 metal can containing unknown residue
MF 76 metal can containing unknown residue
MF 77 metal can containing unknown residue
MF 78 metal can containing unknown residue
MF 79 cardboard box of wire and a plastic bag
MF 80 cardboard container within one metal can
MF 81 plastic container
MF 82 misc. pipes, metal rod and a tire tool
MF 83 black powder and smokeless powder
MF 84 loose metal parts
MF 85 plastic bucket containing thick black material
MF 86 paper bag containing metal container with metal tops and wire
MF 87 one plastic bag containing various drill bits and other metal items
MF 88 metal container of black granular material
MF 89 metal container containing white powder material
MF 90 three plastic bottles labeled "alcohol," containing liquid
MF 91 two metal fragments

MF	92	one white plastic container of white powder
MF	93	one metal can containing keys and twine
MF	94	plastic container of white powder
MF	95	two samples, one from each paint can
MF	96	sample of ash taken from pot
MF	97	sample of ash taken from wood stove
MF	98	ammunition for .22-cal.
MF	99	ammunition
MF	100	green notebook
MF	101	vacuum debris
MF	102	vacuum debris
MF	103	wood
OC	1	tool made with rebar
OC	2	sample of cabin wall
OC	3	staples removed from homemade ladder
OC	4	corroded metal-like substance
OC	5	paint can with acetone can in it
OC	6	screen wire
OC	7	paint can with acetone
OC	8	piece of green license plate
OC	9	sample of screen
OC	10	paint scrapings
OC	11	paint scrapings
OC	12	can of adhesive
OC	13	glazing compound
OC	14	can labeled "acetone"
R	1	ceramic bowl
R	2	ceramic bowl
R	3	ceramic bowl
R	4	ceramic bowl
R	5	rusted sheet metal
R	6	two strips of burnt steel
RSP	1	(IED) partial section of wooden box
RSP	1A	(IED) piece of label from the wooden box
RSP	2a	(IED) piece of label from the wooden box
RSP	2	This item number was not used.
RSP	3	(IED) partial section of wooden box
RSP	4	(IED) packaging material
RSP	5	(IED) misc. debris

The Unabomber's Manifesto

as delivered to the New York *Times*
and Washington *Post* in June 1995

INDUSTRIAL SOCIETY AND ITS FUTURE

INTRODUCTION

1. The Industrial Revolution and its consequences have been a disaster for the human race. They have greatly increased the life-expectancy of those of us who will live in "advanced" countries, but they have destabilized society, have made life unfulfilling, have subjected human beings to indignities, have led to widespread psychological suffering (in the Third World to physical suffering as well) and have inflicted severe damage on the natural world. The continued development of technology will worsen the situation. It will certainly subject human beings to greater indignities and inflict greater damage on the natural world, it will probably lead to greater social disruption and psychological suffering, and it may lead to increased physical suffering even in "advanced" countries.

2. The industrial-technological system may survive or it may break down. If it survives, it MAY eventually achieve a low level of physical and psychological suffering, but only after passing through a long and very painful period of adjustment and only at the cost of permanently reducing human beings and many other living organisms to engineered products and mere cogs in the social machine. Furthermore, if the system survives, the consequences will be inevitable: There is no way of reforming or modifying the system so as to prevent it from depriving people of dignity and autonomy.

3. If the system breaks down the consequences will still be very painful. But the bigger the system grows the more disastrous the

results of its breakdown will be, so if it is to break down it had best break down sooner rather than later.

4. We therefore advocate a revolution against the industrial system. This revolution may or may not make use of violence; it may be sudden or it may be a relatively gradual process spanning a few decades. We can't predict any of that. But we do outline in a very general way the measures that those who hate the industrial system should take in order to prepare the way for a revolution against that form of society. This is not to be a POLITICAL revolution. Its object will be to overthrow not governments but the economic and technological basis of the present society.

5. In this article we give attention to only some of the negative developments that have grown out of the industrial-technological system. Other such developments we mention only briefly or ignore altogether. This does not mean that we regard these other developments as unimportant. For practical reasons we have to confine our discussion to areas that have received insufficient public attention or in which we have something new to say. For example, since there are well-developed environmental and wilderness movements, we have written very little about environmental degradation or the destruction of wild nature, even though we consider these to be highly important.

THE PSYCHOLOGY OF MODERN LEFTISM

6. Almost everyone will agree that we live in a deeply troubled society. One of the most widespread manifestations of the craziness of our world is leftism, so a discussion of the psychology of leftism can serve as an introduction to the discussion of the problems of modern society in general.

7. But what is leftism? During the first half of the 20th century leftism could have been practically identified with socialism. Today the movement is fragmented and it is not clear who can properly be called a leftist. When we speak of leftists in this article we have in mind mainly socialists, collectivists, "politically correct" types, feminists, gay and disability activists, animal rights activists and the like. But not everyone who is associated with one of these movements is a leftist. What we are trying to get at in discussing

leftism is not so much movement or an ideology as a psychological type, or rather a collection of related types. Thus, what we mean by "leftism" will emerge more clearly in the course of our discussion of leftist psychology. (Also, see paragraphs 227-230.)

8. Even so, our conception of leftism will remain a good deal less clear than we would wish, but there doesn't seem to be any remedy for this. All we are trying to do here is indicate in a rough and approximate way the two psychological tendencies that we believe are the main driving force of modern leftism. We by no means claim to be telling the WHOLE truth about leftist psychology. Also, our discussion is meant to apply to modern leftism only. We leave open the question of the extent to which our discussion could be applied to the leftists of the 19th and early 20th centuries.

9. The two psychological tendencies that underlie modern leftism we call "feelings of inferiority" and "oversocialization." Feelings of inferiority are characteristic of modern leftism as a whole, while oversocialization is characteristic only of a certain segment of modern leftism; but this segment is highly influential.

FEELINGS OF INFERIORITY

10. By "feelings of inferiority" we mean not only inferiority feelings in the strict sense but a whole spectrum of related traits; low self-esteem, feelings of powerlessness, depressive tendencies, defeatism, guilt, self-hatred, etc. We argue that modern leftists tend to have some such feelings (possibly more or less repressed) and that these feelings are decisive in determining the direction of modern leftism.

11. When someone interprets as derogatory almost anything that is said about him (or about groups with whom he identifies) we conclude that he has inferiority feelings or low self-esteem. This tendency is pronounced among minority rights activists, whether or not they belong to the minority groups whose rights they defend. They are hypersensitive about the words used to designate minorities and about anything that is said concerning minorities. The terms "negro," "oriental," "handicapped" or "chick" for an African, an Asian, a disabled person or a woman originally had no derogatory connotation. "Broad" and "chick" were merely the feminine equivalents of "guy," "dude," or "fellow." The negative connota-

tions have been attached to these terms by the activists themselves. Some animal rights activists have gone so far as to reject the word "pet" and insist on its replacement by "animal companion." Leftish anthropologists go to great lengths to avoid saying anything about primitive peoples that could conceivably be interpreted as negative. They want to replace the world "primitive" by "nonliterate." They seem almost paranoid about anything that might suggest that any primitive culture is inferior to our own. (We do not mean to imply that primitive cultures ARE inferior to ours. We merely point out the hypersensitivity of leftist anthropologists.)

12. Those who are most sensitive about "politically incorrect" terminology are not the average black ghetto-dweller, Asian immigrant, abused woman or disabled person, but a minority of activists, many of whom do not even belong to any "oppressed" group that come from privileged strata of society. Political correctness has its stronghold among university professors, who have secure employment with comfortable salaries, and the majority of whom are heterosexual white males from middle- to upper-middle-class families.

13. Many leftists have an intense identification with the problems of groups that have an image of being weak (women), defeated (American Indians), repellent (homosexuals) or otherwise inferior. The leftists themselves feel that these groups are inferior. They would never admit to themselves that they have such feelings, but it is precisely because they do see these groups as inferior that they identify with their problems. (We do not mean to suggest that women, Indians, etc. ARE inferior; we are only making a point about leftist psychology.)

14. Feminists are desperately anxious to prove that women are as strong and as capable as men. Clearly they are nagged by a fear that women may NOT be as strong and as capable as men.

15. Leftists tend to hate anything that has an image of being strong, good and successful. They hate America, they hate Western civilization, they hate white males, they hate rationality. The reasons that leftists give for hating the West, etc. clearly do not correspond with their real motives. They SAY they hate the West because it is warlike, imperialistic, sexist, ethnocentric and so forth, but where these same faults appear in socialist countries or in primitive cul-

tures, the leftist finds excuses for them, or at best he GRUDGINGLY admits that they exist; whereas he ENTHUSIASTICALLY points out (and often greatly exaggerates) these faults where they appear in Western civilization. Thus it is clear that these faults are not the leftist's real motive for hating America and the West. He hates America and the West because they are strong and successful.

16. Words like "self-confidence," "self-reliance," "initiative," "enterprise," "optimism," etc., play little role in the liberal and leftist vocabulary. The leftist is an anti-individualistic, pro-collectivist. He wants society to solve everyone's problems for them, take care of them. He is not the sort of person who has an inner sense of confidence in his ability to solve his own problems and satisfy his own needs. The leftist is antagonistic to the concept of competition because, deep inside, he feels like a loser.

17. Art forms that appeal to modern leftish intellectuals tend to focus on sordidness, defeat and despair, or else they take an orgiastic tone, throwing off rational control as if there were no hope of accomplishing anything through rational calculation and all that was left was to immerse oneself in the sensations of the moment.

18. Modern leftish philosophers tend to dismiss reason, science, objective reality and to insist that everything is culturally relative. It is true that one can ask serious questions about the foundations of scientific knowledge and about how, if at all, the concept of objective reality can be defined. But it is obvious that modern leftish philosophers are not simply cool-headed logicians systematically analyzing the foundations of knowledge. They are deeply involved emotionally in their attack on truth and reality. They attack these concepts because of their own psychological needs. For one thing, their attack is an outlet for hostility, and, to the extent that it is successful, it satisfies the drive for power. More importantly, the leftist hates science and rationality because they classify certain beliefs as true (i.e., successful, superior) and other beliefs as false (i.e., failed, inferior). The leftist's feelings of inferiority run so deep that he cannot tolerate any classification of some things as successful or superior and other things as failed or inferior. This also underlies the rejection by many leftists of the concept of mental illness and of the utility of IQ tests. Leftists are antagonistic to genetic explanations

of human abilities or behavior because such explanations tend to make some persons appear superior or inferior to others. Leftists prefer to give society the credit or blame for an individual's ability or lack of it. Thus if a person is "inferior" it is not his fault, but society's, because he has not been brought up properly.

19. The leftist is not typically the kind of person whose feelings of inferiority make him a braggart, an egotist, a bully, a self-promoter, a ruthless competitor. This kind of person has not wholly lost faith in himself. He has a deficit in his sense of power and self-worth, but he can still conceive of himself as having the capacity to be strong, and his efforts to make himself strong produce his unpleasant behavior. [1] But the leftist is too far gone for that. His feelings of inferiority are so ingrained that he cannot conceive of himself as individually strong and valuable. Hence the collectivism of the leftist. He can feel strong only as a member of a large organization or a mass movement with which he identifies himself.

20. Notice the masochistic tendency of leftist tactics. Leftists protest by lying down in front of vehicles, they intentionally provoke police or racists to abuse them, etc. These tactics may often be effective, but many leftists use them not as a means to an end but because they PREFER masochistic tactics. Self-hatred is a leftist trait.

21. Leftists may claim that their activism is motivated by compassion or by moral principles, and moral principle does play a role for the leftist of the oversocialized type. But compassion and moral principle cannot be the main motives for leftist activism. Hostility is too prominent a component of leftist behavior; so is the drive for power. Moreover, much leftist behavior is not rationally calculated to be of benefit to the people whom the leftists claim to be trying to help. For example, if one believes that affirmative action is good for black people, does it make sense to demand affirmative action in hostile or dogmatic terms? Obviously it would be more productive to take a diplomatic and conciliatory approach that would make at least verbal and symbolic concessions to white people who think that affirmative action discriminates against them. But leftist activists do not take such an approach because it would not satisfy their emotional needs. Helping black people is not their real goal. Instead, race problems serve as an excuse for them to express their

own hostility and frustrated need for power. In doing so they actually harm black people, because the activists' hostile attitude toward the white majority tends to intensify race hatred.

22. If our society had no social problems at all, the leftists would have to INVENT problems in order to provide themselves with an excuse for making a fuss.

23. We emphasize that the foregoing does not pretend to be an accurate description of everyone who might be considered a leftist. It is only a rough indication of a general tendency of leftism.

OVERSOCIALIZATION

24. Psychologists use the term "socialization" to designate the process by which children are trained to think and act as society demands. A person is said to be well socialized if he believes in and obeys the moral code of his society and fits in well as a functioning part of that society. It may seem senseless to say that many leftists are over-socialized, since the leftist is perceived as a rebel. Nevertheless, the position can be defended. Many leftists are not such rebels as they seem.

25. The moral code of our society is so demanding that no one can think, feel and act in a complete moral way. For example, we are not supposed to hate anyone, yet almost everyone hates somebody at some time or other, whether he admits it to himself or not. Some people are so highly socialized that the attempt to think, feel and act morally imposes a severe burden on them. In order to avoid feelings of guilt, they continually have to deceive themselves about their own motives and find moral explanations for feelings and actions that in reality have a non-moral origin. We use the term "oversocialized" to describe such people. [2]

26. Oversocialization can lead to low self-esteem, a sense of powerlessness, defeatism, guilt, etc. One of the most important means by which our society socializes children is by making them feel ashamed of behavior or speech that is contrary to society's expectations. If this is overdone, or if a particular child is especially susceptible to such feelings, he ends by feeling ashamed of HIMSELF. Moreover the thought and the behavior of the oversocialized person are more restricted by society's expectations than are those of the lightly socialized person. The majority of people engage in a signif-

icant amount of naughty behavior. They lie, they commit petty thefts, they break traffic laws, they goof off at work, they hate someone, they say spiteful things or they use some underhanded trick to get ahead of the other guy. The oversocialized person cannot do these things, or if he does do them he generates in himself a sense of shame and self-hatred. The oversocialized person cannot even experience, without guilt, thoughts or feelings that are contrary to the accepted morality; he cannot think "unclean" thoughts. And socialization is not just a matter of morality; we are socialized to conform to many norms of behavior that do not fall under the heading of morality. Thus the oversocialized person is kept on a psychological leash and spends his life running on rails that society has laid down for him. In many oversocialized people this results in a sense of constraint and powerlessness that can be a severe hardship. We suggest that oversocialization is among the more serious cruelties that human beings inflict on one another.

27. We argue that a very important and influential segment of the modern left is oversocialized and that their oversocialization is of great importance in determining the direction of modern leftism. Leftists of the oversocialized type tend to be intellectuals or members of the upper-middle class. Notice that university intellectuals [3] constitute the most highly socialized segment of our society and also the most left-wing segment.

28. The leftist of the oversocialized type tries to get off his psychological leash and assert his autonomy by rebelling. But usually he is not strong enough to rebel against the most basic values of society. Generally speaking, the goals of today's leftists are NOT in conflict with the accepted morality. On the contrary, the left takes an accepted moral principle, adopts it as it own, and then accuses mainstream society of violating that principle. Examples: racial equality, equality of the sexes, helping poor people, peace as opposed to war, nonviolence generally, freedom of expression, kindness to animals. More fundamentally, the duty of the individual to serve society and the duty of society to take care of the individual. All these have been deeply rooted values of our society (or at least of its middle and upper classes [4] for a long time. These values are explicitly or implicitly expressed or presupposed in most of

the material presented to us by the mainstream communications media and the educational system. Leftists, especially those of the oversocialized type, usually do not rebel against these principles but justify their hostility to society by claiming (with some degree of truth) that society is not living up to these principles.

29. Here is an illustration of the way in which the oversocialized leftist shows his real attachment to the conventional attitudes of our society while pretending to be in rebellion against it. Many leftists push for affirmative action, for moving black people into high-prestige jobs, for improved education in black schools and more money for such schools; the way of life of the black "underclass" they regard as a social disgrace. They want to integrate the black man into the system, make him a business executive, a lawyer, a scientist just like upper-middle-class white people. The leftists will reply that the last thing they want is to make the black man into a copy of the white man; instead, they want to preserve African American culture. But in what does this preservation of African American culture consist? It can hardly consist in anything more than eating black-style food, listening to black-style music, wearing black-style clothing and going to a black-style church or mosque. In other words, it can express itself only in superficial matters. In all ESSENTIAL respects most leftists of the oversocialized type want to make the black man conform to white, middle-class ideals. They want to make him study technical subjects, become an executive or a scientist, spend his life climbing the status ladder to prove that black people are as good as white. They want to make black fathers "responsible," they want black gangs to become nonviolent, etc. But these are exactly the values of the industrial-technological system. The system couldn't care less what kind of music a man listens to, what kind of clothes he wears or what religion he believes in as long as he studies in school, holds a respectable job, climbs the status ladder, is a "responsible" parent, is nonviolent and so forth. In effect, however much he may deny it, the oversocialized leftist wants to integrate the black man into the system and make him adopt its values.

30. We certainly do not claim that leftists, even of the oversocialized type, NEVER rebel against the fundamental values of our society. Clearly they sometimes do. Some oversocialized leftists have

gone so far as to rebel against one of modern society's most important principles by engaging in physical violence. By their own account, violence is for them a form of "liberation." In other words, by committing violence they break through the psychological restraints that have been trained into them. Because they are oversocialized these restraints have been more confining for them than for others; hence their need to break free of them. But they usually justify their rebellion in terms of mainstream values. If they engage in violence they claim to be fighting against racism or the like.

31. We realize that many objections could be raised to the foregoing thumbnail sketch of leftist psychology. The real situation is complex, and anything like a complete description of it would take several volumes even if the necessary data were available. We claim only to have indicated very roughly the two most important tendencies in the psychology of modern leftism.

32. The problems of the leftist are indicative of the problems of our society as a whole. Low self-esteem, depressive tendencies and defeatism are not restricted to the left. Though they are especially noticeable in the left, they are widespread in our society. And today's society tries to socialize us to a greater extent than any previous society. We are even told by experts how to eat, how to exercise, how to make love, how to raise our kids and so forth.

THE POWER PROCESS

33. Human beings have a need (probably based in biology) for something that we will call the "power process." This is closely related to the need for power (which is widely recognized) but is not quite the same thing. The power process has four elements. The three most clear-cut of these we call goal, effort and attainment of goal. (Everyone needs to have goals whose attainment requires effort, and needs to succeed in attaining at least some of his goals). The fourth element is more difficult to define and may not be necessary for everyone. We call it autonomy and will discuss it later (paragraphs 42-44).

34. Consider the hypothetical case of a man who can have anything he wants just by wishing for it. Such a man has power, but he will develop serious psychological problems. At first he will have a lot of fun, but by and by he will become eventually bored and demoral-

ized. Eventually he may become clinically depressed. History shows that leisured aristocracies tend to become decadent. This is not true of fighting aristocracies that have to struggle to maintain their power. But leisured, secure aristocracies that have no need to exert themselves usually become bored, hedonistic and demoralized, even though they have power. This shows that power is not enough. One must have goals toward which to exercise one's power.

35. Everyone has goals: if nothing else, to obtain the physical necessities of life: food, water and whatever clothing and shelter are made necessary by the climate. But the leisured aristocrat obtains these things without effort. Hence his boredom and demoralization.

36. Nonattainment of important goals results in death if the goals are physical necessities, and in frustration if nonattainment of the goals is compatible with survival. Consistent failure to attain goals throughout life results in defeatism, low self-esteem or depression.

37. Thus, in order to avoid serious psychological problems, a human being needs goals whose attainment requires effort, and he must have a reasonable rate of success in attaining his goals.

SURROGATE ACTIVITIES

38. But not every leisured aristocrat become bored and demoralized. For example, the emperor Hirohito, instead of sinking into decadent hedonism, devoted himself to marine biology, a field in which he became distinguished. When people do not have to exert themselves to satisfy their physical needs they often set up artificial goals for themselves. In many cases they then pursue these goals with the same energy and emotional involvement that they otherwise would have put into the search for physical necessities. Thus the aristocrats of the Roman Empire had their literary pretensions; many European aristocrats a few centuries ago invested tremendous time and energy in hunting, though they certainly didn't need the meat; other aristocracies have competed for status through elaborate displays of wealth; and a few aristocrats, like Hirohito, have turned to science.

39. We use the term "surrogate activity" to designate an activity that is directed toward an artificial goal that people set up for themselves merely in order to have some goal to work toward, or let us say, merely for the sake of the "fulfillment" that they get from pur-

suing the goal. Here is a rule of thumb for the identification of surrogate activities. Given a person who devotes much time and energy to the pursuit of goal X, ask yourself this: If he had to devote most of his time and energy to satisfy his biological needs, and if that effort required him to use his physical and mental faculties in a varied and interesting way, would he feel seriously deprived because he did not attain goal X? If the answer is no, then the person's pursuit of goal X is a surrogate activity. Hirohito's studies in marine biology clearly constituted a surrogate activity, since it is pretty certain that if Hirohito had had to spend his time working at interesting non-scientific task in order to obtain the necessities of life, he would not have felt deprived because he didn't know all about the anatomy and life-cycles of marine animals. On the other hand the pursuit of sex and love (for example) is not a surrogate activity, because most people, even if their existence were otherwise satisfactory, would feel deprived if they passed their lives without ever having a relationship with a member of the opposite sex. (But pursuit of an excessive amount of sex, more than one really needs, can be a surrogate activity.)

40. In modern industrial society only minimal effort is necessary to satisfy one's physical needs. It is enough to go through a training program to acquire some petty technical skill, then come to work on time and exert the very modest effort needed to hold a job. The only requirements are a moderate amount of intelligence and, most of all, simple OBEDIENCE. If one has those, society takes care of one from cradle to grave. (Yes, there is an underclass that cannot take the physical necessities for granted, but we are speaking here of mainstream society.) Thus it is not surprising that modern society is full of surrogate activities. These include scientific work, athletic achievement, humanitarian work, artistic and literary creation, climbing the corporate ladder, acquisition of money and material goods far beyond the point at which they cease to give any additional physical satisfaction, and social activism when it addresses issues that are not important for the activist personally, as in the case of white activists who work for the rights of nonwhite minorities. These are not always PURE surrogate activities, since for many people they may be motivated in part by needs other than the

need to have some goal to pursue. Scientific work may be motivated in part by a drive for prestige, artistic creation by a need to express feelings, militant social activism by hostility. But for most people who pursue them, these activities are in large part surrogate activities. For example the majority of scientists will probably agree that the "fulfillment" they get from their work is more important than the money and prestige they earn.

41. For many if not most people, surrogate activities are less satisfying than the pursuit of real goals (that is, goals that people would want to attain even if their need for the power process were already fulfilled). One indication of this is the fact that, in many or most cases, people who are deeply involved in surrogate activities are never satisfied, never at rest. Thus the money-maker constantly strives for more and more wealth. The scientist no sooner solves one problem than he moves on to the next. The long-distance runner drives himself to run always farther and faster. Many people who pursue surrogate activities will say that they get far more fulfillment from these activities than they do from the "mundane" business of satisfying their biological needs, but that is because in our society the effort needed to satisfy the biological needs has been reduced to triviality. More importantly, in our society people do not satisfy their biological needs AUTONOMOUSLY but by functioning as parts of an immense social machine. In contrast, people generally have a great deal of autonomy in pursuing their surrogate activities.

AUTONOMY

42. Autonomy as a part of the power process may not be necessary for every individual. But most people need a greater or lesser degree of autonomy in working toward their goals. Their efforts must be undertaken on their own initiative and must be under their own direction and control. Yet most people do not have to exert this initiative, direction and control as single individuals. It is usually enough to act as a member of a SMALL group. Thus if half a dozen people discuss a goal among themselves and make a successful joint effort to attain that goal, their need for the power process will be served. But if they work under rigid orders handed down from above that leave them no room for autonomous decision and initia-

tive, then their need for the power process will not be served. The same is true when decisions are made on a collective basis if the group making the collective decision is so large that the role of each individual is insignificant. [5]

43. It is true that some individuals seem to have little need for autonomy. Either their drive for power is weak or they satisfy it by identifying themselves with some powerful organization to which they belong. And then there are unthinking, animal types who seem to be satisfied with a purely physical sense of power (the good combat soldier, who gets his sense of power by developing fighting skills that he is quite content to use in blind obedience to his superiors).

44. But for most people it is through the power process—having a goal, making an AUTONOMOUS effort and attaining the goal—that self-esteem, self-confidence and a sense of power are acquired. When one does not have adequate opportunity to go through the power process the consequences are (depending on the individual and on the way the power process is disrupted) boredom, demoralization, low self-esteem, inferiority feelings, defeatism, depression, anxiety, guilt, frustration, hostility, spouse or child abuse, insatiable hedonism, abnormal sexual behavior, sleep disorders, eating disorders, etc. [6]

SOURCES OF SOCIAL PROBLEMS

45. Any of the foregoing symptoms can occur in any society, but in modern industrial society they are present on a massive scale. We aren't the first to mention that the world today seems to be going crazy. This sort of thing is not normal for human societies. There is good reason to believe that primitive man suffered from less stress and frustration and was better satisfied with his way of life than modern man is. It is true that not all was sweetness and light in primitive societies. Abuse of women was common among the Australian aborigines, transsexuality was fairly common among some of the American Indian tribes. But it does appear that GENERALLY SPEAKING the kinds of problems that we have listed in the preceding paragraph were far less common among primitive peoples than they are in modern society.

46. We attribute the social and psychological problems of modern society to the fact that that society requires people to live under

conditions radically different from those under which the human race evolved and to behave in ways that conflict with the patterns of behavior that the human race developed while living under the earlier conditions. It is clear from what we have already written that we consider lack of opportunity to properly experience the power process as the most important of the abnormal conditions to which modern society subjects people. But it is not the only one. Before dealing with disruption of the power process as a source of social problems we will discuss some of the other sources.

47. Among the abnormal conditions present in modern industrial society are excessive density of population, isolation of man from nature, excessive rapidity of social change and the breakdown of natural small-scale communities such as the extended family, the village or the tribe.

48. It is well known that crowding increases stress and aggression. The degree of crowding that exists today and the isolation of man from nature are consequences of technological progress. All pre-industrial societies were predominantly rural. The Industrial Revolution vastly increased the size of cities and the proportion of the population that lives in them, and modern agricultural technology has made it possible for the Earth to support a far denser population than it ever did before. (Also, technology exacerbates the effects of crowding because it puts increased disruptive powers in people's hands. For example, a variety of noise-making devices: power mowers, radios, motorcycles, etc. If the use of these devices is unrestricted, people who want peace and quiet are frustrated by the noise. If their use is restricted, people who use the devices are frustrated by the regulations. But if these machines had never been invented there would have been no conflict and no frustration generated by them.)

49. For primitive societies the natural world (which usually changes only slowly) provided a stable framework and therefore a sense of security. In the modern world it is human society that dominates nature rather than the other way around, and modern society changes very rapidly owing to technological change. Thus there is no stable framework.

50. The conservatives are fools: They whine about the decay of traditional values, yet they enthusiastically support technological

progress and economic growth. Apparently it never occurs to them that you can't make rapid, drastic changes in the technology and the economy of a society without causing rapid changes in all other aspects of the society as well, and that such rapid changes inevitably break down traditional values.

51. The breakdown of traditional values to some extent implies the breakdown of the bonds that hold together traditional small-scale social groups. The disintegration of small-scale social groups is also promoted by the fact that modern conditions often require or tempt individuals to move to new locations, separating themselves from their communities. Beyond that, a technological society HAS TO weaken family ties and local communities if it is to function efficiently. In modern society an individual's loyalty must be first to the system and only secondarily to a small-scale community, because if the internal loyalties of small-scale communities were stronger than loyalty to the system, such communities would pursue their own advantage at the expense of the system.

52. Suppose that a public official or a corporation executive appoints his cousin, his friend or his co-religionist to a position rather than appointing the person best qualified for the job. He has permitted personal loyalty to supersede his loyalty to the system, and that is "nepotism" or "discrimination," both of which are terrible sins in modern society. Would be industrial societies that have done a poor job of subordinating personal or local loyalties to loyalty to the system are usually very inefficient. (Look at Latin America.) Thus an advanced industrial society can tolerate only those small-scale communities that are emasculated, tame and made into tools of the system. [7]

53. Crowding, rapid change and the breakdown of communities have been widely recognized as sources of social problems. But we do not believe they are enough to account for the extent of the problems that are seen today.

54. A few pre-industrial cities were very large and crowded, yet their inhabitants do not seem to have suffered from psychological problems to the same extent as modern man. In America today there still are uncrowded rural areas, and we find there the same problems as in

urban areas, though the problems tend to be less acute in the rural areas. Thus crowding does not seem to be the decisive factor.

55. On the growing edge of the American frontier during the 19th century, the mobility of the population probably broke down extended families and small-scale social groups to at least the same extent as these are broken down today. In fact, many nuclear families lived by choice in such isolation, having no neighbors within several miles, that they belonged to no community at all, yet they do not seem to have developed problems as a result.

56. Furthermore, change in American frontier society was very rapid and deep. A man might be born and raised in a log cabin, outside the reach of law and order and fed largely on wild meat; and by the time he arrived at old age he might be working at a regular job and living in an ordered community with effective law enforcement. This was a deeper change than that which typically occurs in the life of a modern individual, yet it does not seem to have led to psychological problems. In fact, 19th century American society had an optimistic and self-confident tone, quite unlike that of today's society. [8]

57. The difference, we argue, is that modern man has the sense (largely justified) that change is IMPOSED on him, whereas the 19th century frontiersman had the sense (also largely justified) that he created change himself, by his own choice. Thus a pioneer settled on a piece of land of his own choosing and made it into a farm through his own effort. In those days an entire county might have only a couple of hundred inhabitants and was a far more isolated and autonomous entity than a modern county is. Hence the pioneer farmer participated as a member of a relatively small group in the creation of a new, ordered community. One may well question whether the creation of this community was an improvement, but at any rate it satisfied the pioneer's need for the power process.

58. It would be possible to give other examples of societies in which there has been rapid change and/or lack of close community ties without the kind of massive behavioral aberration that is seen in today's industrial society. We contend that the most important cause of social and psychological problems in modern society is the fact that people have insufficient opportunity to go through the power process in a normal way. We don't mean to say that modern

society is the only one in which the power process has been disrupted. Probably most if not all civilized societies have interfered with the power process to a greater or lesser extent. But in modern industrial society the problem has become particularly acute. Leftism, at least in its recent (mid- to late-20th century) form, is in part a symptom of deprivation with respect to the power process.

DISRUPTION OF THE POWER PROCESS IN MODERN SOCIETY

59. We divide human drives into three groups: (1) those drives that can be satisfied with minimal effort; (2) those that can be satisfied but only at the cost of serious effort; (3) those that cannot be adequately satisfied no matter how much effort one makes. The power process is the process of satisfying the drives of the second group. The more drives there are in the third group, the more there is frustration, anger, eventually defeatism, depression, etc.

60. In modern industrial society natural human drives tend to be pushed into the first and third groups, and the second group tends to consist increasingly of artificially created drives.

61. In primitive societies, physical necessities generally fall into group 2: They can be obtained, but only at the cost of serious effort. But modern society tends to guaranty the physical necessities to everyone [9] in exchange for only minimal effort, hence physical needs are pushed into group 1. (There may be disagreement about whether the effort needed to hold a job is "minimal"; but usually, in lower- to middle-level jobs, whatever effort is required is merely that of OBEDIENCE. You sit or stand where you are told to sit or stand and do what you are told to do in the way you are told to do it. Seldom do you have to exert yourself seriously, and in any case you have hardly any autonomy in work, so that the need for the power process is not well served.)

62. Social needs, such as sex, love and status, often remain in group 2 in modern society, depending on the situation of the individual. [10] But, except for people who have a particularly strong drive for status, the effort required to fulfill the social drives in insufficient to satisfy adequately the need for the power process.

63. So certain artificial needs have been created that fall into group 2,

hence serve the need for the power process. Advertising and marketing techniques have been developed that make many people feel they need things that their grandparents never desired or even dreamed of. It requires serious effort to earn enough money to satisfy these artificial needs, hence they fall into group 2. (But see paragraphs 80-82.) Modern man must satisfy his need for the power process largely through pursuit of the artificial needs created by the advertising and marketing industry [11], and through surrogate activities.

64. It seems that for many people, maybe the majority, these artificial forms of the power process are insufficient. A theme that appears repeatedly in the writings of the social critics of the second half of the 20th century is the sense of purposelessness that afflicts many people in modern society. (This purposelessness is often called by other names such as "anomic" or "middle-class vacuity.") We suggest that the so-called "identity crisis" is actually a search for a sense of purpose, often for commitment to a suitable surrogate activity. It may be that existentialism is in large part a response to the purposelessness of modern life. [12] Very widespread in modern society is the search for "fulfillment." But we think that for the majority of people an activity whose main goal is fulfillment (that is, a surrogate activity) does not bring completely satisfactory fulfillment. In other words, it does not fully satisfy the need for the power process. (See paragraph 41.) That need can be fully satisfied only through activities that have some external goal, such as physical necessities, sex, love, status, revenge, etc.

65. Moreover, where goals are pursued through earning money, climbing the status ladder or functioning as part of the system in some other way, most people are not in a position to pursue their goals AUTONOMOUSLY. Most workers are someone else's employee and, as we pointed out in paragraph 61, must spend their days doing what they are told to do in the way they are told to do it. Even people who are in business for themselves have only limited autonomy. It is a chronic complaint of small-business persons and entrepreneurs that their hands are tied by excess government regulation. Some of these regulations are doubtless unnecessary, but for the most part government regulations are essential and inevitable parts of our extremely complex society. A large portion of small

business today operates on the franchise system. It was reported in the Wall Street Journal a few years ago that many of the franchise-granting companies require applicants for franchises to take a personality test that is designed to EXCLUDE those who have creativity and initiative, because such persons are not sufficiently docile to go along obediently with the franchise system. This excludes from small business many of the people who most need autonomy.

66. Today people live more by virtue of what the system does FOR them or TO them than by virtue of what they do for themselves. And what they do for themselves is done more and more along channels laid down by the system. Opportunities tend to be those that the system provides, the opportunities must be exploited in accord with rules and regulations [13], and techniques prescribed by experts must be followed if there is to be a chance of success.

67. Thus the power process is disrupted in our society through a deficiency of real goals and a deficiency of autonomy in the pursuit of goals. But it is also disrupted because of those human drives that fall into group 3: the drives that one cannot adequately satisfy no matter how much effort one makes. One of these drives is the need for security. Our lives depend on decisions made by other people; we have no control over these decisions and usually we do not even know the people who make them. ("We live in a world in which relatively few people–maybe 500 or 1,000—make the important decisions"—Philip B. Heymann of Harvard Law School, quoted by Anthony Lewis, New York Times, April 21, 1995.) Our lives depend on whether safety standards at a nuclear power plant are properly maintained; on how much pesticide is allowed to get into our food or how much pollution into our air; on how skillful (or incompetent) our doctor is; whether we lose or get a job may depend on decisions made by government economists or corporation executives; and so forth. Most individuals are not in a position to secure themselves against these threats to more [than] a very limited extent. The individual's search for security is therefore frustrated, which leads to a sense of powerlessness.

68. It may be objected that primitive man is physically less secure than modern man, as is shown by his shorter life expectancy; hence modern man suffers from less, not more than the amount of insecu-

rity that is normal of human beings. But psychological security does not closely correspond with physical security. What makes us FEEL secure is not so much objective security as a sense of confidence in our ability to take care of ourselves. Primitive man, threatened by a fierce animal or by hunger, can fight in self-defense or travel in search of food. He has no certainty of success in these efforts, but he is by no means helpless against the thing that threaten him. The modern individual on the other hand is threatened by many things against which he is helpless: nuclear accidents, carcinogens in food, environmental pollution, war, increasing taxes, invasion of his privacy by large organizations, nationwide social or economic phenomena that may disrupt his way of life.

69. It is true that primitive man is powerless against some of the things that threaten him; disease for example. But he can accept the risk of disease stoically. It is part of the nature of things, it is no one's fault, unless it is the fault of some imaginary, impersonal demon. But threats to the modern individual tend to be MAN-MADE. They are not the result of chance but are IMPOSED on him by other persons whose decisions he, as an individual, is unable to influence. Consequently he feels frustrated, humiliated and angry.

70. Thus primitive man for the most part has his security in his own hands (either as an individual or as a member of a SMALL group) whereas the security of modern man is in the hands of persons or organizations that are too remote or too large for him to be able personally to influence them. So modern man's drive for security tends to fall into groups 1 and 3; in some areas (food, shelter etc.) his security is assured at the cost of only trivial effort, whereas in other areas he CANNOT attain security. (The foregoing greatly simplifies the real situation, but it does indicate in a rough, general way how the condition of modern man differs from that of primitive man.)

71. People have many transitory drives or impulses that are necessarily frustrated in modern life, hence fall into group 3. One may become angry, but modern society cannot permit fighting. In many situations it does not even permit verbal aggression. When going somewhere one may be in a hurry, or one may be in a mood to travel slowly, but one generally has no choice but to move with the flow of traffic and obey the traffic signals. One may want to do

one's work in a different way, but usually one can work only according to the rules laid down by one's employer. In many other ways as well, modern man is strapped down by a network of rules and regulations (explicit or implicit) that frustrate many of his impulses and thus interfere with the power process. Most of these regulations cannot be dispensed with, because they are necessary for the functioning of industrial society.

72. Modern society is in certain respects extremely permissive. In matters that are irrelevant to the functioning of the system we can generally do what we please. We can believe in any religion we like (as long as it does not encourage behavior that is dangerous to the system). We can go to bed with anyone we like (as long as we practice "safe sex"). We can do anything we like as long as it is UNIMPORTANT. But in all IMPORTANT matters the system tends increasingly to regulate our behavior.

73. Behavior is regulated not only through explicit rules and not only by the government. Control is often exercised through indirect coercion or through psychological pressure or manipulation, and by organizations other than the government, or by the system as a whole. Most large organizations use some form of propaganda [14] to manipulate public attitudes or behavior. Propaganda is not limited to "commercials" and advertisements, and sometimes it is not even consciously intended as propaganda by the people who make it. For instance, the content of entertainment programming is a powerful form of propaganda. An example of indirect coercion: There is no law that says we have to go to work every day and follow our employer's orders. Legally there is nothing to prevent us from going to live in the wild like primitive people or from going into business for ourselves. But in practice there is very little wild country left, and there is room in the economy for only a limited number of small business owners. Hence most of us can survive only as someone else's employee.

74. We suggest that modern man's obsession with longevity, and with maintaining physical vigor and sexual attractiveness to an advanced age, is a symptom of unfulfillment resulting from deprivation with respect to the power process. The "mid-life crisis" also is such a symp-

tom. So is the lack of interest in having children that is fairly common in modern society but almost unheard-of in primitive societies.

75. In primitive societies life is a succession of stages. The needs and purposes of one stage having been fulfilled, there is no particular reluctance about passing on to the next stage. A young man goes through the power process by becoming a hunter, hunting not for sport or for fulfillment but to get meat that is necessary for food. (In young women the process is more complex, with greater emphasis on social power; we won't discuss that here.) This phase having been successfully passed through, the young man has no reluctance about settling down to the responsibilities of raising a family. (In contrast, some modern people indefinitely postpone having children because they are too busy seeking some kind of "fulfillment." We suggest that the fulfillment they need is adequate experience of the power process—with real goals instead of the artificial goals of surrogate activities.) Again, having successfully raised his children, going through the power process by providing them with the physical necessities, the primitive man feels that his work is done and he is prepared to accept old age (if he survives that long) and death. Many modern people, on the other hand, are disturbed by the prospect of physical deterioration and death, as is shown by the amount of effort they expend trying to maintain their physical condition, appearance and health. We argue that this is due to unfulfillment resulting from the fact that they have never put their physical powers to any practical use, have never gone through the power process using their bodies in a serious way. It is not the primitive man, who has used his body daily for practical purposes, who fears the deterioration of age, but the modern man, who has never had a practical use for his body beyond walking from his car to his house. It is the man whose need for the power process has been satisfied during his life who is best prepared to accept the end of that life.

76. In response to the arguments of this section someone will say, "Society must find a way to give people the opportunity to go through the power process." For such people the value of the opportunity is destroyed by the very fact that society gives it to them. What they need is to find or make their own opportunities. As

long as the system GIVES them their opportunities it still has them on a leash. To attain autonomy they must get off that leash.

HOW SOME PEOPLE ADJUST

77. Not everyone in industrial-technological society suffers from psychological problems. Some people even profess to be quite satisfied with society as it is. We now discuss some of the reasons why people differ so greatly in their response to modern society.

78. First, there doubtless are differences in the strength of the drive for power. Individuals with a weak drive for power may have relatively little need to go through the power process, or at least relatively little need for autonomy in the power process. These are docile types who would have been happy as plantation darkies in the Old South. (We don't mean to sneer at the "plantation darkies" of the Old South. To their credit, most of the slaves were NOT content with their servitude. We do sneer at people who ARE content with servitude.)

79. Some people may have some exceptional drive, in pursuing which they satisfy their need for the power process. For example, those who have an unusually strong drive for social status may spend their whole lives climbing the status ladder without ever getting bored with that game.

80. People vary in their susceptibility to advertising and marketing techniques. Some are so susceptible that, even if they make a great deal of money, they cannot satisfy their constant craving for the shiny new toys that the marketing industry dangles before their eyes. So they always feel hard-pressed financially even if their income is large, and their cravings are frustrated.

81. Some people have low susceptibility to advertising and marketing techniques. These are the people who aren't interested in money. Material acquisition does not serve their need for the power. process.

82. People who have medium susceptibility to advertising and marketing techniques are able to earn enough money to satisfy their craving for goods and services, but only at the cost of serious effort (putting in overtime, taking a second job earning promotions, etc.). Thus material acquisition serves their need for the power process. But it does not necessarily follow that their need is fully satisfied. They may have insufficient autonomy in the power process (their

work may consist of following orders) and some of their drives may be frustrated (e.g., security, aggression). (We are guilty of oversimplification in paragraphs 80-82 because we have assumed that the desire for material acquisition is entirely a creation of the advertising and marketing industry. Of course it's not that simple. [11]

83. Some people partly satisfy their need for power by identifying themselves with a powerful organization or mass movement. An individual lacking goals or power joins a movement or an organization, adopts its goals as his own, then works toward those goals. When some of the goals are attained, the individual, even though his personal efforts have played only an insignificant part in the attainment of the goals, feels (through his identification with the movement or organization) as if he had gone through the power process. This phenomenon was exploited by the fascists, nazis and communists. Our society uses it too, though less crudely. Example: Manuel Noriega was an irritant to the U.S. (goal: punish Noriega). The U.S. invaded Panama (effort) and punished Noriega (attainment of goal). Thus the U.S went through the power process and many Americans, because of their identification with the U S., experienced the power process vicariously. Hence the widespread public approval of the Panama invasion; it gave people as sense of power. [15] We see the same phenomenon in armies, corporations, political parties, humanitarian organizations, religious or ideological movements. In particular, leftist movements tend to attract people who are seeking to satisfy their need for power. But for most people identification with a large organization or a mass movement does not fully satisfy the need for power.

84. Another way in which people satisfy their need for the power process is through surrogate activities. As we explained in paragraphs 38-40, a surrogate activity is an activity that is directed toward an artificial goal that the individual pursues for the sake of the "fulfillment" that he gets from pursuing the goal, not because he needs to attain the goal itself. For instance, there is no practical motive for building enormous muscles, hitting a little ball into a hole or acquiring a complete series of postage stamps. Yet many people in our society devote themselves with passion to bodybuilding, golf or stamp-collecting. Some people are more "other-direct-

ed" than others, and therefore will more readily attach importance to a surrogate activity simply because the people around them treat it as important or because society tells them it is important. That is why some people get very serious about essentially trivial activities such as sports, or bridge, or chess, or arcane scholarly pursuits, whereas others who are more clear-sighted never see these things as anything but the surrogate activities that they are, and consequently never attach enough importance to them to satisfy their need for the power process in that way. It only remains to point out that in many cases a person's way of earning a living is also a surrogate activity. Not a PURE surrogate activity, since part of the motive for the activity is to gain the physical necessities and (for some people) social status and the luxuries that advertising makes them want. But many people put into their work far more effort than is necessary to earn whatever money and status they require, and this extra effort constitutes a surrogate activity. This extra effort, together with the emotional investment that accompanies it, is one of the most potent forces acting toward the continual development and perfecting of the system, with negative consequences for individual freedom (see paragraph 131). Especially, for the most creative scientists and engineers, work tends to be largely a surrogate activity. This point is so important that it deserves a separate discussion, which we shall give in a moment (paragraphs 87-92).

85. In this section we have explained how many people in modern society do satisfy their need for the power process to a greater or lesser extent. But we think that for the majority of people the need for the power process is not fully satisfied. In the first place, those who have an insatiable drive for status, or who get firmly "hook" on a surrogate activity, or who identify strongly enough with a movement or organization to satisfy their need for power in that way, are exceptional personalities. Others are not fully satisfied with surrogate activities or by identification with an organization (see paragraphs 41, 64). In the second place, too much control is imposed by the system through explicit regulation or through socialization, which results in a deficiency of autonomy, and in frustration due to the impossibility of attaining certain goals and the necessity of restraining too many impulses.

86. But even if most people in industrial-technological society were well satisfied, we (FC) would still be opposed to that form of society, because (among other reasons) we consider it demeaning to fulfill one's need for the power process through surrogate activities or through identification with an organization, rather than through pursuit of real goals.

THE MOTIVE OF SCIENTISTS

87. Science and technology provide the most important example of surrogate activities. Some scientists claim that they are motivated by "curiosity" or by a desire to "benefit humanity." But it is easy to see that neither of these can be the principal motive of most scientists. As for "curiosity," that notion is simply absurd. Most scientists work on highly specialized problems that are not the object of any normal curiosity. For example, is an astronomer, a mathematician or an entomologist curious about the properties of isopropyltrimethylmethane? Of course not. Only a chemist is curious about such a thing, and he is curious about it only because chemistry is his surrogate activity. Is the chemist curious about the appropriate classification of a new species of beetle? No. That question is of interest only to the entomologist, and he is interested in it only because entomology is his surrogate activity. If the chemist and the entomologist had to exert themselves seriously to obtain the physical necessities, and if that effort exercised their abilities in an interesting way but in some nonscientific pursuit, then they wouldn't give a damn about isopropyltrimethylmethane or the classification of beetles. Suppose that lack of funds for postgraduate education had led the chemist to become an insurance broker instead of a chemist. In that case he would have been very interested in insurance matters but would have cared nothing about isopropyltrimethylmethane. In any case it is not normal to put into the satisfaction of mere curiosity the amount of time and effort that scientists put into their work. The "curiosity" explanation for the scientists' motive just doesn't stand up.

88. The "benefit of humanity" explanation doesn't work any better. Some scientific work has no conceivable relation to the welfare of the human race—most of archaeology or comparative linguistics for example. Some other areas of science present obviously dangerous

possibilities. Yet scientists in these areas are just as enthusiastic about their work as those who develop vaccines or study air pollution. Consider the case of Dr. Edward Teller, who had an obvious emotional involvement in promoting nuclear power plants. Did this involvement stem from a desire to benefit humanity? If so, then why didn't Dr. Teller get emotional about other "humanitarian" causes? If he was such a humanitarian then why did he help to develop the H-bomb? As with many other scientific achievements, it is very much open to question whether nuclear power plants actually do benefit humanity. Does the cheap electricity outweigh the accumulating waste and the risk of accidents? Dr. Teller saw only one side of the question. Clearly his emotional involvement with nuclear power arose not from a desire to "benefit humanity" but from a personal fulfillment he got from his work and from seeing it put to practical use.

89. The same is true of scientists generally. With possible rare exceptions, their motive is neither curiosity nor a desire to benefit humanity but the need to go through the power process: to have a goal (a scientific problem to solve), to make an effort (research) and to attain the goal (solution of the problem.) Science is a surrogate activity because scientists work mainly for the fulfillment they get out of the work itself.

90. Of course, it's not that simple. Other motives do play a role for many scientists. Money and status for example. Some scientists may be persons of the type who have an insatiable drive for status (see paragraph 79) and this may provide much of the motivation for their work. No doubt the majority of scientists, like the majority of the general population, are more or less susceptible to advertising and marketing techniques and need money to satisfy their craving for goods and services. Thus science is not a PURE surrogate activity. But it is in large part a surrogate activity.

91. Also, science and technology constitute a power mass movement, and many scientists gratify their need for power through identification with this mass movement (see paragraph 83).

92. Thus science marches on blindly, without regard to the real welfare of the human race or to any other standard, obedient only to the psychological needs of the scientists and of the government officials and corporation executives who provide the funds for research.

THE NATURE OF FREEDOM

93. We are going to argue that industrial-technological society cannot be reformed in such a way as to prevent it from progressively narrowing the sphere of human freedom. But, because "freedom" is a word that can be interpreted in many ways, we must first make clear what kind of freedom we are concerned with.

94. By "freedom" we mean the opportunity to go through the power process, with real goals not the artificial goals of surrogate activities, and without interference, manipulation or supervision from anyone, especially from any large organization. Freedom means being in control (either as an individual or as a member of a SMALL group) of the life-and-death issues of one's existence; food, clothing, shelter and defense against whatever threats there may be in one's environment. Freedom means having power; not the power to control other people but the power to control the circumstances of one's own life. One does not have freedom if anyone else (especially a large organization) has power over one, no matter how benevolently, tolerantly and permissively that power may be exercised. It is important not to confuse freedom with mere permissiveness (see paragraph 72).

95. It is said that we live in a free society because we have a certain number of constitutionally guaranteed rights. But these are not as important as they seem. The degree of personal freedom that exists in a society is determined more by the economic and technological structure of the society than by its laws or its form of government. [16] Most of the Indian nations of New England were monarchies, and many of the cities of the Italian Renaissance were controlled by dictators. But in reading about these societies one gets the impression that they allowed far more personal freedom than our society does. In part this was because they lacked efficient mechanisms for enforcing the ruler's will: There were no modern, well-organized police forces, no rapid long-distance communications, no surveillance cameras, no dossiers of information about the lives of average citizens. Hence it was relatively easy to evade control.

96. As for our constitutional rights, consider for example that of freedom of the press. We certainly don't mean to knock that right; it is very important tool for limiting concentration of political power

and for keeping those who do have political power in line by publicly exposing any misbehavior on their part. But freedom of the press is of very little use to the average citizen as an individual. The mass media are mostly under the control of large organizations that are integrated into the system. Anyone who has a little money can have something printed, or can distribute it on the Internet or in some such way, but what he has to say will be swamped by the vast volume of material put out by the media, hence it will have no practical effect. To make an impression on society with words is therefore almost impossible for most individuals and small groups. Take us (FC) for example. If we had never done anything violent and had submitted the present writings to a publisher, they probably would not have been accepted. If they had been been accepted and published, they probably would not have attracted many readers, because it's more fun to watch the entertainment put out by the media than to read a sober essay. Even if these writings had had many readers, most of these readers would soon have forgotten what they had read as their minds were flooded by the mass of material to which the media expose them. In order to get our message before the public with some chance of making a lasting impression, we've had to kill people.

97. Constitutional rights are useful up to a point, but they do not serve to guarantee much more than what might be called the bourgeois conception of freedom. According to the bourgeois conception, a "free" man is essentially an element of a social machine and has only a certain set of prescribed and delimited freedoms; freedoms that are designed to serve the needs of the social machine more than those of the individual. Thus the bourgeois's "free" man has economic freedom because that promotes growth and progress; he has freedom of the press because public criticism restrains misbehavior by political leaders; he has a right to a fair trial because imprisonment at the whim of the powerful would be bad for the system. This was clearly the attitude of Simon Bolivar. To him, people deserved liberty only if they used it to promote progress (progress as conceived by the bourgeois). Other bourgeois thinkers have taken a similar view of freedom as a mere means to collective ends. Chester C. Tan, "Chinese Political Thought in the Twentieth

Century," page 202, explains the philosophy of the Kuomintang leader Hu Han-min. "An individual is granted rights because he is a member of society and his community life requires such rights. By community Hu meant the whole society of the nation." And on page 259 Tan states that according to Carsum Chang (Chang Chun-mai, head of the State Socialist Party in China) freedom had to be used in the interest of the state and of the people as a whole. But what kind of freedom does one have if one can use it only as someone else prescribes? FC's conception of freedom is not that of Bolivar, Hu, Change or other bourgeois theorists. The trouble with such theorists is that they have made the development and application of social theories their surrogate activity. Consequently the theories are designed to serve the needs of the theorists more than the needs of any people who may be unlucky enough to live in a society on which the theories are imposed.

98. One more point to be made in this section: It should not be assumed that a person has enough freedom just because he SAYS he has enough. Freedom is restricted in part by psychological controls of which people are unconscious, and moreover many people's ideas of what constitutes freedom are governed more by social convention than by their real needs. For example, it's likely that many leftists of the oversocialized type would say that most people, including themselves, are socialized too little rather than too much, yet the oversocialized leftist pays a heavy psychological price for his high level of socialization.

SOME PRINCIPLES OF HISTORY

99. Think of history as being the sum of two components: an erratic component that consists of unpredictable events that follow no discernible pattern, and a regular component that consists of long-term historical trends. Here we are concerned with the long-term trends.

100. FIRST PRINCIPLE. If a SMALL change is made that affects a long-term historical trend, then the effect of that change will almost always be transitory—the trend will soon revert to its original state. (Example: A reform movement designed to clean up political corruption in a society rarely has more than a short-term effect; sooner or later the reformers relax and corruption creeps back in.

The level of political corruption in a given society tends to remain constant, or to change only slowly with the evolution of the society. Normally, a political cleanup will be permanent only if accompanied by widespread social changes; a SMALL change in the society won't be enough.) If a small change in a long-term historical trend appears to be permanent, it is only because the change acts in the direction in which the trend is already moving, so that the trend is not altered by only pushed a step ahead.

101. The first principle is almost a tautology. If a trend were not stable with respect to small changes, it would wander at random rather than following a definite direction; in other words it would not be a long-term trend at all.

102. SECOND PRINCIPLE. If a change is made that is sufficiently large to alter permanently a long-term historical trend, then it will alter the society as a whole. In other words, a society is a system in which all parts are interrelated, and you can't permanently change any important part without changing all other parts as well.

103. THIRD PRINCIPLE. If a change is made that is large enough to alter permanently a long-term trend, then the consequences for the society as a whole cannot be predicted in advance. (Unless various other societies have passed through the same change and have all experienced the same consequences, in which case one can predict on empirical grounds that another society that passes through the same change will be like to experience similar consequences.)

104. FOURTH PRINCIPLE. A new kind of society cannot be designed on paper. That is, you cannot plan out a new form of society in advance, then set it up and expect it to function as it was designed to do.

105. The third and fourth principles result from the complexity of human societies. A change in human behavior will affect the economy of a society and its physical environment; the economy will affect the environment and vice versa, and the changes in the economy and the environment will affect human behavior in complex, unpredictable ways; and so forth. The network of causes and effects is far to complex to be untangled and understood.

106. FIFTH PRINCIPLE. People do not consciously and rationally

choose the form of their society. Societies develop through processes of social evolution that are not under rational human control.

107. The fifth principle is a consequence of the other four.

108. To illustrate: By the first principle, generally speaking an attempt at social reform either acts in the direction in which the society is developing anyway (so that it merely accelerates a change that would have occurred in any case) or else it has only a transitory effect, so that the society soon slips back into its old groove. To make a lasting change in the direction of development of any important aspect of a society, reform is insufficient and revolution is required. (A revolution does not necessarily involve an armed uprising or the overthrow of a government.) By the second principle, a revolution never changes only one aspect of a society, it changes the whole society; and by the third principle changes occur that were never expected or desired by the revolutionaries. By the fourth principle, when revolutionaries or utopians set up a new kind of society, it never works out as planned.

109. The American Revolution does not provide a counterexample. The American "Revolution" was not a revolution in our sense of the word, but a war of independence followed by a rather far-reaching political reform. The Founding Fathers did not change the direction of development of American society, nor did they aspire to do so. They only freed the development of American society from the retarding effect of British rule. Their political reform did not change any basic trend, but only pushed American political culture along its natural direction of development. British society, of which American society was an off-shoot, had been moving for a long time in the direction of representative democracy. And prior to the War of Independence the Americans were already practicing a significant degree of representative democracy in the colonial assemblies. The political system established by the Constitution was modeled on the British system and on the colonial assemblies. With major alteration, to be sure—there is no doubt that the Founding Fathers took a very important step. But it was a step along the road that English-speaking world was already traveling. The proof is that Britain and all of its colonies that were populated predominantly by people of British descent ended up with systems

of representative democracy essentially similar to that of the United States. If the Founding Fathers had lost their nerve and declined to sign the Declaration of Independence, our way of life today would not have been significantly different. Maybe we would have had somewhat closer ties to Britain, and would have had a parliament and Prime Minister instead of a Congress and President. No big deal. Thus the American Revolution provides not a counterexample to our principles but a good illustration of them.

110. Still, one has to use common sense in applying the principles. They are expressed in imprecise language that allows latitude for interpretation, and exceptions to them can be found. So we present these principles not as inviolable laws but as rules of thumb, or guides to thinking, that may provide a partial antidote to naive ideas about the future of society. The principles should be borne constantly in mind, and whenever one reaches a conclusion that conflicts with them one should carefully reexamine one's thinking and retain the conclusion only if one has good, solid reasons for doing so.

INDUSTRIAL-TECHNOLOGICAL SOCIETY CANNOT BE REFORMED

111. The foregoing principles help to show how hopelessly difficult it would be to reform the industrial system in such a way as to prevent it from progressively narrowing our sphere of freedom. There has been a consistent tendency, going back at least to the Industrial Revolution for technology to strengthen the system at a high cost in individual freedom and local autonomy. Hence any change designed to protect freedom from technology would be contrary to a fundamental trend in the development of our society. Consequently, such a change either would be a transitory one—soon swamped by the tide of history—or, if large enough to be permanent would alter the nature of our whole society. This by the first and second principles. Moreover, since society would be altered in a way that could not be predicted in advance (third principle) there would be great risk. Changes large enough to make a lasting difference in favor of freedom would not be initiated because it would be realized that they would gravely disrupt the system. So any attempts at reform would be too timid to be effective. Even if

changes large enough to make a lasting difference were initiated, they would be retracted when their disruptive effects became apparent. Thus, permanent changes in favor of freedom could be brought about only by persons prepared to accept radical, dangerous and unpredictable alteration of the entire system. In other words by revolutionaries, not reformers.

112. People anxious to rescue freedom without sacrificing the supposed benefits of technology will suggest naive schemes for some new form of society that would reconcile freedom with technology. Apart from the fact that people who make such suggestions seldom propose any practical means by which the new form of society could be set up in the first place, it follows from the fourth principle that even if the new form of society could be once established, it either would collapse or would give results very different from those expected.

113. So even on very general grounds it seems highly improbable that any way of changing society could be found that would reconcile freedom with modern technology. In the next few sections we will give more specific reasons for concluding that freedom and technological progress are incompatible.

RESTRICTION OF FREEDOM IS UNAVOIDABLE IN INDUSTRIAL SOCIETY

114. As explained in paragraphs 65-67 70-73, modern man is strapped down by a network of rules and regulations, and his fate depends on the actions of persons remote from him whose decisions he cannot influence. This is not accidental or as a result of the arbitrariness of arrogant bureaucrats. It is necessary and inevitable in any technologically advanced society. The system HAS TO regulate human behavior closely in order to function. At work people have to do what they are told to do, otherwise production would be thrown into chaos. Bureaucracies HAVE TO be run according to rigid rules. To allow any substantial personal discretion to lower-level bureaucrats would disrupt the system and lead to charges of unfairness due to differences in the way individual bureaucrats exercised their discretion. It is true that some restrictions on our freedom could be eliminated, but GENERALLY SPEAKING the regulation of our lives by large organizations is necessary for the

functioning of industrial-technological society. The result is a sense of powerlessness on the part of the average person. It may be, however, that formal regulations will tend increasingly to be replaced by psychological tools that make us want to do what the system requires of us. (Propaganda [14], educational techniques, "mental health" programs, etc.)

115. The system HAS TO force people to behave in ways that are increasingly remote from the natural pattern of human behavior. For example, the system needs scientists, mathematicians and engineers. It can't function without them. So heavy pressure is put on children to excel in these fields. It isn't natural for an adolescent human being to spend the bulk of his time sitting at a desk absorbed in study. A normal adolescent wants to spend his time in active contact with the real world. Among primitive peoples the things that children are trained to do tend to be in reasonable harmony with natural human impulses. Among the American Indians, for example, boys were trained in active outdoor pursuits—just the sort of thing that boys like. But in our society children are pushed into studying technical subjects, which most do grudgingly.

116. Because of the constant pressure that the system exerts to modify human behavior, there is a gradual increase in the number of people who cannot or will not adjust to society's requirements: welfare leeches, youth-gang members, cultists, anti-government rebels, radical environmentalist saboteurs, dropouts and resisters of various kinds.

117. In any technologically advanced society the individual's fate MUST depend on decisions that he personally cannot influence to any great extent. A technological society cannot be broken down into small, autonomous communities, because production depends on the cooperation of very large numbers of people and machines. Such a society MUST be highly organized and decisions HAVE TO be made that affect very large numbers of people

118. Conservatives and some others advocate more "local autonomy." Local communities once did have autonomy, but such autonomy becomes less and less possible as local communities become more enmeshed with and dependent on large-scale systems like public utilities, computer networks, highway systems, the mass communications media, the modern health care system. Also oper-

ating against autonomy is the fact that technology applied in one location often affects people at other locations far away. Thus pesticide or chemical use near a creek may contaminate the water supply hundreds of miles downstream, and the greenhouse effect affects the whole world.

119. The system does not and cannot exist to satisfy human needs. Instead, it is human behavior that has to be modified to fit the needs of the system. This has nothing to do with the political or social ideology that may pretend to guide the technological system. It is the fault of technology, because the system is guided not by ideology but by technical necessity. [18] Of course the system does satisfy many human needs, but generally speaking it does this only to the extend that it is to the advantage of the system to do it. It is the needs of the system that are paramount, not those of the human being. For example, the system provides people with food because the system couldn't function if everyone starved; it attends to people's psychological needs whenever it can CONVENIENTLY do so, because it couldn't function if too many people became depressed or rebellious. But the system, for good, solid, practical reasons, must exert constant pressure on people to mold their behavior to the needs of the system. To much waste accumulating? The government, the media, the educational system, environmentalists, everyone inundates us with a mass of propaganda about recycling. Need more technical personnel? A chorus of voices exhorts kids to study science. No one stops to ask whether it is inhumane to force adolescents to spend the bulk of their time studying subjects most of them hate. When skilled workers are put out of a job by technical advances and have to undergo "retraining," no one asks whether it is humiliating for them to be pushed around in this way. It is simply taken for granted that everyone must bow to technical necessity, and for good reason: If human needs were put before technical necessity there would be economic problems, unemployment, shortages or worse. The concept of "mental health" in our society is defined largely by the extent to which an individual behaves in accord with the needs of the system and does so without showing signs of stress.

120. Efforts to make room for a sense of purpose and for autonomy

within the system are no better than a joke. For example, one company, instead of having each of its employees assemble only one section of a catalogue, had each assemble a whole catalogue, and this was supposed to give them a sense of purpose and achievement. Some companies have tried to give their employees more autonomy in their work, but for practical reasons this usually can be done only to a very limited extent, and in any case employees are never given autonomy as to ultimate goals—their "autonomous" efforts can never be directed toward goals that they select personally, but only toward their employer's goals, such as the survival and growth of the company. Any company would soon go out of business if it permitted its employees to act otherwise. Similarly, in any enterprise within a socialist system, workers must direct their efforts toward the goals of the enterprise, otherwise the enterprise will not serve its purpose as part of the system. Once again, for purely technical reasons it is not possible for most individuals or small groups to have much autonomy in industrial society. Even the small-business owner commonly has only limited autonomy. Apart from the necessity of government regulations, he is restricted by the fact that he must fit into the economic system and conform to its requirements. For instance, when someone develops a new technology, the small-business person often has to use that technology whether he wants to or not, in order to remain competitive.

THE 'BAD' PARTS OF TECHNOLOGY CANNOT BE SEPARATED FROM THE 'GOOD' PARTS

121. A further reason why industrial society cannot be reformed in favor of freedom is that modern technology is a unified system in which all parts are dependent on one another. You can't get rid of the "bad" parts of technology and retain only the "good" parts. Take modern medicine, for example. Progress in medical science depends on progress in chemistry, physics, biology, computer science and other fields. Advanced medical treatments require expensive, high-tech equipment that can be made available only by a technologically progressive, economically rich society. Clearly you can't have much progress in medicine without the whole technological system and everything that goes with it.

122. Even if medical progress could be maintained without the rest of the technological systems, it would by itself bring certain evils. Suppose for example that a cure for diabetes is discovered. People with a genetic tendency to diabetes will then be able to survive and reproduce as well as anyone else. Natural selection against genes for diabetes will cease and such genes will spread throughout the population. (This may be occurring to some extent already, since diabetes, while not curable, can be controlled through use of insulin.) The same thing will happen with many other diseases susceptibility to which is affected by genetic degradation of the population. The only solution will be some sort of eugenics program or extensive genetic engineering of human beings, so that man in the future will no longer be a creation of nature, or of chance, or of God (depending on your religious or philosophical opinions), but a manufactured product.

123. If you think that big government interferes in your life too much NOW, just wait till the government starts regulating the genetic constitution of your children. Such regulation will inevitably follow the introduction of genetic engineering of human beings, because the consequences of unregulated genetic engineering would be disastrous. [19]

124. The usual response to such concerns is to talk about "medical ethics." But a code of ethics would not serve to protect freedom in the face of medical progress; it would only make matters worse. A code of ethics applicable to genetic engineering would be in effect a means of regulating the genetic constitution of human beings. Somebody (probably the upper-middle class, mostly) would decide that such and such applications of genetic engineering were "ethical" and others were not, so that in effect they would be imposing their own values on the genetic constitution of the population at large. Even if a code of ethics were chosen on a completely democratic basis, the majority would be imposing their own values on any minorities who might have a different idea of what constituted an "ethical" use of genetic engineering. The only code of ethics that would truly protect freedom would be one that prohibited ANY genetic engineering of human beings, and you can be sure that no such code will ever be applied in a technological society. No code that reduced genetic engineering to a minor role could stand up for

long, because the temptation presented by the immense power of biotechnology would be irresistible, especially since to the majority of people many of its applications will seem obviously and unequivocally good (eliminating physical and mental disease, giving people the abilities they need to get along in today's world). Inevitably, genetic engineering will be used extensively, but only in ways consistent with the needs of the industrial-technological system. [20]

TECHNOLOGY IS MORE POWERFUL SOCIAL FORCE THAN THE ASPIRATION FOR FREEDOM

125. It is not possible to make a LASTING compromise between technology and freedom, because technology is by far the more powerful social force and continually encroaches on freedom through REPEATED compromises. Imagine the case of two neighbors, each of whom at the outset owns the same amount of land, but one of whom is more powerful than the other. The powerful one demands a piece of the other's land. The weak on refuses. The powerful one says, "OK, let's compromise. Give me half of what I asked." The weak one has little choice but to give in. Some time later the powerful neighbor demands another piece of land, again there is a compromise, and so forth. By forcing a long series of compromises on the weaker man, the powerful one eventually gets all of his land. So it goes in the conflict between technology and freedom.

126. Let us explain why technology is a more powerful social force than the aspiration for freedom.

127. A technological advance that appears not to threaten freedom often turns out to threaten it very seriously later on. For example, consider motorized transport. A walking man formerly could go where he pleased, go at his own pace without observing any traffic regulations, and was independent of technological support-systems. When motor vehicles were introduced they appeared to increase man's freedom. They took no freedom away from the walking man, no one had to have an automobile if he didn't want one, and anyone who did choose to buy an automobile could travel much faster and farther than a walking man. But the introduction of motorized transport soon changed society in such a way as to restrict greatly man's freedom of locomotion. When automobiles became numerous, it

became necessary to regulate their use extensively. In a car, especially in densely populated areas, one cannot just go where one likes at one's own pace one's movement is governed by the flow of traffic and by various traffic laws. One is tied down by various obligations: license requirements, driver test, renewing registration, insurance, maintenance required for safety, monthly payments on purchase price. Moreover, the use of motorized transport is no longer optional. Since the introduction of motorized transport the arrangement of our cities has changed in such a way that the majority of people no longer live within walking distance of their place of employment, shopping areas and recreational opportunities, so that they HAVE TO depend on the automobile for transportation. Or else they must use public transportation, in which case they have even less control over their own movement than when driving a car. Even the walker's freedom is now greatly restricted. In the city he continually has to stop to wait for traffic lights that are designed mainly to serve auto traffic. In the country, motor traffic makes it dangerous and unpleasant to walk along the highway. (Note this important point that we have just illustrated with the case of motorized transport: When a new item of technology is introduced as an option that an individual can accept or not as he chooses, it does not necessarily REMAIN optional. In many cases the new technology changes society in such a way that people eventually find themselves FORCED to use it.)

128. While technological progress AS A WHOLE continually narrows our sphere of freedom, each new technical advance CONSIDERED BY ITSELF appears to be desirable. Electricity, indoor plumbing, rapid long-distance communications ... how could one argue against any of these things, or against any other of the innumerable technical advances that have made modern society? It would have been absurd to resist the introduction of the telephone, for example. It offered many advantages and no disadvantages. Yet, as we explained in paragraphs 59-76, all these technical advances taken together have created a world in which the average man's fate is no longer in his own hands or in the hands of his neighbors and friends, but in those of politicians, corporation executives and remote, anonymous technicians and bureaucrats whom he as an

individual has no power to influence. [21] The same process will continue in the future. Take genetic engineering, for example. Few people will resist the introduction of a genetic technique that eliminates a hereditary disease. It does no apparent harm and prevents much suffering. Yet a large number of genetic improvements taken together will make the human being into an engineered product rather than a free creation of chance (or of God, of whatever, depending on your religious beliefs).

129. Another reason why technology is such a powerful social force is that, within the context of a given society, technological progress marches in only one direction; it can never be reversed. Once a technical innovation has been introduced, people usually become dependent on it, so that they can never again do without it, unless it is replaced by some still more advanced innovation. Not only do people become dependent as individuals on a new item of technology, but, even more, the system as a whole becomes dependent on it. (Imagine what would happen to the system today if computers, for examples, were eliminated). Thus the system can move in only one direction, toward greater technologization. Technology repeatedly forces freedom to take a step back, but technology can never take a step back—short of the overthrow of the whole technological system.

130. Technology advances with great rapidity and threatens freedom at many different points at the same time (crowding, rules and regulations, increasing dependence of individuals on large organizations, propaganda and other psychological techniques, genetic engineering, invasion of privacy through surveillance devices and computers, etc.). To hold back any ONE of the threats to freedom would require a long and difficult social struggle. Those who want to protect freedom are overwhelmed by the sheer number of new attacks and the rapidity with which they develop, hence they become apathetic and no longer resist. To fight each of the threats separately would be futile. Success can be hoped for only by fighting the technological system as a whole; but that is revolution, not reform.

131. Technicians (we use this term in its broad sense to describe all those who perform a specialized task that requires training) tend to be so involved in their work (their surrogate activity) that when a conflict arises between their technical work and freedom, they

almost always decide in favor of their technical work. This is obvious in the case of scientists, but it also appears elsewhere: Educators, humanitarian groups, conservation organizations do not hesitate to use propaganda or other psychological techniques to help them achieve their laudable ends. Corporations and government agencies, when they find it useful, do not hesitate to collect information about individuals without regard to their privacy. Law enforcement agencies are frequently inconvenienced by the constitutional rights of suspects and often of completely innocent persons, and they do whatever they can do legally (or sometimes illegally) to restrict or circumvent those rights. Most of these educators, government officials and law officers believe in freedom, privacy and constitutional rights, but when these conflict with their work, they usually feel that their work is more important.

132. It is well known that people generally work better and more persistently when striving for a reward than when attempting to avoid a punishment or negative outcome. Scientists and other technicians are motivated mainly by the rewards they get through their work. But those who oppose technological invasions of freedom are working to avoid a negative outcome, consequently there are few who work persistently and well at this discouraging task. If reformers ever achieved a signal victory that seemed to set up a solid barrier against further erosion of freedom through technical progress, most would tend to relax and turn their attention to more agreeable pursuits. But the scientists would remain busy in their laboratories, and technology as it progresses would find ways, in spite of any barriers, to exert more and more control over individuals and make them always more dependent on the system.

133. No social arrangements, whether laws, institutions, customs or ethical codes, can provide permanent protection against technology. History shows that all social arrangements are transitory; they all change or break down eventually. But technological advances are permanent within the context of a given civilization. Suppose for example that it were possible to arrive at some social arrangements that would prevent genetic engineering from being applied to human beings, or prevent it from being applied in such a way as to threaten freedom and dignity. Still, the technology would remain waiting.

Sooner or later the social arrangement would break down. Probably sooner, given the pace of change in our society. Then genetic engineering would begin to invade our sphere of freedom, and this invasion would be irreversible (short of a breakdown of technological civilization itself). Any illusions about achieving anything permanent through social arrangements should be dispelled by what is currently happening with environmental legislation. A few years ago its seemed that there were secure legal barriers preventing at least SOME of the worst forms of environmental degradation. A change in the political wind, and those barriers begin to crumble.

134. For all of the foregoing reasons, technology is a more powerful social force than the aspiration for freedom. But this statement requires an important qualification. It appears that during the next several decades the industrial-technological system will be undergoing severe stresses due to economic and environmental problems, and especially due to problems of human behavior (alienation, rebellion, hostility, a variety of social and psychological difficulties). We hope that the stresses through which the system is likely to pass will cause it to break down, or at least will weaken it sufficiently so that a revolution against it becomes possible. If such a revolution occurs and is successful, then at that particular moment the aspiration for freedom will have proved more powerful than technology.

135. In paragraph 125 we used an analogy of a weak neighbor who is left destitute by a strong neighbor who takes all his land by forcing on him a series of compromises. But suppose now that the strong neighbor gets sick, so that he is unable to defend himself. The weak neighbor can force the strong one to give him his land back, or he can kill him. If he lets the strong man survive and only forces him to give the land back, he is a fool, because when the strong man gets well he will again take all the land for himself. The only sensible alternative for the weaker man is to kill the strong one while he has the chance. In the same way, while the industrial system is sick we must destroy it. If we compromise with it and let it recover from its sickness, it will eventually wipe out all of our freedom.

SIMPLER SOCIAL PROBLEMS HAVE PROVED INTRACTABLE

136. If anyone still imagines that it would be possible to reform the system in such a way as to protect freedom from technology, let him consider how clumsily and for the most part unsuccessfully our society has dealt with other social problems, that are far more simple and straightforward. Among other things, the system has failed to stop environmental degradation, political corruption, drug trafficking or domestic abuse.

137. Take our environmental problems, for example. Here the conflict of values is straightforward: economic expedience now versus saving some of our natural resources for our grandchildren. [22] But on this subject we get only a lot of blather and obfuscation from the people who have power, and nothing like a clear, consistent line of action, and we keep on piling up environmental problems that our grandchildren will have to live with. Attempts to resolve the environmental issue consist of struggles and compromises between different factions, some of which are ascendant at one moment, others at another moment. The line of struggle changes with the shifting currents of public opinion. This is not a rational process, nor is it one that is likely to lead to a timely and successful solution to the problem. Major social problems, if they get "solved" at all, are rarely or never solved through any rational, comprehensive plan. They just work themselves out through a process in which various competing groups pursuing their own (usually short-term) self-interest [23] arrive (mainly by luck) at some more or less stable modus vivendi. In fact, the principles we formulated in paragraphs 100-106 make it seem doubtful that rational, long-term social planning can EVER be successful.

138. Thus it is clear that the human race has at best a very limited capacity for solving even relatively straightforward social problems. How then is it going to solve the far more difficult and subtle problem of reconciling freedom with technology? Technology presents clear-cut material advantages, whereas freedom is an abstraction that means different things to different people, and its loss is easily obscured by propaganda and fancy talk.

139. And note this important difference: It is conceivable that our

environmental problems (for example) may some day be settled through a rational, comprehensive plan, but if this happens it will be only because it is in the long-term interest of the system to solve these problems. But it is NOT in the interest of the system to preserve freedom or small-group autonomy. On the contrary, it is in the interest of the system to bring human behavior under control to the greatest possible extent. [24] Thus, while practical considerations may eventually force the system to take a rational, prudent approach to environmental problems, equally practical considerations will force the system to regulate human behavior ever more closely (preferably by indirect means that will disguise the encroachment on freedom). This isn't just our opinion. Eminent social scientists (e.g. James Q. Wilson) have stressed the importance of "socializing" people more effectively.

REVOLUTION IS EASIER THAN REFORM

140. We hope we have convinced the reader that the system cannot be reformed in such a way as to reconcile freedom with technology. The only way out is to dispense with the industrial-technological system altogether. This implies revolution, not necessarily an armed uprising, but certainly a radical and fundamental change in the nature of society.

141. People tend to assume that because a revolution involves a much greater change that reform does, it is more difficult to bring about than reform is. Actually, under certain circumstances revolution is much easier than reform. The reason is that a revolutionary movement can inspire an intensive of commitment that a reform movement cannot inspire. A reform movement merely offers to solve a particular social problem. A revolutionary movement offers to solve all problems at one stroke and create a whole new world; it provides the kind of ideal for which people will take great risks and make great sacrifices. For this reasons it would be much easier to overthrow the whole technological system than to put effective, permanent restraints on the development or application of any one segment of technology, such as genetic engineering, for example. Not any people will devote themselves with single-minded passion to imposing and maintaining restraints on genetic engineering, but under suitable conditions large numbers of people may devote

themselves passionately to a revolution against the industrial-technological system. As we noted in paragraph 132, reformers seeking to limit certain aspects of technology would be working to avoid a negative outcome. But revolutionaries work to gain a powerful reward—fulfillment of their revolutionary vision—and therefore work harder and more persistently than reformers do.

142. Reform is always restrained by the fear of painful consequences if changes go too far. But once a revolutionary fever has taken hold of a society, people are willing to undergo unlimited hardships for the sake of their revolution. This was clearly shown in the French and Russian Revolutions. It may be that in such cases only a minority of the population is really committed to the revolution, but this minority is sufficiently large and active so that it becomes the dominant force in society. We will have more to say about revolution in paragraphs 180-205.

CONTROL OF HUMAN BEHAVIOR

143. Since the beginning of civilization, organized societies have had to put pressures on human beings of the sake of the functioning of the social organism. The kinds of pressures vary greatly from one society to another. Some the pressures are physical (poor diet, excessive labor, environmental pollution), some are psychological (noise, crowding, forcing human behavior into the mold that society requires). In the past, human nature has been appropriately constant, or at any rate has varied only with certain bounds. Consequently, societies have been able to push people only up to certain limits. When the limit of human endurance has been passed, things start going wrong: rebellion, or crime. or corruption, or evasion of work, or depression and other mental problems, or an elevated death rate, or a declining birth rate of something else, so that either the society breaks down, or its functioning becomes to inefficient and it is (quickly or gradually, through conquest, attrition or evolution) replaced by some more efficient form of society. [25]

144. Thus human nature has in the past put certain limits on the development of societies. People could be pushed only so far and no father. But today this may be changing, because modern technology is developing ways for modifying human beings.

145. Imagine a society that subjects people to conditions that make them terribly unhappy, then gives them drugs to take away their unhappiness. Science fiction? It is already happening to some extent in our own society. It is well known that the rate of clinical depression has been greatly increasing in recent decades. We believe that this is due to disruption of the power process, as explained in paragraphs 59-76. But even if we are wrong, the increasing rate of depression is certainly the result of SOME conditions that exist in today's society. Instead of removing the conditions that make people depressed, modern society gives them antidepressant drugs. In effect, antidepressants are a means of modifying an individual's internal state in such a way as to enable him to tolerate social conditions that he would otherwise find intolerable. (Yes, we know that depression is often of purely genetic origin. We are referring here to those cases in which environment plays the predominant role.)

146. Drugs that affect the mind are only one example of the new methods of controlling human behavior that modern society is developing. Let us look at some of the other methods.

147. To start with, there are the techniques of surveillance. Hidden video cameras are now used in most stores and in many other places, computers are used to collect and process vast amounts of information about individuals. Information so obtained greatly increases the effectiveness of physical coercion (i.e., law enforcement.) [26] Then there are the methods of propaganda, for which the mass communication media provide effective vehicles. Effective techniques have been developed for winning elections, selling products, influencing public opinion. The entertainment industry serves as an important psychological tool of the system, possibly even when it is dished out large amounts of sex and violence. Entertainment provides modern man with an essential means of escape. While absorbed in television, videos, etc., he can forget stress, anxiety, frustration, dissatisfaction. Many primitive peoples, when they don't have work to do, are quite content to sit for hours at a time doing nothing at all, because they are at peace with themselves and their world. But most modern people must be constantly occupied or entertained, otherwise they get "bored," i.e., they get fidgety, uneasy, irritable.

148. Other techniques strike deeper than the foregoing. Education is no longer a simple affair of paddling a kid's behind when he doesn't know his lessons and patting him on the head when he does know them. It is becoming a scientific technique for controlling the child's development. Sylvan Learning Centers, for example, have had great success in motivating children to study, and psychological techniques are also used with more or less success in many conventional schools. "Parenting" techniques that are taught to parents are designed to make children accept fundamental values of the system and behave in ways that the system finds desirable. "Mental health" programs, "intervention" techniques, psychotherapy and so forth are ostensibly designed to benefit individuals, but in practice they usually serve as methods for inducing individuals to think and behave as the system requires. (There is no contradiction here; an individual those attitudes or behavior bring him into conflict with the system is up against a force that is too powerful for him to conquer or escape from, hence he is likely to suffer from stress, frustration, defeat. His path will be much easier if he thinks and behaves as the system requires. In that sense the system is acting for the benefit of the individual when it brainwashes him into conformity.) Child abuse in its gross and obvious forms is disapproved in most if not all cultures. Tormenting a child for a trivial reason or no reason at all is something that appalls almost everyone. But may psychologists interpret the concept of abuse much more broadly. Is spanking, when used as part of a rational and consistent system of discipline, a form of abuse? The question will ultimately be decided by whether or not spanking tends to produce behavior that makes a person fit in well with the existing system of society. In practice, the word "abuse" tends to be interpreted to include any method of child-rearing that produces behavior inconvenient for the system. Thus, when they go beyond the prevention of obvious, senseless cruelty, programs for preventing "child abuse" are directed toward the control of human behavior on behalf of the system.

149. Presumably, research will continue to increase the effectiveness of psychological techniques for controlling human behavior. But we think it is unlikely that psychological techniques alone will be sufficient to adjust human beings to the kind of society that tech-

nology is creating. Biological methods probably will have to be used. We have already mentioned the use of drugs in this connection. Neurology may provide other avenues for modifying the human mind. Genetic engineering of human beings is already beginning to occur in the form of "gene therapy," and there is no reason to assume that such methods will not eventually be used to modify those aspects of the body that affect mental functioning.

150. As we mentioned in paragraph 134, industrial society seems likely to be entering a period of severe stress, due in part to problems of human behavior and in part to economic and environmental problems. And a considerable proportion of the system's economic and environmental problems result from the way human beings behave. Alienation, low self-esteem, depression, hostility, rebellion; children who won't study, youth gangs, illegal drug use, rape, child abuse, other crimes, unsafe sex, teen pregnancy, population growth, political corruption, race hatred, ethnic rivalry, bitter ideological conflict (e.g., pro-choice vs. pro-life), political extremism, terrorism, sabotage, anti-government groups, hate groups. All these threaten the very survival of the system. The system will therefore be FORCED to use every practical means of controlling human behavior.

151. The social disruption that we see today is certainly not the result of mere chance. It can only be a result of the conditions of life that the system imposes on people. (We have argued that the most important of these conditions is disruption of the power process.) If the systems succeeds in imposing sufficient control over human behavior to assure its own survival, a new watershed in human history will have been passed. Whereas formerly the limits of human endurance have imposed limits on the development of societies (as we explained in paragraphs 143, 144), industrial-technological society will be able to pass those limits by modifying human beings, whether by psychological methods or biological methods or both. In the future, social systems will not be adjusted to suit the needs of human beings. Instead, human being will be adjusted to suit the needs of the system. [27]

152. Generally speaking, technological control over human behavior will probably not be introduced with a totalitarian intention or even through a conscious desire to restrict human freedom. [28]

Each new step in the assertion of control over the human mind will be taken as a rational response to a problem that faces society, such as curing alcoholism, reducing the crime rate or inducing young people to study science and engineering. In many cases there will be a humanitarian justification. For example, when a psychiatrist prescribes an anti-depressant for a depressed patient, he is clearing doing that individual a favor. It would be inhumane to withhold the drug from someone who needs it. When parents send their children to Sylvan Learning Centers to have them manipulated into becoming enthusiastic about their studies, they do so from concern for their children's welfare. It may be that some of these parents wish that one didn't have to have specialized training to get a job and that their kid didn't have to be brainwashed into becoming a computer nerd. But what can they do? They can't change society, and their child may be unemployable if he doesn't have certain skills. So they send him to Sylvan.

153. Thus control over human behavior will be introduced not by a calculated decision of the authorities but through a process of social evolution (RAPID evolution, however). The process will be impossible to resist, because each advance, considered by itself, will appear to be beneficial, or at least the evil involved in making the advance will appear to be beneficial, or at least the evil involved in making the advance will seem to be less than that which would result from not making it (see paragraph 127). Propaganda for example is used for many good purposes, such as discouraging child abuse or race hatred. [14] Sex education is obviously useful, yet the effect of sex education (to the extent that it is successful) is to take the shaping of sexual attitudes away from the family and put it into the hands of the state as represented by the public school system.

154. Suppose a biological trait is discovered that increases the likelihood that a child will grow up to be a criminal, and suppose some sort of gene therapy can remove this trait. [29] Of course most parents whose children possess the trait will have them undergo the therapy. It would be inhumane to do otherwise, since the child would probably have a miserable life if he grew up to be a criminal. But many or most primitive societies have a low crime rate in comparison with that of our society, even though they have neither

high-tech methods of child-rearing nor harsh systems of punishment. Since there is no reason to suppose that more modern men than primitive men have innate predatory tendencies, the high crime rate of our society must be due to the pressures that modern conditions put on people, to which many cannot or will not adjust. Thus a treatment designed to remove potential criminal tendencies is at least in part a way of re-engineering people so that they suit the requirements of the system.

155. Our society tends to regard as a "sickness" any mode of thought or behavior that is inconvenient for the system, and this is plausible because when an individual doesn't fit into the system it causes pain to the individual as well as problems for the system. Thus the manipulation of an individual to adjust him to the system is seen as a "cure" for a "sickness" and therefore as good.

156. In paragraph 127 we pointed out that if the use of a new item of technology is INITIALLY optional, it does not necessarily REMAIN optional, because the new technology tends to change society in such a way that it becomes difficult or impossible for an individual to function without using that technology. This applies also to the technology of human behavior. In a world in which most children are put through a program to make then enthusiastic about studying, a parent will almost be forced to put his kid through such a program, because if he does not, then the kid will grow up to be, comparatively speaking, an ignoramus and therefore unemployable. Or suppose a biological treatment is discovered that, without undesirable side-effects, will greatly reduce the psychological stress from which so many people suffer in our society. If large number of people choose to undergo the treatment, then the general level of stress in society will be reduced, so that it will be possible for the system to increase the stress-producing pressures. In fact, something like this seems to have happened already with one of our society's most important psychological tools for enabling people to reduce (or at least temporarily escape from) stress, namely, mass entertainment (see paragraph 147). Our use of mass entertainment is "optional": No law requires us to watch television, listen to the radio, read magazines. Yet mass entertainment is a means of escape and stress-reduction on which most of us have become dependent. Everyone complains about the trashiness of tele-

vision, but almost everyone watches it. A few have kicked the TV habit, but it would be a rare person who could get along today without using ANY form of mass entertainment. (Yet until quite recently in human history most people got along very nicely with no other entertainment than that which each local community created for itself.) Without the entertainment industry the system probably would not have been able to get away with putting as much stress-producing pressure on us as it does.

157. Assuming that industrial society survives, it is likely that technology will eventually acquire something approaching complete control over human behavior. It has been established beyond any rational doubt that human thought and behavior have a largely biological basis. As experimenters have demonstrated, feelings such as hunger, pleasure, anger and fear can be turned on and off by electrical stimulation and appropriate parts of the brain. Memories can be destroyed by damaging parts of the brain or they can be brought to the surface by electrical stimulation. Hallucinations can be induced or moods changed by drugs. There may or may not be an immaterial human soul, but if there is one it clearly is less powerful that the biological mechanisms of human behavior. For if that were not the case then researchers would not be able so easily to manipulate human feelings and behavior with drugs and electrical currents.

158. It presumably would be impractical for all people to have electrodes inserted in their heads so that they could be controlled by the authorities. But the fact that human thoughts and feelings are so open to biological intervention shows that the problem of controlling human behavior is mainly a technical problem; a problem of neurons, hormones and complex molecules; the kind of problem that is accessible to scientific attack. Given the outstanding record of our society in solving technical problems, it is overwhelmingly probable that great advances will be made in the control of human behavior.

159. Will public resistance prevent the introduction of technological control of human behavior? It certainly would if an attempt were made to introduce such control all at once. But since technological control will be introduced through a long sequence of small advances, there will be no rational and effective public resistance. (See paragraphs 127, 132, 153.)

160. To those who think that all this sounds like science fiction, we point out that yesterday's science fiction is today's fact. The Industrial Revolution has radically altered man's environment and way of life, and it is only to be expected that as technology is increasingly applied to the human body and mind, man himself will be altered as radically as his environment and way of life have been.

HUMAN RACE AT A CROSSROADS

161. But we have gotten ahead of our story. It is one thing to develop in the laboratory a series of psychological or biological techniques for manipulating human behavior and quite another to integrate these techniques into a functioning social system. The latter problem is the more difficult of the two. For example, while the techniques of educational psychology doubtless work quite well in the "lab schools" where they are developed, it is not necessarily easy to apply them effectively throughout our educational system. We all know what many of our schools are like. The teachers are too busy taking knives and guns away from the kids to subject them to the latest techniques for making them into computer nerds. Thus, in spite of all its technical advances relating to human behavior, the system to date has not been impressively successful in controlling human beings. The people whose behavior is fairly well under the control of the system are those of the type that might be called "bourgeois." But there are growing numbers of people who in one way or another are rebels against the system: welfare leaches, youth gangs, cultists, satanists, nazis, radical environmentalists, militiamen, etc.

162. The system is currently engaged in a desperate struggle to overcome certain problems that threaten its survival, among which the problems of human behavior are the most important. If the system succeeds in acquiring sufficient control over human behavior quickly enough, it will probably survive. Otherwise it will most likely be resolved within the next several decades, say 40 to 100 years.

163. Suppose the system survives the crisis of the next several decades. By that time it will to have solved, or at least brought under control, the principal problems that confront it, in particular that of "socializing" human beings: that is, making people sufficiently docile so that their behavior no longer threatens the system.

That being accomplished, it does not appear that there would be any further obstacle to the development of technology, and it would presumably advance toward its local conclusion, which is complete control over everything on Earth, including human beings and all other important organisms. The system may become a unitary, monolithic organization, or it may be more or less fragmented and consist of a number of organizations coexisting in a relationship that includes elements of both cooperation and competition, just as today the government, the corporations and other large organizations both cooperate and compete with one another. Human freedom mostly will have vanished, because individuals and small groups will be impotent vis-a-vis large organizations armed with supertechnology and an arsenal of advanced psychological and biological tools for manipulating human beings, besides instruments of surveillance and physical coercion. Only a small number of people will have any real power, and even these probably will have only very limited freedom, because their behavior too will be regulated, just as today our politicians and corporation executives can retain their positions of power only as long as their behavior remains within certain fairly narrow limits.

164. Don't imagine that the systems will stop developing further techniques for controlling human beings and nature once the crisis of the next few decades is over and increasing control is no longer necessary for the system's survival. On the contrary, once the hard times are over the system will increase its control over people and nature more rapidly, because it will no longer be hampered by difficulties of the kind that it is currently experiencing. Survival is not the principal motive for extending control. As we explained in paragraphs 87-90, technicians and scientists carry on their work largely as a surrogate activity; that is, they satisfy their need for power by solving technical problems. They will continue to do this with unabated enthusiasm, and among the most interesting and challenging problems for them to solve will be those of understanding the human body and mind and intervening in their development. For the "good of humanity," of course.

165. But suppose on the other hand that the stresses of the coming decades prove to be too much for the system. If the system breaks

down there may be a period of chaos, a "time of troubles" such as those that history has recorded at various epochs in the past. It is impossible to predict what would emerge from such a time of troubles, but at any rate the human race would be given a new chance. The greatest danger is that industrial society may begin to reconstitute itself within the first few years after the breakdown. Certainly there will be many people (power-hungry types especially) who will be anxious to get the factories running again.

166. Therefore two tasks confront those who hate the servitude to which the industrial system is reducing the human race. First, we must work to heighten the social stresses within the system to as to increase the likelihood that it will break down or be weakened sufficiently so that a revolution against it becomes possible. Second, it is necessary to develop and propagate an ideology that opposes technology and the industrial society if and when the system becomes sufficiently weakened. And such an ideology will help to assure that, if and when industrial society breaks down, its remnants will be smashed beyond repair, so that the system cannot be reconstituted. The factories should be destroyed, technical books burned, etc.

HUMAN SUFFERING

167. The industrial system will not break down purely as a result of revolutionary action. It will not be vulnerable to revolutionary attack unless its own internal problems of development lead it into very serious difficulties. So if the system breaks down it will do so either spontaneously, or through a process that is in part spontaneous but helped along by revolutionaries. If the breakdown is sudden, many people will die, since the world's population has become so overblown that it cannot even feed itself any longer without advanced technology. Even if the breakdown is gradual enough so that reduction of the population can occur more through lowering of the birth rate than through elevation of the death rate, the process of de-industrialization probably will be very chaotic and involve much suffering. It is naive to think it likely that technology can be phased out in a smoothly managed, orderly way, especially since the technophiles will fight stubbornly at every step. Is it therefore cruel to work for the breakdown of the system? Maybe, but maybe

not. In the first place, revolutionaries will not be able to beak the system down unless it is already in enough trouble so that there would be a good chance of its eventually breaking down by itself anyway; and the bigger the system grows, the more disastrous the consequences of its breakdown will be; so it may be that revolutionaries, by hastening the onset of the breakdown, will be reducing the extent of the disaster.

168. In the second place, one has to balance struggle and death against the loss of freedom and dignity. To many of us, freedom and dignity are more important than a long life or avoidance of physical pain. Besides, we all have to die some time, and it may be better to die fighting for survival, or for a cause, than to live a long but empty and purposeless life.

169. In the third place, it is not at all certain that survival of the system will lead to less suffering than breakdown of the system would. The system has already caused, and is continuing to cause, immense suffering all over the world. Ancient cultures, that for hundreds of years gave people a satisfactory relationship with each other and with their environment, have been shattered by contact with industrial society, and the result has been a whole catalogue of economic, environmental, social and psychological problems. One of the effects of the intrusion of industrial society has been that over much of the world traditional controls on population have been thrown out of balance. Hence the population explosion, with all that that implies. Then there is the psychological suffering that is widespread throughout the supposedly fortunate countries of the West (see paragraphs 44, 45). No one knows what will happen as a result of ozone depletion, the greenhouse effect and other environmental problems that cannot yet be foreseen. And, as nuclear proliferation has shown, new technology cannot be kept out of the hands of dictators and irresponsible Third World nations. Would you like to speculate about what Iraq or North Korea will do with genetic engineering?

170. "Oh!" says the technophiles, "Science is going to fix all that! We will conquer famine, eliminate psychological suffering, make everybody healthy and happy!" Yeah, sure. That's what they said 200 years ago. The Industrial Revolution was supposed to eliminate poverty, make everybody happy, etc. The actual result has been quite

different. The technophiles are hopelessly naive (or self-deceiving) in their understanding of social problems. They are unaware of (or choose to ignore) the fact that when large changes, even seemingly beneficial ones, are introduced into a society, they lead to a long sequence of other changes, most of which are impossible to predict (paragraph 103). The result is disruption of the society. So it is very probable that in their attempts to end poverty and disease, engineer docile, happy personalities and so forth, the technophiles will create social systems that are terribly troubled, even more so than the present once. For example, the scientists boast that they will end famine by creating new, genetically engineered food plants. But this will allow the human population to keep expanding indefinitely, and it is well known that crowding leads to increased stress and aggression. This is merely one example of the PREDICTABLE problems that will arise. We emphasize that, as past experience has shown, technical progress will lead to other new problems that CANNOT be predicted in advance (paragraph 103). In fact, ever since the Industrial Revolution, technology has been creating new problems for society far more rapidly than it has been solving old ones. Thus it will take a long and difficult period of trial and error for the technophiles to work the bugs out of their Brave New World (if they every do). In the meantime there will be great suffering. So it is not at all clear that the survival of industrial society would involve less suffering than the breakdown of that society would. Technology has gotten the human race into a fix from which there is not likely to be any easy escape.

THE FUTURE

171. But suppose now that industrial society does survive the next several decades and that the bugs do eventually get worked out of the system, so that it functions smoothly. What kind of system will it be? We will consider several possibilities.

172. First let us postulate that the computer scientists succeed in developing intelligent machines that can do all things better than human beings can do them. In the case presumably all work will be done by vast, highly organized systems of machines and no human effort will be necessary. Either of two cases might occur. The machines might be

permitted to make all of their own decisions without human oversight, or else human control over the machines might be retained.

173. If the machines are permitted to make all their own decisions, we can't make any conjectures as to the results, because it is impossible to guess how such machines might behave. We only point out that the fate of the human race would be at the mercy of the machines. It might be argued that the human race would never be foolish enough to hand over all power to the machines. But we are suggesting neither that the human race would voluntarily turn power over to the machines nor that the machines would willfully seize power. What we do suggest is that the human race might easily permit itself to drift into a position of such dependence on the machines that it would have no practical choice but to accept all of the machines' decisions. As society and the problems that face it become more and more complex and as machines become more and more intelligent, people will let machines make more and more of their decisions for them, simply because machine-made decisions will bring better results than man-made ones. Eventually a stage may be reached at which the decisions necessary to keep the system running will be so complex that human beings will be incapable of making them intelligently. At that stage the machines will be in effective control. People won't be able to just turn the machines off, because they will be so dependent on them that turning them off would amount to suicide.

174. On the other hand it is possible that human control over the machines may be retained. In that case that average man may have control over certain private machines of his own, such as his car or his personal computer, but control over large systems of machines will be in the hands of a tiny elite—just as it is today, but with two differences. Due to improved techniques the elite will have greater control over the masses; and because human work will no longer be necessary the masses will be superfluous, a useless burden on the system. If the elite is ruthless they may simply decide to exterminate the mass of humanity. If they are humane they may use propaganda or other psychological or biological techniques to reduce the birth rate until the mass of humanity becomes extinct, leaving the world to the elite. Or, if the elite consists of soft-hearted liberals,

they may decide to play the role of good shepherds to the rest of the human race. They will see to it that everyone's physical needs are satisfied, that all children are raised under psychologically hygienic conditions, that everyone has a wholesome hobby to keep him busy, and that anyone who may become dissatisfied undergoes "treatment" to cure his "problem." Of course, life will be so purposeless that people will have to be biologically or psychologically engineered either to remove their need for the power process or to make them "sublimate" their drive for power into some harmless hobby. These engineered human beings may be happy in such a society, but they most certainly will not be free. They will have been reduced to the status of domestic animals.

175. But suppose now that the computer scientists do not succeed in developing artificial intelligence, so that human work remains necessary. Even so, machines will take care of more and more of the simpler tasks so that there will be an increasing surplus of human workers at the lower levels of ability. (We see this happening already. There are many people who find it difficult or impossible to get work, because for intellectual or psychological reasons they cannot acquire the level of training necessary to make themselves useful in the present system.) On those who are employed, ever-increasing demands will be placed: They will need more and more training, more and more ability, and will have to be ever more reliable, confirming and docile, because they will be more and more like cells of a giant organism. Their tasks will be increasingly specialized, so that their work will be, in a sense, out of touch with the real world, being concentrated on one tiny slice of reality. The system will have to use any means that it can, whether psychological or biological, to engineer people to be docile, to have the abilities that the system requires and to "sublimate" their drive for power into some specialized task. But the statement that the people of such a society will have to be docile may require qualification. The society may find competitiveness useful, provided that ways are found of directing competitiveness into channels that serve the needs of the system. We can imagine a future society in which there is endless competition for positions of prestige and power. But no more than a very few people will ever reach the top, where the only

real power is (see end of paragraph 163). Very repellent is a society in which a person can satisfy his need for power only by pushing large numbers of other people out of the way and depriving them of THEIR opportunity for power.

176. One can envision scenarios that incorporate aspects of more than one of the possibilities that we have just discussed. For instance, it may be that machines will take over most of the work that is of real, practical importance, but that human being will be kept busy by being given relatively unimportant work. It has been suggested, for example, that a great development of the service industries might provide work for human beings. Thus people would spent their time shining each other shoes, driving each other around in taxicabs, making handicrafts for one another, waiting on each other's tables, etc. This seems to us a thoroughly contemptible way for the human race to end up, and we doubt that many people would find fulfilling lives in such pointless busy-work. They would seek other, dangerous outlets (drugs, crime, "cults," hate groups) unless they are biologically or psychologically engineered to adapt them to such a way of life.

177. Needless to say, the scenarios outlines above do not exhaust all the possibilities. They only indicate the kinds of outcomes that seem to us most likely. But we can envision no plausible scenarios that are any more palatable than the ones we've just described. It is overwhelmingly probable that if the industrial-technological system survives the next 40 to 100 years, it will by that time have developed certain general characteristics: Individuals (at least those of the "bourgeois" type, who are integrated into the system and make it run, and who therefore have all the power) will be more dependent than ever on large organizations; they will be more "socialized" than ever and their physical and mental qualities to a significant extent (possibly to a very great extent) will be those that are engineered into them rather than being the results of chance (or of God's will, or whatever); and whatever may be left of wild nature will be reduced to remnants preserved for scientific study and kept under the supervision and management of scientists (hence it will no longer be truly wild). In the long run (say a few centuries from now) it is likely that neither the human race nor any other important organisms will exist

as we know them today, because once you start modifying organisms through genetic engineering there is no reason to stop at any particular point, so that the modifications will probably continue until man and other organisms have been utterly transformed.

178. Whatever else may be the case, it is certain that a technology is creating for human beings a new physical and social environment radically different from the spectrum of environments to which natural selection has adapted the human race physically and psychologically. If man is not adjusted to this new environment by being artificially re-engineered, then he will be adapted to it through a long and painful process of natural selection. The former is far more likely than the latter.

179. It would be better to dump the whole stinking system and take the consequences.

STRATEGY

180. The technophiles are taking us all on an utterly reckless ride into the unknown. Many people understand something of what technological progress is doing to us yet take a passive attitude toward it because they think it is inevitable. But we (FC) don't think it is inevitable. We think it can be stopped, and we will give here some indications of how to go about stopping it.

181. As we stated in paragraph 166, the two main tasks for the present are to promote social stress and instability in industrial society and to develop and propagate an ideology that opposes technology and the industrial system. When the system becomes sufficiently stressed and unstable, a revolution against technology may be possible. The pattern would be similar to that of the French and Russian Revolutions. French society and Russian society, for several decades prior to their respective revolutions, showed increasing signs of stress and weakness. Meanwhile, ideologies were being developed that offered a new world view that was quite different from the old one. In the Russian case, revolutionaries were actively working to undermine the old order. Then, when the old system was put under sufficient additional stress (by financial crisis in France, by military defeat in Russia) it was swept away by revolution. What we propose is something along the same lines.

182. It will be objected that the French and Russian Revolutions were failures. But most revolutions have two goals. One is to destroy an old form of society and the other is to set up the new form of society envisioned by the revolutionaries. The French and Russian revolutionaries failed (fortunately!) to create the new kind of society of which they dreamed, but they were quite successful in destroying the old society. We have no illusions about the feasibility of creating a new, ideal form of society. Our goal is only to destroy the existing form of society.

183. But an ideology, in order to gain enthusiastic support, must have a positive ideal as well as a negative one; it must be FOR something as well as AGAINST something. The positive ideal that we propose is Nature. That is, WILD nature: those aspects of the functioning of the Earth and its living things that are independent of human management and free of human interference and control. And with wild nature we include human nature, by which we mean those aspects of the functioning of the human individual that are not subject to regulation by organized society but are products of chance, or free will, or God (depending on your religious or philosophical opinions).

184. Nature makes a perfect counter-ideal to technology for several reasons. Nature (that which is outside the power of the system) is the opposite of technology (which seeks to expand indefinitely the power of the system). Most people will agree that nature is beautiful; certainly it has tremendous popular appeal. The radical environmentalists ALREADY hold an ideology that exalts nature and opposes technology. [30] It is not necessary for the sake of nature to set up some chimerical utopia or any new kind of social order. Nature takes care of itself. It was a spontaneous creation that existed long before any human society, and for countless centuries many different kinds of human societies coexisted with nature without doing it an excessive amount of damages. Only with the Industrial Revolution did the effect of human society on nature become really devastating. To relieve the pressure on nature it is not necessary to create a special kind of social system, it is only necessary to get rid of industrial society. Granted, this will not solve all problems. Industrial society has already done tremendous damage to nature and it will take a very long time for the scars to heal. Besides, even

pre-industrial societies can do significant damage to nature. Nevertheless, getting rid of industrial society will accomplish a great deal. It will relieve the worst of the pressure on nature so that the scars can begin to heal. It will remove the capacity of organized society to keep increasing its control over nature (including human nature). Whatever kind of society may exist after the demise of the industrial system, it is certain that most people will live close to nature, because in the absence of advanced technology there is no other way that people CAN live. To feed themselves they must be peasants or herdsmen of fishermen or hunters, etc. And, generally speaking, local autonomy should tend to increase, because lack of advanced technology and rapid communications will limit the capacity of governments or other large organizations to control local communities.

185. As for the negative consequences of eliminating industrial society—well, you can't eat your cake and have it too. To gain one thing you have to sacrifice another.

186. Most people hate psychological conflict. For this reason they avoid doing any serious thinking about difficult social issues, and they like to have such issues presented to them in simple, black-and-white terms: THIS is all good and THAT is all bad. The revolutionary ideology should therefore be developed on two levels.

187. On the more sophisticated level the ideology should address itself to people who are intelligent, thoughtful and rational. The object should be to create a core of people who will be opposed to the industrial system on a rational, thought-out bases, with full appreciation of the problems and ambiguities involved, and of the price that has to be paid for getting rid of the system. It is particularly important to attract people of this type, as they are capable people and will be instrumental in influencing others. These people should be addressed on as rational a level as possible. Facts should never intentionally be distorted and intemperate language should be avoided. This does not mean that no appeal can be made to the emotions, but in making such appeal care should be taken to avoid misrepresenting the truth or doing anything else that would destroy the intellectual respectability of the ideology.

188. On a second level, the ideology should be propagated in a

simplified form that will enable the unthinking majority to see the conflict of technology vs. nature in unambiguous terms. But even on this second level the ideology should not be expressed in language that is so cheap, intemperate or irrational that it alienates people of the thoughtful and rational type. Cheap, intemperate propaganda sometimes achieves impressive short-term gains, but it will be more advantageous in the long run to keep the loyalty of a small number of intelligently committed people than to arouse the passions of an unthinking, fickle mob who will change their attitude as soon as someone comes along with a better propaganda gimmick. However, propaganda of the rabble-rousing type may be necessary when the system is nearing the point of collapse and there is a final struggle between rival ideologies to determine which will become dominant when the old world-view goes under.

189. Prior to that final struggle, the revolutionaries should not expect to have a majority of people on their side. History is made by active, determined minorities, not by the majority, which seldom has a clear and consistent idea of what it really wants. Until the time comes for the final push toward revolution [31], the task of revolutionaries will be less to win the shallow support of the majority than to build a small core of deeply committed people. As for the majority, it will be enough to make them aware of the existence of the new ideology and remind them of it frequently; though of course it will be desirable to get majority support to the extent that this can be done without weakening the core of seriously committed people.

190. Any kind of social conflicts helps to destabilize the system, but one should be careful about what kinds of conflict one encourages. The line of conflict should be drawn between the mass of the people and the power-holding elite of industrial society (politicians, scientists, upper-level business executives, government officials, etc). It should NOT be drawn between the revolutionaries and the mass of the people. For example, it would be bad strategy for the revolutionaries to condemn Americans for their habits of consumption. Instead, the average American should be portrayed as a victim of the advertising and marketing industry, which has suckered him into buying a lot of junk that he doesn't need and that is very poor compensation for his lost freedom. Either approach is consistent

with the facts. It is merely a matter of attitude whether you blame the advertising industry for manipulating the public or blame the public for allowing itself to be manipulated. As a matter of strategy one should generally avoid blaming the public.

191. One should think twice before encouraging any other social conflict than that between the power-holding elite (which wields technology) and the general public (over which technology exerts its power). For one thing, other conflicts tend to distract attention from the important conflicts (between power-elite and ordinary people, between technology and nature); for another thing, other conflicts may actually tend to encourage technologization, because each side in such a conflicts wants to use technological power to gain advantages over its adversary. This is clearly seen in rivalries between nations. It also appears in ethnic conflicts within nations. For example, in America many black leaders are anxious to gain power for African Americans by placing black individuals in the technological power-elite. They want there to be many black government officials, scientists, corporation executives and so forth. In this way they are helping to absorb the African American subculture into the technological system. Generally speaking, one should encourage only those social conflicts that can be fitted into the framework of the conflicts of power-elite vs. ordinary people, technology vs. nature.

192. But the way to discourage ethnic conflict is NOT through militant advocacy of minority rights (sees paragraphs 21, 29). Instead, the revolutionaries should emphasize that although minorities do suffer more or less disadvantage, this disadvantage is of peripheral significance. Our real enemy is the industrial-technological system, and in the struggle against the system, ethnic distinctions are of no importance.

193. The kind of revolution we have in mind will not necessarily involve an armed uprising against any government. It may or may not involve physical violence, but it will not be a POLITICAL revolution. Its focus will be on technology and economics, not politics. [32]

194. Probably the revolutionaries should even AVOID assuming political power, whether by legal or illegal means, until the industrial system is stressed to the danger point and has proved itself to be a failure in the eyes of most people. Suppose for example that some "green" party should win control of the United States

Congress in an election. In order to avoid betraying or watering down their own ideology they would have to take vigorous measures to turn economic growth into economic shrinkage. To the average man the results would appear disastrous: There would be massive unemployment, shortages of commodities, etc. Even if the grosser ill effects could be avoided through superhumanly skillful management, still people would have to begin giving up the luxuries to which they have become addicted. Dissatisfaction would grow, the "green" party would be voted out of office and the revolutionaries would have suffered a severe setback. For this reason the revolutionaries should not try to acquire political power until the system has gotten itself into such a mess that any hardships will be seen as resulting from the failures of the industrial system itself and not from the policies of the revolutionaries. The revolution against technology will probably have to be a revolution by outsiders, a revolution from below and not from above.

195. The revolution must be international and worldwide. It cannot be carried out on a nation-by-nation basis. Whenever is it suggested that the United States, for example, should cut back on technological progress or economic growth, people get hysterical and start screaming that if we fall behind in technology the Japanese will get ahead of us. Holy robots! The world will fly off its orbit if the Japanese ever sell more cars than we do! (Nationalism is a great promoter of technology). More reasonably, it is argued that if the relatively democratic nations of the world fall behind in technology while nasty, dictatorial nations like China, Vietnam and North Korea continue to progress, eventually the dictators may come to dominate the world. That is why the industrial system should be attacked in all nations simultaneously, to the extent that this may be possible. True, there is no assurance that the industrial system can be destroyed at approximately the same time all over the world, and it is even conceivable that the attempt to overthrow the system could lead instead to the domination of the system by dictators. That is a risk that has to be taken. And it is worth taking, since the difference between a "democratic" industrial system and one controlled by dictators is small compared with the difference between an industrial system and a non-industrial one. [33] It might even be argued that an indus-

trial system controlled by dictators would be preferable because dictator-controlled systems usually have proved inefficient, hence they are presumably more likely to break down. Look at Cuba.

196. Revolutionaries might consider favoring measures that tend to bind the world economy into a unified whole. Free trade agreements like NAFTA and GATT are probably harmful to the environment in the short run, but in the long run they may perhaps be advantageous because they foster economic interdependence between nations. It will be easier to destroy the industrial system on a worldwide basis if the world economy is so unified that its breakdown in any one major nation will lead to its breakdown in all industrialized nations.

197. Some people take the line that modern man has too much power, too much control over nature; they argue for a more passive attitude on the part of the human race. At best these people are expressing themselves unclearly, because they fail to distinguish between power for LARGE ORGANIZATIONS and power for INDIVIDUALS and SMALL GROUPS. It is a mistake to argue for powerlessness and passivity, because people NEED power. Modern man as a collective entity—that is, the industrial system—has immense power over nature, and we (FC) regard this as evil, but modern INDIVIDUALS and SMALL GROUPS OF INDIVIDUALS have far less power than primitive man ever did. Generally speaking, the vast power of "modern man" over nature is exercised not by individuals or small groups but by large organizations. To the extent that the average modern INDIVIDUAL can wield the power of technology, he is permitted to do so only within narrow limits and only under the supervision and control of the system. (You need a license for everything and with the license come rules and regulations.) The individual has only those technological powers with which the system chooses to provide him. His PERSONAL power over nature is slight.

198. Primitive INDIVIDUALS and SMALL GROUPS actually had considerable power over nature; or maybe it would be better to say power WITHIN nature. When primitive man needed food he knew how to find and prepare edible roots, how to track game and take it with homemade weapons. He knew how to protect himself from heat, cold, rain, dangerous animals, etc. But primitive man did

relatively little damage to nature because the COLLECTIVE power of primitive society was negligible compared to the COLLECTIVE power of industrial society.

199. Instead of arguing for powerlessness and passivity, one should argue that the power of the INDUSTRIAL SYSTEM should be broken, and that this will greatly INCREASE the power and freedom of INDIVIDUALS and SMALL GROUPS.

200. Until the industrial system has been thoroughly wrecked, the destruction of that system must be revolutionaries' ONLY goal. Other goals would distract attention and energy from the main goal. More importantly, if the revolutionaries permit themselves to have any other goal than the destruction of technology, they will be tempted to use technology as a tool for reaching that other goal. If they give in to that temptation, they will fall right back into the technological trap, because modern technology is a unified, tightly organized system, so that, in order to retain SOME technology, one finds oneself obliged to retain MOST technology, hence one ends up sacrificing only token amounts of technology.

201. Suppose for example that the revolutionaries took "social justice" as a goal. Human nature being what it is, social justice would not come about spontaneously; it would have to be enforced. In order to enforce it the revolutionaries would have to retain central organization and control. For that they would need rapid long-distance transportation and communications, and therefore all the technology needed to support the transportation and communication systems. To feed and clothe poor people they would have to use agricultural and manufacturing technology. And so forth. So that the attempt to insure social justice would force them to retain most parts of the technological system. Not that we have anything against social justice, but it must not be allowed to interfere with the effort to get rid of the technological system.

202. It would be hopeless for revolutionaries to try to attack the system without using SOME modern technology. If nothing else they must use the communications media to spread their message. But they should use modern technology for only ONE purpose: to attack the technological system.

203. Imagine an alcoholic sitting with a barrel of wine in front of him.

Suppose he starts saying to himself, "Wine isn't bad for you if used in moderation. Why, they say small amounts of wine are even good for you! It won't do me any harm if I take just one little drink ..." Well you know what is going to happen. Never forget that the human race with technology is just like an alcoholic with a barrel of wine.

204. Revolutionaries should have as many children as they can. There is strong scientific evidence that social attitudes are to a significant extent inherited. No one suggests that a social attitude is a direct outcome of a person's genetic constitution, but it appears that personality traits are partly inherited and that certain personality traits tend, within the context of our society, to make a person more likely to hold this or that social attitude. Objections to these findings have been raised, but the objections are feeble and seem to be ideologically motivated. In any event, no one denies that children tend on the average to hold social attitudes similar to those of their parents. From our point of view it doesn't matter all that much whether the attitudes are passed on genetically or through childhood training. In either case they ARE passed on.

205. The trouble is that many of the people who are inclined to rebel against the industrial system are also concerned about the population problems, hence they are apt to have few or no children. In this way they may be handing the world over to the sort of people who support or at least accept the industrial system. To insure the strength of the next generation of revolutionaries the present generation should reproduce itself abundantly. In doing so they will be worsening the population problem only slightly. And the important problem is to get rid of the industrial system, because once the industrial system is gone the world's population necessarily will decrease (see paragraph 167); whereas, if the industrial system survives, it will continue developing new techniques of food production that may enable the world's population to keep increasing almost indefinitely.

206. With regard to revolutionary strategy, the only point on which we absolutely insist are that the single overriding goal must be the elimination of modern technology, and that no other goal can be allowed to compete with this one. For the rest, revolutionaries should take an empirical approach. If experience indicates that some of the

recommendations made in the foregoing paragraphs are not going to give good results, then those recommendations should be discarded.

TWO KINDS OF TECHNOLOGY

207. An argument likely to be raised against our proposed revolution is that it is bound to fail, because (it is claimed) throughout history technology has always progressed, never regressed, hence technological regression is impossible. But this claim is false.

208. We distinguish between two kinds of technology, which we will call small-scale technology and organization-dependent technology. Small-scale technology is technology that can be used by small-scale communities without outside assistance. Organization-dependent technology is technology that depends on large-scale social organization. We are aware of no significant cases of regression in small-scale technology. But organization-dependent technology DOES regress when the social organization on which it depends breaks down. Example: When the Roman Empire fell apart the Romans' small-scale technology survived because any clever village craftsman could build, for instance, a water wheel, any skilled smith could make steel by Roman methods, and so forth. But the Romans' organization-dependent technology DID regress. Their aqueducts fell into disrepair and were never rebuilt. Their techniques of road construction were lost. The Roman'system of urban sanitation was forgotten, so that not until rather recent times did the sanitation of European cities equal that of Ancient Rome.

209. The reason why technology has seemed always to progress is that, until perhaps a century or two before the industrial Revolution, most technology was small-scale technology. But most of the technology developed since the Industrial Revolution is organization-dependent technology. Take the refrigerator for example. Without factory-made parts or the facilities of a post-industrial machine shop it would be virtually impossible for a handful of local craftsmen to build a refrigerator. If by some miracle they did succeed in building one it would be useless to them without a reliable source of electric power. So they would have to dam a stream and build a generator. Generators require large amounts of copper wire. Imagine trying to make that wire without modern machinery. And

where would they get a gas suitable for refrigeration? It would be much easier to build an icehouse or preserve food by drying or picking, as was done before the invention of the refrigerator.

210. So it is clear that if the industrial system were once thoroughly broken down, refrigeration technology would quickly be lost. The same is true of other organization-dependent technology. And once this technology had been lost for a generation or so it would take centuries to rebuild it, just as it took centuries to build it the first time around. Surviving technical books would be few and scattered. An industrial society, if built from scratch without outside help, can only be built in a series of stages: You need tools to make tools to make tools to make tools ... A long process of economic development and progress in social organization is required. And, even in the absence of an ideology opposed to technology, there is no reason to believe that anyone would be interested in rebuilding industrial society. The enthusiasm for "progress" is a phenomenon peculiar to the modern form of society, and it seems not to have existed prior to the 17th century or thereabouts.

211. In the late Middle Ages there were four main civilizations that were about equally "advanced": Europe, the Islamic world, India, and the Far East (China, Japan, Korea). Three of those civilizations remained more or less stable, and only Europe became dynamic. No one knows why Europe became dynamic at that time; historians have their theories but these are only speculation. At any rate, it is clear that rapid development toward a technological form of society occurs only under special conditions. So there is no reason to assume that a long-lasting technological regression cannot be brought about.

212. Would society EVENTUALLY develop again toward an industrial-technological form? Maybe, but there is no use in worrying about it, since we can't predict or control events 500 or 1,000 years in the future. Those problems must be dealt with by the people who will live at that time.

THE DANGER OF LEFTISM

213. Because of their need for rebellion and for membership in a movement, leftists or persons of similar psychological type often are unattracted to a rebellious or activist movement whose goals and

membership are not initially leftist. The resulting influx of leftish types can easily turn a non-leftist movement into a leftist one, so that leftist goals replace or distort the original goals of the movement.

214. To avoid this, a movement that exalts nature and opposes technology must take a resolutely anti-leftist stance and must avoid all collaboration with leftists. Leftism is in the long run inconsistent with the wild nature, with human freedom and with the elimination of modern technology. Leftism is collectivist; it seems to bind together the entire world (both nature and the human race) into a unified whole. But this implies management of nature and of human life by organized society, and it requires advanced technology. You can't have a united world without rapid transportation and communication, you can't make all people love one another without sophisticated psychological techniques, you can't have a "planned society" without the necessary technological base. Above all, leftism is driven by the need for power, and the leftist seeks power on a collective basis, through identification, with a mass movement or an organization. Leftism is unlikely ever to give up technology, because technology is too valuable a source of collective power.

215. The anarchist [34] too seeks power, but he seeks it on an individual or small-group basis; he wants individuals and small groups to be able to control the circumstances of their own lives. He opposes technology because it make small groups dependent on large organizations.

216. Some leftists may seem to oppose technology, but they will oppose it only so long as they are outsiders and the technological system is controlled by non-leftists. If leftism ever becomes dominant in society, so that the technological system becomes a tool in the hands of leftists, they will enthusiastically use it and promote its growth. In doing this they will be repeating a pattern that leftism has shown again and again in the past. When the Bolsheviks in Russia were outsiders, they vigorously opposed censorship and the secret police, they advocated self-determination for ethnic minorities, and so forth; but as soon as they came into power themselves, they imposed a tighter censorship and created a more ruthless secret police than any that had existed under the tsars, and they oppressed ethnic minorities at least as much as the tsars had done. In the

United States, a couple of decades ago when leftists were a minority in our universities, leftist professors were vigorous proponents of academic freedom, but today, in those of our universities where leftists have become dominant, they have shown themselves ready to take away from everyone else's academic freedom. (This is "political correctness.") The same will happen with leftists and technology: They will use it to oppress everyone else if they ever get it under their own control.

217. In earlier revolutions, leftists of the most power-hungry type, repeatedly, have first cooperated with non-leftist revolutionaries, as well as with leftists of a more libertarian inclination, and later have double-crossed them to seize power for themselves. Robespierre did this in the French Revolution, the Bolsheviks did it in the Russian Revolution, the communists did it in Spain in 1938 and Castro and his followers did it in Cuba. Given the past history of leftism, it would be utterly foolish for non-leftists revolutionaries today to collaborate with leftists.

218. Various thinkers have pointed out that leftism is a kind of religion. Leftism is not a religion in the strict sense because leftist doctrine does not postulate the existence of any supernatural being. But, for the leftist, leftism plays a psychological role much like that which religion plays for some people. The leftist NEEDS to believe in leftism; it plays a vital role in his psychological economy. His beliefs are not easily modified by logic or facts. He has a deep conviction that leftism is morally Right with a capital R, and that he has not only a right but a duty to impose leftist morality on everyone. (However, many of the people we are referring to as "leftists" do not think of themselves as leftists and would not describe their system of beliefs as leftism. We use the term "leftism" because we don't know of any better words to designate the spectrum of related creeds that includes the feminist, gay rights, political correctness, etc., movements, and because these movements have a strong affinity with the old left. See paragraphs 227-230.)

219. Leftism is a totalitarian force. Wherever leftism is in a position of power it tends to invade every private corner and force every thought into a leftist mold. In part this is because of the quasi-religious character of leftism; everything contrary to leftist beliefs repre-

sents Sin. More importantly, leftism is a totalitarian force because of the leftists' drive for power. The leftist seeks to satisfy his need for power through identification with a social movement and he tries to go through the power process by helping to pursue and attain the goals of the movement (see paragraph 83). But no matter how far the movement has gone in attaining its goals the leftist is never satisfied, because his activism is a surrogate activity (see paragraph 41). That is, the leftist's real motive is not to attain the ostensible goals of leftism; in reality he is motivated by the sense of power he gets from struggling for and then reaching a social goal. [35] Consequently the leftist is never satisfied with the goals he has already attained; his need for the power process leads him always to pursue some new goal. The leftist wants equal opportunities for minorities. When that is attained he insist on statistical equality of achievement by minorities. And as long as anyone harbors in some corner of his mind a negative attitude toward some minority, the leftist has to re-educated him. And ethnic minorities are not enough; no one can be allowed to have a negative attitude toward homosexuals, disabled people, fat people, old people, ugly people, and on and on and on. It's not enough that the public should be informed about the hazards of smoking; a warning has to be stamped on every package of cigarettes. Then cigarette advertising has to be restricted if not banned. The activists will never be satisfied until tobacco is outlawed, and after that it will be alcohol, then junk food, etc. Activists have fought gross child abuse, which is reasonable. But now they want to stop all spanking. When they have done that they will want to ban something else they consider unwholesome, then another thing and then another. They will never be satisfied until they have complete control over all child rearing practices. And then they will move on to another cause.

220. Suppose you asked leftists to make a list of ALL the things that were wrong with society, and then suppose you instituted EVERY social change that they demanded. It is safe to say that within a couple of years the majority of leftists would find something new to complain about, some new social "evil" to correct because, once again, the leftist is motivated less by distress at society's ills than by the need to satisfy his drive for power by imposing his solutions on society.

221. Because of the restrictions placed on their thoughts and behav-

ior by their high level of socialization, many leftists of the over-socialized type cannot pursue power in the ways that other people do. For them the drive for power has only one morally acceptable outlet, and that is in the struggle to impose their morality on everyone.

222. Leftists, especially those of the oversocialized type, are True Believers in the sense of Eric Hoffer's book, "The True Believer." But not all True Believers are of the same psychological type as leftists. Presumably a true-believing nazi, for instance, is very different psychologically from a true-believing leftist. Because of their capacity for single-minded devotion to a cause, True Believers are a useful, perhaps a necessary, ingredient of any revolutionary movement. This presents a problem with which we must admit we don't know how to deal. We aren't sure how to harness the energies of the True Believer to a revolution against technology. At present all we can say is that no True Believer will make a safe recruit to the revolution unless his commitment is exclusively to the destruction of technology. If he is committed also to another ideal, he may want to use technology as a tool for pursuing that other ideal (see paragraphs 220, 221).

223. Some readers may say, "This stuff about leftism is a lot of crap. I know John and Jane who are leftish types and they don't have all these totalitarian tendencies." It's quite true that many leftists, possibly even a numerical majority, are decent people who sincerely believe in tolerating others' values (up to a point) and wouldn't want to use high-handed methods to reach their social goals. Our remarks about leftism are not meant to apply to every individual leftist but to describe the general character of leftism as a movement. And the general character of a movement is not necessarily determined by the numerical proportions of the various kinds of people involved in the movement.

224. The people who rise to positions of power in leftist movements tend to be leftists of the most power-hungry type, because power-hungry people are those who strive hardest to get into positions of power. Once the power-hungry types have captured control of the movement, there are many leftists of a gentler breed who inwardly disapprove of many of the actions of the leaders, but cannot bring themselves to oppose them. They NEED their faith in the movement, and because

they cannot give up this faith they go along with the leaders. True, SOME leftists do have the guts to oppose the totalitarian tendencies that emerge, but they generally lose, because the power-hungry types are better organized, are more ruthless and Machiavellian and have take care to build themselves a strong power base.

225. These phenomena appeared clearly in Russia and other countries that were taken over by leftists. Similarly, before the breakdown of communism in the USSR, leftish types in the West would seldom criticize that country. If prodded they would admit that the USSR did many wrong things, but then they would try to find excuses for the communists and begin talking about the faults of the West. They always opposed Western military resistance to communist aggression. Leftish types all over the world vigorously protested the U.S. military action in Vietnam, but when the USSR invaded Afghanistan they did nothing. Not that they approved of the Soviet actions; but because of their leftist faith, they just couldn't bear to put themselves in opposition to communism. Today, in those of our universities where "political correctness" has become dominant, there are probably many leftish types who privately disapprove of the suppression of academic freedom, but they go along with it anyway.

226. Thus the fact that many individual leftists are personally mild and fairly tolerant people by no means prevents leftism as a whole from having a totalitarian tendency.

227. Our discussion of leftism has a serious weakness. It is still far from clear what we mean by the word "leftist." There doesn't seem to be much we can do about this. Today leftism is fragmented into a whole spectrum of activist movements. Yet not all activist movements are leftist, and some activist movements (e.g., radical environmentalism) seem to include both personalities of the leftist type and personalities of thoroughly un-leftist types who ought to know better than to collaborate with leftists. Varieties of leftists fade out gradually into varieties of non-leftists and we ourselves would often be hard-pressed to decide whether a given individual is or is not a leftist. To the extent that it is defined at all, our conception of leftism is defined by the discussion of it that we have given in this

article, and we can only advise the reader to use his own judgment in deciding who is a leftist.

228. But it will be helpful to list some criteria for diagnosing leftism. These criteria cannot be applied in a cut and dried manner. Some individuals may meet some of the criteria without being leftists, some leftists may not meet any of the criteria. Again, you just have to use your judgment.

229. The leftist is oriented toward large-scale collectivism. He emphasizes the duty of the individual to serve society and the duty of society to take care of the individual. He has a negative attitude toward individualism. He often takes a moralistic tone. He tends to be for gun control, for sex education and other psychologically "enlightened" educational methods, for social planning, for affirmative action, for multiculturalism. He tends to identify with victims. He tends to be against competition and against violence, but he often finds excuses for those leftists who do commit violence. He is fond of using the common catch-phrases on the left, like "racism," "sexism," "homophobia," "capitalism," "imperialism," "neocolonialism," "genocide," "social change," "social justice," "social responsibility." Maybe the best diagnostic trait of the leftist is his tendency to sympathize with the following movements; feminism, gay rights, ethnic rights, disability rights, animal rights, political correctness. Anyone who strongly sympathizes with ALL of these movements is almost certainly a leftist. [36]

230. The more dangerous leftists, that is, those who are most power-hungry, are often characterized by arrogance or by a dogmatic approach to ideology. However, the most dangerous leftists of all may be certain oversocialized types who avoid irritating displays of aggressiveness and refrain from advertising their leftism, but work quietly and unobtrusively to promote collectivist values, "enlightened" psychological techniques for socializing children, dependence of the individual on the system, and so forth. These crypto-leftists (as we may call them) approximate certain bourgeois types as far as practical action is concerned, but differ from them in psychology, ideology and motivation. The ordinary bourgeois tries to bring people under control of the system in order to protect his way of life, or he does so simply because his attitudes are conventional. The cryp-

to-leftist tries to bring people under control of the system because he is a True Believer in a collectivistic ideology. The crypto-leftist is differentiated from the average leftist of the oversocialized type by the fact that his rebellious impulse is weaker and he is more securely socialized. He is differentiated from the ordinary well-socialized bourgeois by the fact that there is some deep lack within him that makes it necessary for him to devote himself to a cause and immerse himself in a collectivity. And maybe his (well-sublimated) drive for power is stronger than that of the average bourgeois.

FINAL NOTE

231. Throughout this article we've made imprecise statements and statements that ought to have had all sorts of qualifications and reservations attached to them; and some of our statements may be flatly false. Lack of sufficient information and the need for brevity made it impossible for us to formulate our assertions more precisely or add all the necessary qualifications. And of course in a discussion of this kind one must rely heavily on intuitive judgment, and that can sometimes be wrong. So we don't claim that this article expresses more than a crude approximation to the truth.

232. All the same, we are reasonably confident that the general outlines of the picture we have pointed here are roughly correct. Just one possible weak point needs to be mentioned. We have portrayed leftism in its modern form as a phenomenon peculiar to our time and as a symptom of the disruption of the power process. But we might possibly be wrong about this. Oversocialized types who try to satisfy their drive for power by imposing their morality on everyone have certainly been around for a long time. But we THINK that the decisive role played by feelings of inferiority, low self-esteem, powerlessness, identification with victims by people who are not themselves victims, is a peculiarity of modern leftism. Identification with victims by people not themselves victims can be seen to some extent in 19th century leftism and early Christianity but as far as we can make out, symptoms of low self-esteem etc., were not nearly so evident in these movements, or in any other movements, as they are in modern leftism. But we are not in a position to assert confidently that no such movements have existed

prior to modern leftism. This is a significant question to which historians ought to give their attention.

NOTES

1. (Paragraph 19) We are asserting that ALL, or even most, bullies and ruthless competitors suffer from feelings of inferiority.
2. (Paragraph 25) During the Victorian period many oversocialized people suffered from serious psychological problems as a result of repressing or trying to repress their sexual feelings. Freud apparently based his theories on people of this type. Today the focus of socialization has shifted from sex to aggression.
3. (Paragraph 27) Not necessarily including specialists in engineering or the "hard" sciences.
4. (Paragraph 28) There are many individuals of the middle and upper classes who resist some of these values, but usually their resistance is more or less covert. Such resistance appears in the mass media only to a very limited extent. The main thrust of propaganda in our society is in favor of the stand values.

The main reason why these values have become, so to speak, the official values of our society is that they are useful to the industrial system. Violence is discouraged because it disrupts the functioning of the system. Racism is discouraged because ethnic conflicts also disrupt the system, and discrimination wastes the talents of minority-group members who could be useful to the system. Poverty must be "cured" because the underclass causes problems for the system and contact with the underclass lowers the morale of the other classes. Women are encouraged to have careers because their talents are useful to the system and, more importantly, because by having regular jobs women become better integrated into the system and tied directly to it rather than to their families. This helps to weaken family solidarity. (The leaders of the system say they want to strengthen the family, but they really mean is that they want the family to serve as an effective tool for socializing children in accord with the needs of the system. We argue in paragraphs 51, 52 that the system cannot afford to let the family or other small scale social groups be strong or autonomous.)

5. (Paragraph 42) It may be argued that the majority of people don't

want to make their own decisions but want leaders to do their thinking for them. There is an element of truth in this. People like to make their own decisions in small matters, but making decisions on difficult, fundamental questions requires facing up to psychological conflict, and most people hate psychological conflict. Hence they tend to lean on others in making difficult decisions. But it does not follow that they like to have decisions imposed upon them without having any opportunity to influence those decisions. The majority of people are natural followers, not leaders, but they like to have direct personal access to their leaders, they want to be able to influence the leaders and participate to some extent in making even the difficult decisions. At least to that degree they need autonomy.

6. (Paragraph 44) Some of the symptoms listed are similar to those shown by caged animals.

To explain how these symptoms arise from deprivation with respect to the power process:

Common-sense understanding of human nature tells one that lack of goals whose attainment requires effort leads to boredom and that boredom, long continued, often leads eventually to depression. Failure to attain goals leads to frustration and lowering of self-esteem. Frustration leads to anger, anger to aggression, often in the form of spouse or child abuse. It has been shown that long-continued frustration commonly leads to depression and that depression tends to cause guilt, sleep disorders, eating disorders and bad feelings about oneself. Those who are tending toward depression seek pleasure as an antidote; hence insatiable hedonism and excessive sex, with perversions as a means of getting new kicks. Boredom too tends to cause excessive pleasure-seeking since, lacking other goals, people often use pleasure as a goal. See accompanying diagram.

The foregoing is a simplification. Realty is more complex, and of course, deprivation with respect to the power process is not the ONLY cause of the symptoms described.

By the way, when we mention depression we do not necessarily mean depression that is severe enough to be treated by a psychiatrist. Often only mild forms of depression are involved. And when we speak of goals we do not necessarily mean long-term, thought-out goals. For many or most people through much of human histo-

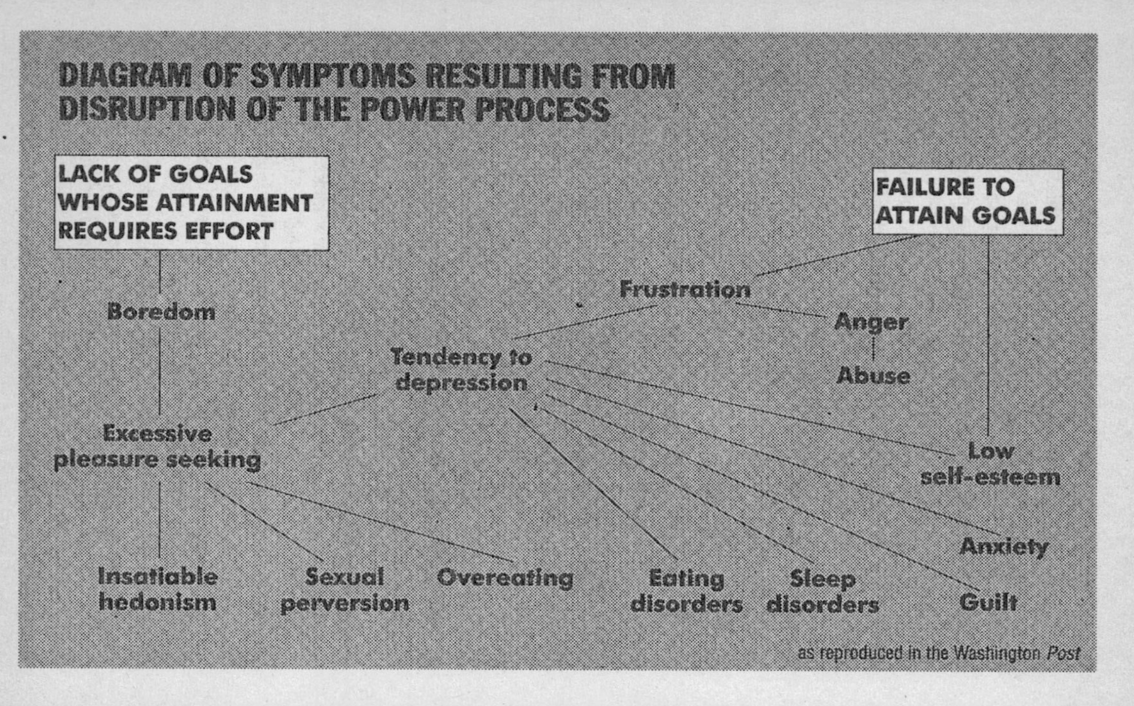

as reproduced in the Washington *Post*

ry, the goals of a hand-to-mouth existence (merely providing oneself and one's family with food from day to day) have been quite sufficient.

7. (Paragraph 52) A partial exception may be made for a few passive, inward-looking groups, such as the Amish, which have little effect on the wider society. Apart from these, some genuine small-scale communities do exist in America today. For instance, youth gangs and "cults." Everyone regards them as dangerous, and so they are, because the members of these groups are loyal primarily to one another rather than to the system, hence the system cannot control them.

Or take the gypsies. The gypsies commonly get away with theft and fraud because their loyalties are such that they can always get other gypsies to give testimony that "proves" their innocence. Obviously the system would be in serious trouble if too many people belonged to such groups.

Some of the early-20th century Chinese thinkers who were concerned with modernizing China recognized the necessity breaking down small-scale social groups such as the family: "(According to Sun Yat-sen) the Chinese people needed a new surge of patriotism, which would lead to a transfer of loyalty from the family to the state ... (According to Li Huang) traditional attachments, particularly to the family had to be abandoned if nationalism were to develop in China." (Chester C. Tan, "Chinese Political Thought in the Twentieth Century," page 125, page 297.)

8. (Paragraph 56) Yes, we know that 19th century America had its problems, and serous ones, but for the sake of brevity we have to express ourselves in simplified terms.

9. (Paragraph 61) We leave aside the "underclass." We are speaking of the mainstream.

10. (Paragraph 62) Some social scientists, educators, "mental health" professionals and the like are doing their best to push the social drives into group 1 by trying to see to it that everyone has a satisfactory social life.

11. (Paragraphs 63, 82) Is the drive for endless material acquisition really an artificial creation of the advertising and marketing industry? Certainly there is no innate human drive for material acquisition. There have been many cultures in which people have desired

little material wealth beyond what was necessary to satisfy their basic physical needs (Australian aborigines, traditional Mexican peasant culture, some African cultures). On the other hand there have also been many pre-industrial cultures in which material acquisition has played an important role. So we can't claim that today's acquisition-oriented culture is exclusively a creation of the advertising and marketing industry. But it is clear that the advertising and marketing industry has had an important part in creating that culture. The big corporations that spend millions on advertising wouldn't be spending that kind of money without solid proof that they were getting it back in increased sales. One member of FC met a sales manager a couple of years ago who was frank enough to tell him, "Our job is to make people buy things they don't want and don't need." He the described how an untrained novice could present people with the facts about a product, and make no sales at all, while a trained and experienced professional salesman would make lots of sales to the same people. This shows that people are manipulated into buying things they don't really want.

12. (Paragraph 64) The problem of purposelessness seems to have become less serious during the last 15 years or so, because people now feel less secure physically and economically than they did earlier, and the need for security provides them with a goal. But purposelessness has been replaced by frustration over the difficulty of attaining security. We emphasize the problem of purposelessness because the liberals and leftists would wish to solve our social problems by having society guarantee everyone's security; but if that could be done it would only bring back the problem of purposelessness. The real issue is not whether society provides well or poorly for people's security; the trouble is that people are dependent on the system for their security rather that having it in their own hands. This, by the way, is part of the reason why some people get worked up about the right to bear arms; possession of a gun puts that aspect of their security in their own hands.

13. (Paragraph 66) Conservatives' efforts to decrease the amount of government regulation are of little benefit to the average man. For one thing, only a fraction of the regulations can be eliminated because most regulations are necessary. For another thing, most of

the deregulation affects business rather than the average individual, so that its main effect is to take power from the government and give it to private corporations. What this means for the average man is that government interference in his life is replaced by interference from big corporations, which may be permitted, for example, to dump more chemicals that get into his water supply and give him cancer. The conservatives are just taking the average man for a sucker, exploiting his resentment of Big Government to promote the power of Big Business.

14. (Paragraph 73) When someone approves of the purpose for which propaganda is being used in a given case, he generally calls it "education" or applies to it some similar euphemism. But propaganda is propaganda regardless of the purpose for which it is used.

15. (Paragraph 83) We are not expressing approval or disapproval of the Panama invasion. We only use it to illustrate a point.

16. (Paragraph 95) When the American colonies were under British rule there were fewer and less effective legal guarantees of freedom than there were after the American Constitution went into effect, yet there was more personal freedom in pre-industrial America, both before and after the War of Independence, than there was after the Industrial Revolution took hold in this country. We quote from "Violence in America: Historical and Comparative Perspectives," edited by Hugh Davis Graham and Ted Robert Gurr, Chapter 12 by Roger Lane, pages 476-478: "The progressive heightening of standards of propriety, and with it the increasing reliance on official law enforcement (in 19th century America) ... were common to the whole society ... [The] change in social behavior is so long term and so widespread as to suggest a connection with the most fundamental of contemporary social processes; that of industrial urbanization itself ... Massachusetts in 1835 had a population of some 660,940, 81 percent rural, overwhelmingly preindustrial and native born. Its citizens were used to considerable personal freedom. Whether teamsters, farmers or artisans, they were all accustomed to setting their own schedules, and the nature of their work made them physically independent or each other ... Individual problems, sins or even crimes, were not generally cause for wider social concern ..." But the impact of the twin movements to the city and to the factory, both

just gathering force in 1835, had a progressive effect on personal behavior throughout the 19th century and into the 20th. The factory demanded regularity of behavior, a life governed by obedience to the rhythms of clock and calendar, the demands of foreman and supervisor. In the city or town, the needs of living in closely packed neighborhoods inhibited many action previously unobjectionable. Both blue- and white-collar employees in larger establishments were mutually dependent on their fellows; as one man's work fit into another's, so one man's business was no longer his own.

"The results of the new organization of life and work were apparent by 1900, when some 76 percent of the 2,805,346 inhabitants of Massachusetts were classified as urbanites. Much violent or irregular behavior which had been tolerable in a casual, independent society was no longer acceptable in the more formalized, cooperative atmosphere of the later period ... The move to the cities had, in short, produced a more tractable, more socialized, more 'civilized' generation than its predecessors."

17. (Paragraph 117) Apologists for the system are fond of citing cases in which elections have been decided by one or two votes, but such cases are rare.

18. (Paragraph 119) "Today, in technologically advanced lands, men live very similar lives in spite of geographical, religious, and political difference. The daily lives of a Christian bank clerk in Chicago, a Buddhist bank clerk in Tokyo, and a Communist bank clerk in Moscow are far more alike than the life of any one of them is like that of any single man who lived a thousand years ago. These similarities are the result of a common technology ... " L. Sprague de Camp, "The Ancient Engineers," Ballantine edition, page 17.

The lives of the three bank clerks are not IDENTICAL. Ideology does have SOME effect. But all technological societies, in order to survive, must evolve along APPROXIMATELY the same trajectory.

19. (Paragraph 123) Just think an irresponsible genetic engineer might create a lot of terrorists.

20. (Paragraph 124) For a further example of undesirable consequences of medical progress, suppose a reliable cure for cancer is discovered. Even if the treatment is too expensive to be available to

any but the elite, it will greatly reduce their incentive to stop the escape of carcinogens into the environment.

21. (Paragraph 128) Since many people may find paradoxical the notion that a large number of good things can add up to a bad thing, we illustrate with an analogy. Suppose Mr. A is playing chess with Mr. B. Mr. C, a Grand Master, is looking over Mr. A's shoulder. Mr. A of course wants to win his game, so if Mr. C points out a good move for him to make, he is doing Mr. A a favor. But suppose now that Mr. C. tells Mr. A how to make ALL of his moves. In each particular instance he does Mr. A a favor by showing him his best move, but by making ALL of his moves for him he spoils his game, since there is not point in Mr. A's playing the game at all if someone else makes all his moves.

The situation of modern man is analogous to that of Mr. A. The system makes an individual's life easier for him in innumerable ways, but in doing so it deprives him of control over his own fate.

22. (Paragraph 137) Here we are considering only the conflict of values within the mainstream. For the sake of simplicity we leave out of the picture "outsider" values like the idea that wild nature is more important than human economic welfare.

23. (Paragraph 137) Self-interest is not necessarily MATERIAL self-interest. It can consist in fulfillment of some psychological need, for example, by promoting one's own ideology or religion.

24. (Paragraph 139) A qualification: It is in the interest of the system to permit a certain prescribed degree of freedom in some areas. For example, economic freedom (with suitable limitations and restraints) has proved effective in promoting economic growth. But only planned circumscribed, limited freedom is in the interest of the system.

The individual must always be kept on a leash, even if the leash is sometimes long (see paragraphs 94, 97).

25. (Paragraph 143) We don't mean to suggest that the efficiency or the potential for survival of a society has always been inversely proportional to the amount of pressure or discomfort to which the society subjects people. That certainly is not the case. There is good reason to believe that many primitive societies subjected people to less pressure than European society did, but European society proved far more effi-

cient than any primitive society and always won out in conflicts with such societies because of the advantages conferred by technology.

26. (Paragraph 147) If you think that more effective law enforcement is unequivocally good because it suppresses crime, then remember that crime as defined by the system is not necessarily what YOU would call crime. Today, smoking marijuana is a "crime," and, in some places in the U.S., so is possession of an unregistered handgun. Tomorrow, possession of ANY firearm, registered or not, may be made a crime, and the same thing may happen with disapproved methods of child-rearing, such as spanking. In some countries, expression of dissident political opinions is a crime, and there is no certainty that this will never happen in the U.S., since no constitution or political system lasts forever.

If a society needs a large, powerful law enforcement establishment, then there is something gravely wrong with that society; it must be subjecting people to severe pressures if so many refuse to follow the rules, or follow them only because forced. Many societies in the past have gotten by with little or no formal law-enforcement.

27. (Paragraph 151) To be sure, past societies have had means of influencing human behavior, but these have been primitive and of low effectiveness compared with the technological means that are now being developed.

28. (Paragraph 152) However, some psychologists have publicly expressed opinions indicating their contempt for human freedom. And the mathematician Claude Shannon was quoted in Omni (August 1987) as saying, "I visualize a time when we will be to robots what dogs are to humans, and I'm rooting for the machines."

29. (Paragraph 154) This is no science fiction! After writing paragraph 154 we came across an article in Scientific American according to which scientists are actively developing techniques for identifying possible future criminals and for treating them by a combination of biological and psychological means. Some scientists advocate compulsory application of the treatment, which may be available in the near future. (See "Seeking the Criminal Element," by W. Wayt Gibbs, Scientific American, March 1995.) Maybe you think this is OK because the treatment would be applied to those who might become violent criminals. But of course it won't stop there. Next, a

treatment will be applied to those who might become drunk drivers (they endanger human life too), then perhaps to people who spank their children, then to environmentalists who sabotage logging equipment, eventually to anyone whose behavior is inconvenient for the system.

30. (Paragraph 184) A further advantage of nature as a counter-ideal to technology is that, in many people, nature inspires the kind of reverence that is associated with religion, so that nature could perhaps be idealized on a religious basis. It is true that in many societies religion has served as a support and justification for the established order, but it is also true that religion has often provided a basis for rebellion. Thus it may be useful to introduce a religious element into the rebellion against technology, the more so because Western society today has no strong religious foundation.

Religion, nowadays either is used as cheap and transparent support for narrow, short-sighted selfishness (some conservatives use it this way), or even is cynically exploited to make easy money (by many evangelists), or has degenerated into crude irrationalism (fundamentalist protestant sects, "cults"), or is simply stagnant (Catholicism, main-line Protestantism). The nearest thing to a strong, widespread, dynamic religion that the West has seen in recent times has been the quasi-religion of leftism, but leftism today is fragmented and has no clear, unified, inspiring goal.

Thus there is a religious vacuum in our society that could perhaps be filled by a religion focused on nature in opposition to technology. But it would be a mistake to try to concoct artificially a religion to fill this role. Such an invented religion would probably be a failure. Take the "Gaia" religion for example. Do its adherents REALLY believe in it or are they just play-acting? If they are just play-acting their religion will be a flop in the end.

It is probably best not to try to introduce religion into the conflict of nature vs. technology unless you REALLY believe in that religion yourself and find that it arouses a deep, strong, genuine response in many other people.

31. (Paragraph 189) Assuming that such a final push occurs. Conceivably the industrial system might be eliminated in a somewhat gradual or piecemeal fashion (see paragraphs 4, 167 and Note 4).

32. (Paragraph 193) It is even conceivable (remotely) that the revolution might consist only of a massive change of attitudes toward technology resulting in a relatively gradual and painless disintegration of the industrial system. But if this happens we'll be very lucky. It's far more probably that the transition to a nontechnological society will be very difficult and full of conflicts and disasters.
33. (Paragraph 195) The economic and technological structure of a society are far more important than its political structure in determining the way the average man lives (see paragraphs 95, 119 and Notes 16, 18).
34. (Paragraph 215) This statement refers to our particular brand of anarchism. A wide variety of social attitudes have been called "anarchist," and it may be that many who consider themselves anarchists would not accept our statement of paragraph 215. It should be noted, by the way, that there is a nonviolent anarchist movement whose members probably would not accept FC as anarchist and certainly would not approve of FC's violent methods.
35. (Paragraph 219) Many leftists are motivated also by hostility, but the hostility probably results in part from a frustrated need for power.
36. (Paragraph 229) It is important to understand that we mean someone who sympathizes with these MOVEMENTS as they exist today in our society. One who believes that women, homosexuals, etc., should have equal rights is not necessary a leftist. The feminist, gay rights, etc., movements that exist in our society have the particular ideological tone that characterizes leftism, and if one believes, for example, that women should have equal rights it does not necessarily follow that one must sympathize with the feminist movement as it exists today.
If copyright problems make it impossible for this long quotation to be printed, then please change Note 16 to read as follows:
16. (Paragraph 95) When the American colonies were under British rule there were fewer and less effective legal guarantees of freedom than there were after the American Constitution went into effect, yet there was more personal freedom in pre-industrial America, both before and after the War of Independence, than there was after the industrial Revolution took hold in his country. In "Violence in America: Historical and Comparative Perspectives," edited by Hugh Davis Graham and Ted Robert Gurr, Chapter 12 by

Roger Lane, it is explained how in pre-industrial America the average person had greater independence and autonomy than he does today, and how the process of industrialization necessarily led to the restriction of personal freedom.

The Carrot Package

Nature makes a perfect counter-ideal to technology.

—Manifesto, paragraph 184

Garland's Town and Country Store in Lincoln was founded years ago by Cecil Garland. Back in the '60s, Cecil fought to keep loggers and road builders out of what would become the Scapegoat Wilderness area. Some 20 years ago, Cecil moved to Utah, leaving the store to his daughters.

Teresa and Becky Garland knew Ted Kaczynski probably as well as anyone in Lincoln. Besides the letter he wrote to Becky (page 52), Ted left Teresa Garland one other memento: a packet of wild carrot seeds.

That was in 1994. The packet, which Teresa never opened, was handmade, apparently a couple of years earlier. In its sweeping search through town for possible evidence relevant to the Unabomber case, the FBI subpoenaed the packet, most likely to look for a trace of Ted Kaczynski's DNA on the sealed flap.

The careful instructions for planting and harvesting, a facsimile of which appears on the opposite page, were in Ted's own writing.

WILD CARROT
BIG YELLOW
1992

Plant these just as you would regular carrots. Some will probably put up seed stalks the first year. Pull these out, since the roots get tough as soon as they put up seed stalks.

The white roots have only so-so flavor. The tasty roots are the pale-yellow ones. If you like them and want to grow the seeds, dig around the plants in the fall to see which ones have large, pale-yellow roots. Leave these in the ground over the winter, with soil mounded up over them to prevent mice from getting at them, and the second year they will put up seed stalks.

Supplementary Sources

Associated Press
Boston *Globe*
Chicago *Tribune*
CNN, *Larry King Live*
Daily Northwestern
Daily Southtown
David Fisher, *Hard Evidence*
Donald L. Miller, *City of the Century*
Hartford *Courant*
Helen Lefkowitz Horowitz, *Campus Life*
Los Angeles *Times*
Michigan *Daily*
National Broadcasting Company
National Public Radio
New York *Times*
Newsweek
PEOPLE
Richard Norton Smith's *The Harvard Century*
Sacramento *Bee*
San Francisco *Chronicle*
San Francisco *Examiner*
San Jose *Mercury News*
Theodore John Kaczynski, *Boundary Functions*, (Dissertation, 1967)
United Press International
USA Today
U.S. News & World Report
Washington *Post*